GENDER TRANSFORMATIONS

In this lucid and subtle investigation of the economic, political and cultural condition of women in contemporary society, Sylvia Walby, one of the world's leading authorities on the sociology of gender, shows how undoubted increases in opportunity for women in Europe and America have been accompanied by new forms of inequality. She charts changes in women's employment, education and political representation and the complex relations between gender, class and ethnicity, between local conditions and global pressures which together determine the place of women both in the labour market and in the wider social, political and economic world of today. Individual chapters look at the phenomenon of flexible work and its influence on the total labour market, at gender politics and social theory, at the gendering of citizenship and nationhood and gender in the context of European integration.

The eagerly awaited successor to Walby's classic, *Theorising Patriarchy*, *Gender Transformations* will be essential reading for anyone with an interest in how questions of gender remake and are remade by the social and economic conditions in which they occur.

Sylvia Walby is Professor of Sociology at the University of Leeds and the author of *Theorising Patriarchy* (1990) and *Patriarchy at Work* (1986).

GENDER TRANSFORMATIONS

Sylvia Walby

London and New York

First published 1997
by Routledge
11 New Fetter Lane, London EC4P 4EE

Simultaneously published in the USA and Canada
by Routledge
29 West 35th Street, New York, NY 10001

Typeset in Garamond by Pure Tech India Ltd., Pondicherry
Printed and bound in Great Britain by
Creative Print and Design (Wales), Ebbw Vale

British Library Cataloguing in Publication Data
A catalogue record for this book is available from the British Library

Library of Congress Cataloguing in Publication Data
Walby, Sylvia.
Gender transformations \ Sylvia Walby.
p. cm. – (International library of Sociology)
Includes bibliographical references and index.
1. Women–Social conditions. 2. Women–Economic conditions.
3. Women–Employment. 4. Sex discrimination against Women.
I. Tittle. II. Series.
HQ1206.W2   1997
305.42–dc21   96–46222
                                                         CIP

ISBN 0–415–12080–2 (hbk)
ISBN 0–415–12081–0 (pbk)

CONTENTS

FIGURES

TABLES

ACKNOWLEDGEMENTS

I would like to thank the many individuals who have contributed to the development of my ideas over the time that this research was conducted, and especially: Paul Bagguley, June Greenwell, Joni Lovenduski, Celia Lury, Clare Short, John Urry, Gail Wilson.

The research reported in Chapters 4 and 5 was conducted as part of the Lancaster Locality Study (Grant Number DO4250010) funded under the Economic and Social Research Council's initiative, 'The Changing Urban and Regional System in the UK'. The original versions of these chapters were co-written with Paul Bagguley, for whose thoughtful contributions, as well as permission to publish, I am grateful. Data from the Census of Employment for 1971 and 1981, and from the Census of Population for 1981 was computed from the Manpower Services Commission's National Online Manpower Information Service (NOMIS), programmed and developed in the Department of Geography, University of Durham, by R. Nelson and P. Dodds. I would like to thank D. Shapiro, J. Urry and A. Warde for their comments on earlier versions of these papers.

Earlier versions of some papers have previously been published. I am grateful for permission to publish revised versions of these papers:

(1988) 'Gender politics and social theory', *Sociology*, 22(2): 215–32;

(1989) 'The changing sexual division of labour and flexibility', in Stephen Wood (ed.) *The Transformation of Work? Skill Flexibility and the Labour Process* (Unwin Hyman);

(1989)'Gender restructuring: five labour markets compared', *Environment and Planning D: Society and Space* (Pion Ltd, London);

(1990) 'Sex segregation in local labour markets', *Work Employment and Society*, 4(1): 59–82;

(1991) 'Labour markets and industrial structures in women's working lives', in Shirley Dex (ed.) *Life and Work History Analyses: Qualitative and Quantitative Developments, Sociological Review Monograph* 37 (Routledge);

(1992) 'Woman and nation', in *International Journal of Comparative Sociology* XXXIII (1–2), January–April: 81–100;
(1992) 'Post-post-modernism? Theorising social complexity', in Michele Barrett and Anne Phillips (eds) *Destabilizing Theory: Contemporary Feminist Debates* (Polity Press);
(1993) '"Backlash" in historical context', in Mary Kennedy, Cathy Lubelska and Val Walsh (eds) *Making Connections* (Taylor and Francis);
(1994) 'Is citizenship gendered?', *Sociology*, 28(2): 379–95.

1

INTRODUCTION

FUNDAMENTAL TRANSFORMATIONS

Fundamental transformations of gender relations in the contemporary Western world are affecting the economy and all forms of social relations. The driving forces behind these changes are the increase in women's education and paid employment and new forms of political representation of women's interests. These changes have implications not only for women's positions in wider society, in all their diversity, but also for the overall economy and polity.

For example, women are now almost half of all workers in the contemporary UK. In 1995 they were 49.6 per cent of employees in employment (*Employment Gazette*, April 1996) and indeed in one-third of local labour markets women were the majority of those in work (see Appendix 1). This is a major transformation of gender relations in employment. These transformations are having far-reaching implications not only for gender relations but for social relations in society as a whole, including class relations. However, much of this new employment of women is not performed under conditions equal to those of men. Another example is in education, where girls are passing more exams at schools than boys, creating new possibilities for young women. However, these are achievements for younger women, and older women have significantly fewer qualifications than their male peers.

The system of gender relations is changing, from one which was based on women being largely confined to the domestic sphere, to one in which women are present in the public sphere, but still frequently segregated into unequal positions. This change ultimately derives from the winning of political citizenship by first-wave feminism in the early twentieth century in the context of an increasing demand for women's labour in a developing economy and women's access to education at all levels. The patterns of inequality between women and men have changed as a result, but in complex ways, not simply for better or worse.

Gender restructuring affects women differently according their position, not only in class and ethnic relations, but also within different household forms. Diversity among women is a result not only of class and ethnicity, but also of changes in the forms of patriarchy, of gender regime, giving rise to significant generational differences.

CONVERGENCE AND POLARISATION IN GENDER RELATIONS

Both convergence and polarisation mark the contemporary restructuring of gender relations. Convergence between the genders is occurring among some younger people especially where increased access to education and the labour market for some young women has reduced the differences and inequality between the sexes in qualifications and work. Polarisation is occurring between women of different generations, as young women gain qualifications and labour market positions which are out of reach to older women who built their lives around a different set of patriarchal opportunity structures. Those younger women who do not achieve educational qualifications and entry to good jobs are also disadvantaged, and are especially poor if they become mothers without a supporting partner. To a significant extent women are polarising between those, typically younger, educated and employed, who engage in new patterns of gender relations somewhat convergent with those of men, and those, particularly disadvantaged women, typically older and less educated, who built their life trajectories around patterns of private patriarchy. These new patterns are intertwined with diversities and inequalities generated by social divisions including class, ethnicity and region.

NEW DEVELOPMENTS IN GENDER RELATIONS

Changes have been taking place unevenly in different aspects of gender relations, in the six patriarchal structures outlined in *Theorising Patriarchy*. The leading change has been the increase in women in education and paid employment, though this is tempered by the variable ways in which women are involved, for instance, the poor conditions of the nearly half of employed women who work part-time and by the tenacity of occupational and industrial segregation. The wages gap between women and men full-time workers has narrowed, though not that for part-timers. There has been a dramatic closing of the gap in educational qualifications of young men and women, both at school and University. Changes in these two areas will be explored in detail in the following chapter.

The structure of the typical household has changed, with an increasing propensity for women to live and to rear children outside of marriage, especially as a result of increased rates of divorce and cohabitation. The divorce rate in the UK has risen from 0.5 per 1,000 in 1960, to 3.1 per 1,000 in 1993, and is now the highest in the European Union (EUROSTAT, 1995:

130–1). The proportion of women aged 18–49 who are married has declined from 74 per cent in 1979 to 57 per cent in 1994 (OPCS, 1996b: 34). The proportion of families headed by a lone parent has increased from 8 per cent in 1971 to 23 per cent in 1994 (OPCS, 1996b: 14). Women are more independent from men, but poorer. The meaning of this, in terms of equity and justice for women, is hard to assess, especially since these meanings are culturally and ethnically specific. Different ethnic groups have varied patterns, with South Asian households in the UK the most likely to contain a married couple, and Afro-Caribbean households, followed by White, least likely to contain a married couple.

The political advocacy and representation of women's interests is also subject to complex changes. Since the winning of political citizenship in the early twentieth century not only has there been a significant reduction in legislation which restricts women's activities, but also, since the 1970s a major development of equal opportunities legislation, underpinned by the treaties of the European Union. Further, in social movements and the voluntary sector women are significant actors (Miller, Wilford and Donaghue, 1996), whether these movements are clearly of relevance to women as in many feminist organisations, such as the refuge movement for battered women (Charles, 1995), or more indirectly so such as the Greenham protest against cruise missiles and militarism (Roseneil, 1995), the poll tax protests (Bagguley, 1995), and environmentalism (Cudworth, 1996; Plumwood, 1993). Women are also involved in many voluntary associations such as the Mothers Union, Town's Women's Guild, the Women's Institutes, the National Commission for Women and the National Association of Women's Organisations.

However, women are still significantly underrepresented in the state and many forms of public life, such as Parliament, the institutions of law and order and influential non-governmental bodies. There are very few women in the UK Parliament – only 9.2 per cent of MPs were women following the 1992 election. Women's representation here has increased very slowly, from nil before 1918, to 2.3 per cent in 1929 (the first year in which all women had the vote) to 2.7 per cent in 1951, 4.1 per cent in 1970, 3.5 per cent in 1983, 6.3 per cent in 1987 and 9.2 per cent in the 1992 general election (Norris and Lovenduski, 1995: 103). The greatest changes have occurred in the last decade – only after 1987 have more than 5 per cent of MPs been female. Likewise in senior law and order positions women are notable by their absence – no women Chief Constables until the 1990s, very few senior judges – in 1994, only 4 per cent of High Court judges were women and 6 per cent of circuit judges – while in the lower level of the magistrates' courts women were 47 per cent of lay magistrates. In 1993 only 28 per cent of public appointments in the UK were held by women, though this is an increase on 19 per cent in 1986. Among ambassadors or heads of overseas missions there were only three women in 150 such posts (British Council,

1996: 15). In the corporate sector there are few women chief executives of the large companies. In the second chamber of the British Parliament, the House of Lords, there are very few women as a consequence of the inheritance of titles. There are few women heading the many quangos, or quasi-governmental bodies.

Political pressure during the last two decades has led to significantly more interventionist forms of policing of male violence against women and children including rape, domestic violence and child sex abuse. Pressure, largely from feminists, made male violence into a public issue leading to some significant reforms, such as special training for police dealing with these cases and special units within police stations for example 'rape suites' (Dobash and Dobash, 1992; Hanmer, Radford and Stanko, 1989). However, while there has been an increased number of rapes reported to and recorded by the police, the number of convictions in the courts, while increasing, has risen much more slowly: that is, while there is an increasing rate of reporting of rape, there is a declining rate of conviction (Soothill and Walby, 1991). There is a significant increase in the number of employers with policies and procedures to deal with sexual harassment, following some headline cases in industrial tribunals, but it is hard to assess their impact. In areas such as male violence against women, the existing data makes it hard to interpret changes. There has been a greater public awareness of the impact of sexual harassment in the workplace on women's employment, but we have little evidence on the extent of changes in this. The reported rates of violence against women are increasing but, given that the rate of reporting is low, it is not clear whether this reflects a real increase in the rate of such violence, or merely an increased propensity to report and for the police to record such crimes (Soothill and Walby, 1991).

The forms of sexuality and its representations have changed in complex ways over the last couple of decades. There has been a decline in the discourse and practise of confining sexuality to marriage and an increase in its public presence. Examples include: the increase in extra-marital sexual relations (Lawson and Samson, 1988); increased circulation of pornographic imagery, such as the development of the 'Page 3' first in the *Sun* and then other newspapers; public discussion of the means to control the spread of AIDS; public discussion of the affairs and duties of marriage among royalty.

Cultural representations have changed in complex ways (Franklin, Lury and Stacey, 1991). There is a greater representation of women in positions of authority in some media, such as newscasters, while there has been a backlash against the use of 'politically correct' language. Issues which were previously regarded as private matters are increasingly being represented and debated in the public arena. For instance, in the 1950s and 1960s rape and other forms of sexual attack were seldom reported in the press, while since the 1970s and the development of the tabloids these have increasingly become exposed to the public gaze, albeit in often sensationalist forms,

4

which provide misleading images of the typical pattern of men's attacks on women (Soothill and Walby, 1991). There have been struggles within the Christian churches over whether women can become priests and vicars, with the winning of the right of women to be ordained in the Church of England.

These are tremendous changes in the lives of women and men over the last 20 years or so. There are many areas where some women have gained increasing access to the public domain leading to significantly increased opportunities, but the picture is complicated by the development of new forms of inequality and by the diversity between women.

THEORISING THE DIVERSITY OF GENDER REGIMES

The understanding of the significance of such diversity and inequality has been a driving force in contemporary social theory. This has underlain some of the tension between modernist and postmodernist approaches to the analysis of gender relations which is central to contemporary feminist theorising. Modernist theorising has been criticised as unable to appreciate differences sufficiently and thus easily to become ethnocentric, while the counter criticism of the postmodern alternative is that it has a problematic tendency to relativism. In some instances it has led to any attempt to theorise using the categories of 'women' and 'men' being accused of essentialism. The tension between the rival approaches to the scientific standing of knowledge further underpins this debate: are there systematic ways of reaching closer to reality or truth, or is each discourse equally valid? As I argued in 'Post-post-modernism: theorising social complexity' (Walby, 1992), we need a structural, though not structuralist theorisation of gender, which draws on the insights of discourse analysis in the specification of these structures, in order to conceptualise patterns of continuity and difference.

The significance of diversity in gender relations has led some theorists to abandon attempts at overarching theories of gender relations. Instead of modernist-style elegant explanations we have postmodern complexity of interpretation. However, I do not think that it is necessary to give up on causal explanations in order to take seriously the intersection between different forms of gender, ethnicity and class (Walby, 1992).

In order to grasp the different patterns of gender relations we need to have concepts at different levels of abstraction and which capture the major forms of gender system. In earlier work I have used the notions of 'system of patriarchy'; 'forms of patriarchy'; 'structures of patriarchy'; and 'patriarchal practices' to catch these different levels. A system of patriarchy was conceptualised as a system of social structures and practices in which men dominate, oppress and exploit women. The six structures of patriarchy are: household production; patriarchal relations in paid work; patriarchal relations in the state; male violence; patriarchal relations in sexuality, and patriarchal relations in cultural institutions (Walby, 1990).

There are different forms of gender regime or patriarchy as a result of different articulations and combinations of these structures. These gender regimes are systems of interrelated gendered structures. In earlier work I identified a continuum between two main types of patriarchy: private and public. This may be more elegantly described as more domestic and more public gender regimes. The use of the terms 'gender regime' as well as that of 'system of patriarchy' in this book should not be interpreted as suggesting that systematic gender inequality of patriarchy is over. The domestic gender regime is based upon household production as the main structure and site of women's work activity and the exploitation of her labour and sexuality and upon the exclusion of women from the public. The public gender regime is based, not on excluding women from the public, but on the segregation and subordination of women within the structures of paid employment and the state, as well as within culture, sexuality and violence. The household does not cease to be a relevant structure in the public form, but is no longer the chief one. In the domestic form the beneficiaries are primarily the individual husbands and fathers of the women in the household, while in the public form there is a more collective appropriation. In the domestic form the principle patriarchal strategy is exclusionary, excluding women from the public arena; in the public it is segregationist and subordinating. In both forms all six structures are relevant, but they have a different relationship to each other. In order to understand any particular instance of gender regime it is always necessary to understand the mutual structuring of class and ethnic relations with gender.

In order to analyse the diversity of gender relations and gender inequality it is important to separate analytically the form of gender regime from the degree of gender inequality. Whether a move to a more public form of gender regime leads to a reduction of gender inequality is an empirical question rather than one to be determined in an a priori fashion.

Different forms of gender regime coexist as a result of the diversity in gender relations consequent upon age, class, ethnicity and region. As a result of the recent changes older women will be more likely than younger women to be involved in a more domestic gender regime. Women whose own occupations place them in higher socio-economic groups are more likely to be in a more public form. Women of Pakistani and Bangladeshi descent are more likely to be in a domestic form and Black Caribbean women more likely to be in a more public form than white women. There are complex interactions between these different forms of gender regime, as well as between gender, ethnicity and class.

Social theories which utilise concepts of structure are not infrequently accused of being rigid, and of underestimating the significance of social action. However, this is not a necessary feature of such accounts. I hold that political action is crucial to changes and the maintenance of gendered structures. For instance, the origin of the variety of patterns of occupational segregation cannot be understood outside of an understanding of the balance of gender and class forces in particular locations, as was argued in *Patriarchy at Work*. The transformation from a private to public form of patriarchy, of a domestic to a more public gender regime, was due to the impact of first-wave feminism in a context of increased demand for women's labour (see *Theorising Patriarchy*). The significance of politics for the analysis of gender relations is not to be underestimated.

Social structures are constantly recreated and changed by the social actions of which they are composed, even though they may appear to any historical individual as a rigid institutional force. The duality of structure (Giddens, 1984) is a relevant notion here as well as elsewhere in social science.

It is especially women's collective agency, which is the focus in this book, a concentration on women as political actors, in situations and moments when women's actions have been significant in changing the structures of patriarchy. There is also due recognition to men's collective agency, often, though not always in opposition to feminist action. Further, women's individual agency is found in the myriad ways in which women actively choose options within the constrained opportunities available to them – women act, but not always in circumstances of their choosing.

SPACE

Different patterns of gender relations are found in different spatial locations. These variations are due to the balance of gender and class forces sedimented over time in local gendered institutions including the local industrial structure and the local political institutions. Changes in the economy and the sexual division of labour occur unevenly through time and space. For instance, while women are almost half of employees in employment overall in Britain, in one-third of local labour markets they constitute the majority of such workers. Restructuring depends upon the balance of forces in any particular location. Chapters 4 and 5 on gender restructuring in five local labour markets show how varied can be the outcomes in terms of the extent of women's participation in paid work, the degree to which this is part-time or full-time, and the nature of occupational and industrial segregation. The restructuring of gender relations in any locality depends upon the previous set of social relations which resulted from previous rounds of restructuring. The forces which affect this include among others, organised representation of the gendered interests of women and men, combined worker interests, different ethnic relations, the structure of the employer's interests.

Different gendered structures have different spatial reaches. For instance, some organised religions transcend national boundaries, while systems of industrial relations are more usually restricted to a specific national context. Globalisation is one of the more significant processes affecting the restructuring of local labour markets, with its increased pressures on economic competitiveness, at least partly due to the increased mobility of capital and the speed of international communications. Further, there are changing and overlapping remits of different states and state-like bodies, for instance, with the increasing jurisdiction of EU regulations in the domestic legislation of its Member States. The European Union is emerging as increasingly significant in the restructuring of gender relations in employment in the UK as a result of increasing market integration and the increasing remit of the European Union to regulate labour markets and to ensure equal treatment of women and men in employment. These issues are discussed further in Chapters 10, 'Woman and nation' and 11, 'Gender and European integration'.

TIME

Time is key to the understanding of change and diversity in gender relations. Notions of time as naturalistic – involving a standard movement from one point to another – have been problematised by recent writers. There has been a major increase in interest in time in the theorisation of society for example Adam (1990, 1995), Giddens (1984), Harvey (1990), Lash and Urry (1994), Nowotny (1994). Time is no longer seen as simply the same as that shown on a clock, but as something which is socially perceived, constructed, refracted and implicated in complex and various ways. It is no longer of interest merely as the medium through which social change takes place, but has become an active resource in the creation of this change.

But much of the writing, while sensitive to social variability, has paid little explicit attention to gender relations (though there are notable exceptions, e.g. Adam, 1995; Davies, 1990). Some of the analysis is abstracted in such a way as to make gender legitimately irrelevant. But in many accounts of empirical patterns of social relations and social experiences gender is relevant and the analysis is flawed as a consequence of its omission.

These problems of omission are particularly acute when writers are trying to describe and explain the nature and significance of temporal processes involved in industrialisation and the development of capitalism. Here the major group considered is usually that of wage earners working under the new relations of production. These are disproportionately men, even now. But it is not only the focus which is the problem, for we could simply say that we should merely add on an adjective, male, to restrict the scope of the analysis to one half of society and the description would become accurate. It is more that the experiences of time for women, especially those women for whom child birth and child care are central to the organisation of their lives, are erased by their neglect and with it vital parts of a society's functioning. For many women the key life events have included courtship, marriage, child birth, child care, marriage of children, death. Their work is not organised by the clock, though it has rhythms of its own. The problem in the focus on male workers is the false general-isation from men to the whole society and false assumptions of societal homogeneity in the experience of time. There was not a homogeneous transformation of society from the rhythm of seasonal agriculture to that of the factory and the clock, but rather a coexistence of disparate percep-tions of time, of complex relations between different priorities, rhythms and time scales, and the development of tension and strain between competing ways of ordering and living lives. There are remaining questions of the relation between these different time orders, whether these are harmonious or conflictual, and the circumstances in which one may come to dominate the other.

The issue of time in the analysis of change and diversity of gender relations is addressed in this book in four ways. First, there are major macro-structural changes in the form of patriarchy, in the nature of the gender regime. Second, there is the significance of the intersection of time and space, demonstrated by an analysis of rounds of restructuring of gender relations in employment in spatially specific arenas. Third, there is the question of the significance of the life cycle, where the analysis assesses the balance of importance of life cycle and structural changes on aspects of women's employment and commitment to work in a defined spatial area, addressed especially in Chapter 6, 'Labour markets and industrial structures in women's working lives'. Fourth, there is the intersection of different forms of time, and the different ways that past time impacts on the present. This pushes the consideration of time for gender beyond conventional issues of biography and structural change, and draws attention to the ways in which the past affects the present through the experience of prior patterns of social relations.

The first issue is that of how to conceptualise macro-changes in gender relations. In *Theorising Patriarchy* I differentiated two major forms of patriarchy – private and public – and gave an explanation of the change from private to public in Britain in the twentieth century in terms of the turn-of-the-century feminist movement which won political citizenship for women in the context of an expanding demand for labour. This is a theme which is further developed throughout this book.

Second, there is analysis of the sedimentation of structural change in spatially specific institutional practices. This is conceptualised within the notion of 'rounds of gender restructuring'. This work is concerned not only with change, but with the way that change depends upon previous rounds of restructuring, so that layer upon layer of change is built up. The spatial specificity of such layering of change is important here; a new round of restructuring which appears to have structural similarities will have different outcomes if it is built upon a different foundation. Locality differences can have an impact on the next round of restructuring. The work on the restructuring of employment draws on and develops work done with the Lancaster Regionalism Group and in particular with Paul Bagguley, work which was influenced by Doreen Massey (Bagguley *et al.*, 1990; Lancaster Regionalism Group 1985; Massey, 1984; Walby, 1985, 1986b). In this book the analysis of rounds of restructuring is addressed in chapters on local labour markets and locality-specific forms of occupational segregation. The grounding of the intersection of time and space for gender relations in employment is captured through these analyses of spatially variant patterns of occupational segregation and levels of women's participation in paid work.

Third is the issue of the extent and significance of the life cycle in understanding the patterns of women's and men's lives. The conventional way to analyse women's lives is to focus on life events, such as marriage and child care. However, while these events are clearly of importance, their significance today can be overstated in comparison with other more structural changes. Indeed there is a gender asymmetry here in that while men's lives are often analysed in terms of current social structures, women's are analysed in terms of the impact of a sequence of life events such as marriage, child bearing and child rearing. For men a 'job model' is used while for women there is a 'gender model'.

In Chapter 6, 'Labour markets and industrial structures in women's working lives', the relative significance of labour market structures and life events are explored using two data sets: one a longitudinal study of women's work and life histories in a travel-to-work area; the second, data on changes in the occupational and industrial structures of the same travel-to-work area. By combining both sorts of data it was possible to disentangle and assess the different impacts of life events and of structural change in determining the outcome of aspects of women's current patterns and attachments to employment. This study aimed to assess the extent of women's commitment to specific occupational and industrial niches, despite the disruption caused by leaving the labour market for periods of caring for others. Women remain committed to the occupations and industries of their initial work placements over a life time, especially if they are presented with a choice of full- or part-time working; the new service jobs are largely filled by new entrants to the labour market. This means that direct personal experience of deindustrialisation, of the structural shift from manufacturing to service type employment, is not as great as would be expected from cross-sectional analysis of the changes in the aggregate data on structural change.

A fourth focus on the significance of time for gender relations is that provided by the intersection of structural and biographical change. In this wider approach the question is over the way in which prior events impact upon current events via personal biography in the context of structural change. Here the social medium through which the past connects to the present is not social institutions (as in the second instance), but rather individual biographies. The choices that people make early in their lives affect the range of choices open to them later. This is particularly important for women who early in their lives make crucial life course decisions. For women key decisions as to whether to gain educational qualifications, to marry or not, have children or not, stay in employment or take a break to care, have irrevocable consequences for the rest of their lives and the choices open to them in the future. Even if women appear to face the same opportunity structure now, their realistic range of options is different, depending upon their earlier decisions which set a trajectory which is very hard to change (see Chapter 2).

These life course decisions intersect with structural change in the gender regime. There have been very significant structural changes in gender relations over the twentieth century in most Western societies, with moves from private to public patriarchy. This means that the form of patriarchal relations around which women take crucial life decisions is different now from what it was a few decades ago. Women today will decide on the balance of commitment to education and employment on the one hand and caring and dependence on the other under quite different patterns of gendered opportunities than women of previous age cohorts. Older women will have made these life decisions under a gender regime more private, more domestic, than the more public system of today. Yet once these decisions are made they are hard to undo, a woman's life trajectory is set accordingly, with only very limited room for manoeuvre later. Thus women who face ostensibly similar gendered opportunity structures do so from quite different situations based significantly on age cohorts (as well as obvious differences due to class and ethnicity). Their options and decisions are thus quite different. Women who have adapted their lives to a system of private patriarchy, a domestic gender regime, have a different set of resources and vulnerabilities as compared with those who have grown up in the new forms of more public patriarchy, a more public gendered regime. They will have different values and moralities, different political agendas and priorities.

Women who have built their lives around an experience and expectation of a domestic gender regime are particularly disadvantaged as those structures change to a more public form. For instance, expectations of support for life from a husband were more realistic historically than they are today with the vastly increased divorce rates. Younger women today build their lives around the opportunities and limits of a public gender regime, preparing themselves for a lifetime of paid employment with education and training, delaying or rejecting child birth and marriage. Middle-aged women, who did not gain educational qualifications or labour market experience, who had children and husbands early in life, now face a situation in which they are expected to enter the labour market to support themselves either fully or partially, and find themselves disadvantaged not only as compared with men of their own age, but also with younger women.

Private patriarchy, the domestic gender regime, lives on in the biographies and memories of older women, even as they struggle to live under the current structures of public patriarchy, a public gender regime. The two systems in some sense coexist, one as traces in older women's biographies, the other as current structures.

Age and generation are important then not only in representing different stages of the life cycle, but because people of different ages embody different systems of patriarchy, different gender regimes. Their life trajectories are structured by the different systems. They bring to the present traces of different pasts. It is these different histories, not merely different ages, which are of interest here.

Most of the examples in this section have addressed issues relating to employment and to the relationship of employment to caring in the household. However, many of the issues involved in the layering of time and its embodiment in both biographies and institutions apply also to political institutions. These are explored in chapters on politics, citizenship and nation in the latter part of the book. Here we see the significance of the steady building of women's participation in the public sphere of the state and national politics after the initial impetus and dramatic change brought about by first-wave feminism. There has been a steady spiral of effects in which women's greater public participation in one arena leads to greater public participation in another, linking in particular, the state and employment, over the course of the century. We have not yet seen the end of this spiral of changes. The past affects the present not only as a result of the concatenation of events, not only as a result of the rounds of restructuring of social institutions, but also through traces in individual biographies.

THE GENDERED ECONOMY

Changes in gender relations are central to recent changes in the economy and society. Patterns of inequality and inefficiency in the economy are centrally linked to gender relations. While women are almost as likely to be employed as men, in that they are almost half of employees in employment, they do not receive proportionate benefits, such as pay and pensions, nor have the same levels of job security, nor access to such skilled work. The lack of effective utilisation of women's potential in the market economy reduces the efficiency of the economy and society as a whole. Access to decent labour is fundamental to processes of social inclusion in contemporary Western societies such as the UK.

Women's skills and labour are wasted more than those of men, under-utilised in terms of levels of skill and range of occupations. Under-employment is a chronic disabling feature of many Western economies, that of women being a particularly extreme example. The patterns of inequality which derive from this sexual division of labour have extensive repercussions for both women and men. They contribute to the exertion of power by men over women – in the home, by facilitating violence by men against women and children, and in the polity, where women's voices and interests are underrepresented. In the UK they are deleterious to men because the position of women as vulnerable employees facilitates the development of casualisation and flexibilisation of employment, undermining the position of workers as a whole, and contributing to a cheap labour economic strategy, rather than one based on high skill, high productivity and high wages. Patriarchal relations are inimical to a stakeholder society.

The conditions under which women labour are significantly shaped by the polity, particularly as a result of labour market regulation. These include policies for gender equity and welfare policies which affect women's capacity to combine work and family life effectively. The former reduce the exclusion of women from employment and training, and mitigate the tendency for women's wages to reflect their skill and work contribution insufficiently. The latter policies facilitate the combination of paid work and caring for children and the elderly by women (and men).

The extent to which these policies have been developed depends significantly upon the effective representation of women's interests in political decision making, a process which usually requires their actual political inclusion. Women's acquisition of political citizenship, while formally available after first-wave feminism won the vote for women, is not yet a practical reality for all women. Indeed there is a question as to whether women are able to acquire the full range of citizenship rights while some, especially older women, are positioned more in the domestic sector of society than men.

The economy is structured by political institutions, especially the national state, and increasingly that of the emergent European supra-state. The polity is important in the determination of the trajectory of the economy as a whole. The contrast between the economies of the UK and neighbouring states highlights the importance of politics. The final chapter in this book discusses the increasing importance of the European Union in the regulation of labour markets, and hence of gender relations in the UK.

The traditional view has been that class shapes gender (e.g. Goldthorpe, 1983). I am arguing that in the UK gender shapes class as much as class shapes gender; that gender inequality leads to economic inefficiency; and that the gendered polity impacts on the economy. The divisions in society caused by gender lead to the intensification of other forms of inequality. It is not only that class affects gender, but that the nature of gender inequality exacerbates class and other forms of inequality. This can be seen most clearly in employment, where the increasing utilisation of women as part-time 'flexible' workers, undermines the conditions of employment for all workers. This structured preference leads to an inefficient economy with low levels of capital investment as employers prefer to utilise cheap labour rather than invest in equipment which uses less labour time. That women choose to work part-time rather than full-time, despite the limited and poor nature of much of such employment is at least partly due to the limitation of public child care provision in the UK and to the restricted range of occupations in which part-time work is available.

In these ways the skills of women and other workers are wasted. The UK has a cheap labour economic policy as compared with the high-wage high-skill high-productivity economic policies of comparable nations in the European Union.

THE POLITY AND THE ECONOMY

Gender relations impact on the economy as a whole, and thus on class structure. One of the ways that this impact can be seen is in strategies of flexibilisation and casualisation which increase class inequality. Flexibility depends upon the availability of workers to take flexibilised jobs, and, in the UK in particular, these are disproportionately women. Women, and the forms of employment typically taken by women, have traditionally been outside of the protections developed by the labour movement both within the workplace and by state-enforced regulations. The weakness of women's position, which derives from such patriarchal practices, means that women are easier to employ as cheap labour. In a context where women are being increasingly employed and where there is also high unemployment this leads to a reduction in the terms and conditions and wages for all workers. Women are weaker because they have often been outside the protection of the male-dominated labour movement, which operated both in trade unions and the state (although this has significantly changed in recent years). The lack of representation of women's interests in these organisations was an important factor in facilitating women's disadvantage. If women had been effectively represented in the polity, in the state and major organisations, then it is less likely that such divisions would have occurred. Hence the connection between the gendered nature of the polity and the nature of the economy.

The details of this argument are elucidated in several chapters in this book, following on from those in *Patriarchy at Work*, where they were first developed. In *Patriarchy at Work* the changing representation of gender and class interests in trade unions, the labour movement and the state at both local and national levels constituted a major part of the explanation of the different and changing patterns of occupational and industrial segregation in cotton textiles, engineering and clerical work in nineteenth- and twentieth-century Britain.

The gendered nature of flexible work is the focus of Chapter 3, 'Flexibility and the changing sexual division of labour'. Flexibility is gendered, even though the traditional interpretation of the development of and impact of flexibility has been gender free (NEDO, 1986). One of the major forms of gendered flexible working practices is that of the division between part-time and full-time work. The poorer conditions of work which have traditionally been associated with part-time work, have led to it being highly attractive to employers. Women have taken part-time work because it fits with domestic responsibilities, in the absence of organised child and elder care. It is this combination of interests by women and employers that is important in understanding the growth of part-time employment. Only recently, under the impact of the European Union, have there been major attempts to regulate this work in the same manner as full-time work so that workers receive the same rights and benefits.

The significance of part-time work in the restructuring of the UK economy in labour markets is demonstrated in Chapter 4, 'Localities and gender restructuring'. The rise of part-time workers was greatest in local economies which were the most rapidly declining and those which were the most rapidly growing. Part-timers are not a reserve of labour to be used only when full-time male workers are not available, but are often a preferred option by employers in situations of economic restructuring either up or down. The workers so employed are not only cheaper to employ, but flexible in terms of working hours to suit peak demand. Previous attempts to analyse this phenomenon too quickly tend to interpret gendered patterns of employment as resulting from class relations. Such local variations in restructuring cannot be understood outside of the gendered nature of this work and the conditions in the household which make women available and willing to take such part-time work.

The new feminist literature on the relationship between gender and class is too cautious. The traditional view of the relation between gender and class was that class structures or encompasses gender – since a woman's class position was determined by that of her husband (e.g. Goldthorpe, 1983). However, the critique and rejection of this position is now the dominant understanding (Crompton and Mann, 1986; Marshall *et al.*, 1988; Stanworth, 1984), together with the view that gender and class are interconnected, though situationally specific, rather than theoretically derivable, or structural, ways (Abbott and Wallace, 1990; Afshar and Maynard, 1994). It is important to retain the notion of causal impact of gender and class as social phenomena, rather than adopt a view of interconnection as so complex that causation is irrelevant. Hence my argument that gender and class are mutually causative, and that the form and degree of gender inequality is important in structuring class relations.

Gender relations have an impact on national levels of economic performance. There are two major models of economic performance in contemporary Europe: the stakeholder model and the deregulation model. In the stakeholder version a wide range of groups is seen as having a legitimate interest in the running of economic institutions, not only management and shareholders, but also workers, customers, the local community and others affected – and thus a thick network of representation and negotiation of groups is seen as important in maintaining a stable long-term interest in economic development (Bornschier and Fielder, 1995; Hutton, 1995; Marquand, 1988; Streeck, 1992). In the deregulation model an economy is seen to thrive if competition is encouraged and barriers to free markets removed (European Commission, 1993).

The UK has predominantly followed a deregulation route to economic development since 1979. This itself depends upon the availability of women as cheap, casualised, flexible workers. This results partly from the historical (rather than contemporary) exclusion of women and part-timers from trade union and labour movement protection, both in terms of being organised in the workplace, and in the law. This is an issue of politics and organisation (Walby, 1986b). This policy of economic growth through deregulation and the use of high levels of unemployment to contain inflation creates polarisation and facilitates the development of an 'underclass' of unemployed men.

These processes occur in the context of national government policy to deregulate the labour market in order to increase competitiveness in the context of fierce international competition as a result of globalisation. The general contexts of deregulation and globalisation are highly significant. Other economic and political responses to the challenge of globalisation are possible, as Hutton (1995) has argued and as the social policy of the European Union demonstrates (European Commission, 1994a). The combination of gender restructuring, deregulation and globalisation are transforming the UK economy, and indeed many other Western economies. The outcomes of high unemployment and greater casualisation are not inevitably given from the economic structures, but are altered by political and cultural processes. Economic processes are politically and discursively constructed. Markets are not naturally given but socially constructed and regulated. An example of the discursive construction of the economy can be seen in an analysis of the role of the state in constructing the labour market. This occurs through the direct regulation of appropriate terms and conditions for employment, for instance the recent changes which have reduced the difference in the legal regulation of part-time and full-time work – as a result of the application of EU law in the UK, minimum rates of pay through wages councils or a statutory minimum wage. The labour market is also constructed indirectly, through the regulation of workplace conflict – for instance over the right to organise in trade unions, regulation of picketing, the nature of the legal bodies which try cases such as industrial tribunals. The legal regulation of workplace conflict is extremely important in shaping the outcome of workplace conflicts of interest, for example in determining whether there is a legal right to equity in a particular situation. In this way the state and political struggle plays a vital role in the structuring of workplace social relations and skill. This political arena is inherently conducted through contestation over meaning and through discourse.

In this analysis of gender relations there is a presumption that it is necessary to consider the discursive and political construction of social institutions. A structural analysis need not be structuralist. Political projects are constructed on the basis of current ideas as well as material interests. They usually presume a unit to which they apply, often but not always the nation state, and thus gendered political projects are connected to a wider set of political projects. The long-standing opposition between the 'new' culturalist, postmodernist and poststructuralist view of the world versus the 'old' materialist, modernist structuralist view of the world is rejected here.

POLITICS

Many of the contemporary debates about the economy – for instance, 'stakeholder' versus 'deregulation' strategies – are thus about the proper extent to which the state and other forms of social organisation should be involved in the institutions running the economy. The social relations within these bodies are highly relevant to our understanding of their decision making.

The nature of the polity is very important in the structuring of the economy, and the social relations in employment in particular. In political theory women's interventions are often seen as exceptional, whether as individual politicians or as occasional social movements. Historically however, feminist movements have made a major impact, with turn-of-the-century feminism winning political citizenship for women. These themes are explored in Chapter 7, 'Gender politics and social theory'.

The winning of political citizenship was a major turning point in the nature of gender relations, being crucial for the entry of women into the public sphere, and the reduction in the degree of domestication of women. After women won the vote it was no longer possible for men to use the state to support exclusionary strategies against women at work (Walby, 1986b), and exclusionary practices elsewhere were slowly reduced. After the Victorian era where the domestication of women by confining them to the home was practised whenever financially possible, there was a slow rise in the number of women in paid employment and elsewhere in the public sphere. What did the vote bring? It meant no implementation of legislation restricting women's employment. Despite male demands for a marriage bar during the unemployment of the 1930s and its occurrence in particular industries there was no legislation for one. It brought change in the regulation of divorce and separation so as to make it easier for women to leave marriages which made them unhappy. In the 1960s it brought the decriminalisation of abortion and effective access to contraception. The vote given to women across Europe meant that the Common Market/European Union enshrined equity for women in its founding Treaty of Rome. This treaty led to the Equal Pay Act (1970), the Sex Discrimination Act (1975) and the Equal Value Amendment (1984).

In analysing gender politics it is important to see men as actors as well as women, and to recognise the diversity of practices through which women and men believe they are pursuing their own best interests. A new direction in theorising has been to give greater attention to men's agency (see *Patriarchy at Work*, and Chapter 7 in this volume). Men have historically divided the workforce in pursuit of sectional interests since trade unions often used to prioritise the interests of men. Women have resisted this and contested the form of organisation which has been used for this.

In 'Gender politics and social theory' (Chapter 7) I argue that the analysis of gender politics has long underestimated the significance of men's actions in gender politics. Most theories of gender politics have considered only two options: women are passive; women have struggled around their own interests in particular circumstances. These neglect the opposition to women's struggles to organise around their own interests and to take these interests forward. This opposition is crucial in understanding both the form of women's politics and the limits to their success. This opposition has come largely, but not entirely, from men. Indeed historically, it came from a state from which women were almost entirely excluded, as well as from organised and individual men.

Historically, male political actors have often, but not always, been opposed to women's emancipation. Chapter 8 on 'Backlash' examines some of the specificities of men's opposition to some forms of feminist politics. While opposition to the improvement in women's position in society sometimes takes the form of attempting to push women back into the home, this is not always the case. For instance, Faludi's analysis of such politics in the US in the 1980s should not be transposed to the UK context, where Thatcherism represented a strategy of public rather than private patriarchy (see Faludi 1991, 1992).

Gender politics are often entwined with class projects, thus creating further specificities. For instance, in *Patriarchy at Work*, I showed not only the importance of the opposition of male workers to women's advancement of their interests at work, but also the importance of understanding the balance of class and gender forces intersecting in different place and times. A non-economistic understanding of the economy requires an analysis of politics, organisation, culture and the state. This was the basis of the explanation of the varying patterns of occupational segregation by sex in that text.

Indeed gender politics are almost always situated in relation to other forms of politics. 'Woman and nation', Chapter 10, explores the relationship between national projects and gender politics. National and ethnic projects are always implicitly, if not explicitly gendered, in that they have a model of appropriate womanhood and manhood, which they carry as part of their ideal identity as a nation or ethnic group. Gender politics have to presume some kind of boundary to their project, whether of a local community, ethnic group, nation state or the world. Women have often appeared to be more local, more global and less national in their political agendas than men in Western Europe.

The nature of gender relations and gender politics at the moment of state formation or state restructuring is important in fixing a set of parameters within which state-level politics operate for a period. The nature of gender politics at crucial stages of the development of the European supra-state and its forms of citizenship is thus highly significant. Women were late on the political scene in terms of the formation of the UK state as compared with the establishment of the European supra-state. In the former, women did not have political citizenship when key aspects of the state and the party system were being formed, in the latter women did. This is, perhaps, a factor in the founding agreement of the European Union, The Treaty of Rome (1957), having an article declaring that men and women should have equal treatment. This has been very important in underpinning attempts to provide equal opportunities for women and men in the labour market.

Women's positioning within the change from a domestic to a public gender regime affects their location both in the class structure and also in different gender projects. Differences in the possession of labour market skills are facilitated by different histories within domestic and public gender regimes, positioning women in different occupations and class locations. Further, their location in domestic or public gender regimes affects women's political attitudes towards the politics of the family.

Forms of gender regime vary across time and space, culture and ethnicity, age and generation. Further, these changes in the gender regime occur unevenly across these differences. They generate different forms of politics, of perception of group interests, which further affect the nature of these changes. Older women in the UK are more likely to vote Conservative than men, while younger women are more likely than younger men to vote Labour (Lovenduski, 1995). Gender and generation affect political parties traditionally thought to be based on class divisions. In this way the gendered polity again affects the class and economic structure.

CITIZENSHIP

But can women be full citizens unless they become as public in the way they live their lives as men? Can they be effective stakeholders without full orientation to the market economy? Is the very notion of citizenship gendered (see Chapter 9, 'Is citizenship gendered?')? It is conventional to follow T. H. Marshall (1950) and distinguish three forms of citizenship: civil, political and social. While the provision of these rights does not appear to require employment, in practice in contemporary society it is difficult to acquire sufficient income to achieve social citizenship without a full employment record, since so many benefits are dependent upon it. In this way a domestic orientation by women is incompatible with full citizenship in current forms of social organisation. Either the routes to effective citizenship need to be more plural, or women have to acquire the same employment status as men. The current changes in the sexual division of labour, with the increase in women's educational qualifications and employment, suggest that younger women at least are more able to reach citizenship via the public route. Age is becoming a critical divide among women, since older women without such qualifications or work history are disadvantaged via the public route to citizenship, and derived rights from husbands become more tenuous as the stability of marriage declines. The change in the form of gender regime thus positions younger women more effectively in terms of citizenship than older women who were brought up with a different gendered opportunity structure.

EUROPE

A new dimension to politics, especially in the UK, is provided by the increasing economic and political integration of the European Union. This is potentially of enormous significance to the restructuring of gender and other social relations in the UK, as well as the rest of the European Union, with the potential to affect employment, markets and fiscal regimes. The social and economic policy assumptions underlying these interventions are crucial for the shape of social relations in Europe.

The 'social dimension' of the European Union may be variously regarded as central to this European project, or as a marginal extra to the creation of a single European market (European Commission 1993; European Commission, 1994a; Ziltener and Bornschier, 1995). Nevertheless, the forms of regulation of employment and the equal treatment of women and men in employment, have a clear impact even in the UK, despite the attempt by the UK government to opt out of the Social Chapter of the Maastricht Treaty.

EU policies on equal treatment of women and men, legally underpinned by Article 119 of the founding treaty of the European Union, the Treaty of Rome in 1957, have been important in pushing forward equal opportunities legislation and its implementation in all Member States. For instance, some of the differentiation of the conditions of full- and part-time workers in the UK have been changed as a result of an appeal to European law. Before 1995 those working between eight and sixteen hours had to work five years for an employer in order to gain major employment rights, rather than two years as was the case for those who worked over sixteen hours, while those working less than eight hours did not qualify at all. Employment protection rights from which part-timers have previously been barred include, among others: the right to complain of unfair dismissal; the right to statutory redundancy pay; the right to return to work after maternity leave; the right to a written statement of employment particulars. The European courts and the House of Lords have recently ruled that such differential treatment of workers on the grounds of hours is unlawful because it is discriminatory against women since it is women who are more likely to work shorter hours. Following the defeat of the government in the House of Lords in *R* v *Secretary of State for Employment ex parte Equal Opportunities Commission and another* in 1994, the government was obliged to issue new regulations in February 1995 to remove hours-of-work thresholds from all employment protection legislation in order to remove this unlawful discriminatory treatment of part-time – largely women – workers (*Employment Gazette*, Feb. 1995: 43).

This significant increase in the legal rights of part-time women workers was part of a cluster of changes which has occurred because European law takes precedence over UK law, even that actively supported by the government. The extent to which these European legal concerns with equal treatment may be implemented in the UK is crucial for the future pattern of gender relations in employment. The limitations to the process include that of the balance of political forces in both the UK and the European Union; the development of legal instruments to implement EU concerns in Member States (European Commission, 1994b); and the amenability of a system of labour market governance to centralised legal interventions, in particular, whether the move to a post-Fordist regime limits the impact of such Fordist legal and bureaucratic instruments.

Many employer-based equal opportunities polices depend upon a bureaucratic set of practices for their implementation, which may be less prevalent in a more post-Fordist economic system. They are explored in Chapter 11, 'Gender and European Union integration: towards a political economy of gender'. Further, new policies for deregulation and increased competitiveness may tend to increase hierarchies, probably to the disadvantage of the more vulnerable workers. These concerns illustrate again the significance of the polity for the economy, and the integral nature of gender relations to political economy.

2

RECENT CHANGES IN GENDER RELATIONS IN EMPLOYMENT

INTRODUCTION

The implications of the increase in women's paid employment are potentially massive, but they need to be qualified in relation to new divisions between women based on age, as well as the traditional ones such as those based on class and ethnicity. This increase in paid employment is connected to political, legal and organisational changes in gender relations; the declining significance of domestic activities for women's employment; and the rise in the educational achievements of girls and women. These changes are part of the process of change in the form of gender regime from domestic to public.

That women actively balance their time between household production and paid employment (and leisure) is recognised by theorists from neoclassical economics to radical feminism (see the excellent survey by Folbre, 1994). But the relative significance of household structures and practices, of human capital skills, qualifications and experience, of direct and indirect sex discrimination and of occupational and industrial segregation in determining the exact balance are still controversial. This chapter argues that the recent changes in the employment position of diverse groups of women show the importance of:

- reduced discrimination consequent upon the passing of equal opportunities legislation and introduction of equal opportunities polices by employers and unions since the 1970s;
- the increase in younger women's human capital as a result of increased educational achievements since the 1970s;
- the declining significance of domestic activities for some women, especially younger women in top jobs.

The entry of women into the public sphere is most marked in the areas of employment and education, where there has been both a considerable increase in women's presence and major changes in the patterns of inequality. Women's participation in paid employment has not only risen significantly, but some women, especially those who are younger and well qualified have gained greater entry to the higher skilled and better paid occupations. The wages gap has slowly been reduced for full-time workers, though not for part-timers. Girls at school now achieve more exam passes than boys and participate in similar numbers in undergraduate degree programmes in universities. However, there are continuing and new patterns of poverty and inequality, especially for those who do not effectively participate in the labour market, for instance, lone mothers and older women who build their lives around caring rather than paid employment. It is in the areas of education and employment that we find both the leading edge of the shift from the domestic to the public gender regime, and increased inequality between women.

There are major debates as to whether increased employment significantly impacts on the position of women in society and whether it reduces gender inequality. The United Nations Development Project takes the strong position that the impact of paid employment is both large and positive for women, in that it increases women's capacities and potentials (UNDP, 1992). In its gender sensitive index of human development, the UNDP regards the extent of women's employment and their level of pay relative to men together as one of three major indicators of the position of women (the others being education and longevity). This ambitious and authoritative attempt at the creation of a universal index of human development draws on the work of Sen (1984, 1985) in its view that paid employment is crucial in creating the capacity for women to fulfil their potential.

However, there are arguments that increases in women's paid employment may be merely an extra burden for women, or at least not particularly important for reducing gender inequality. For instance, it has been argued that employment is not the most important area of women's lives, for example, that violence, sexuality and culture are more important sources of inequality (Dworkin, 1981; MacKinnon, 1989); that more paid employment may not lead to greater power for women, especially for women who are working class or from ethnic minorities who only have opportunities to gain relatively poor forms of employment, or are not able to control the product of their work (hooks, 1984); that women's proportion of the total hours worked in the economy (as opposed to jobs held) has not increased significantly (Hakim, 1993a, 1995); and that the changes are not important because women are still segregated from men in poorly paid, insecure work in a narrow range of occupations and, in particular, in part-time work, or do not significantly reduce inequality in other areas of gender relations (Arber and Ginn, 1995).

A middle view is that the impact of work on women's position in society and whether it is a benefit or a burden depends very much on its social context (Boserup, 1970; Elson and Pearson, 1981; Rogers, 1980; Tinker

1990). Further, ethnic diversity and class inequality mediate the impact of employment on gender relations, so that while employment may be a viable route for emancipation for more privileged women, this may not apply to Black and working-class women for whom employment is frequently poorly paid and tedious as compared with the alternative of motherhood (hooks, 1984), hooks further argues that while the family may be a major site of oppression for White women, there should be no generalisation to Black American women for whom the family is also a site of resistance and solidarity against racism. However, there are differences between ethnic minorities, for instance, in the context of South Asian women in Britain, Bhopal (1996) argues that education and employment do play an important role in enhancing the choices of some young ethnic minority women.

The balance that women choose between household production and paid work is affected by the relative amounts of skill and work experience that they bring to the job market. The analysis of the structures and practices which restrict women's access to such skills and employment experience has a long history, from turn-of-the-century materialist feminism (Gilman, 1898; Hamilton, 1909; Schreiner, 1911), through interwar analysis of segregation (Anthony, 1932), to the Chicago 'home economics' (see Folbre 1994 on Reid, 1934 and Kyrk, 1933) and, arguably, to both the neoclassical economic human capital theory of the 'New Home Economics' (Becker, 1965, 1981; Bourke, 1993) and feminist dual-systems theory (Hartmann, 1976). These materialist approaches share a common concern both with housework as work which is an alternative source of livelihood to paid work and the analysis of the relationship between them. They diverge over whether analytic priority should be given to women's choices (or agency?) or to the constraints which structure those choices.

The 'New Home Economics' is linked to Becker's human capital theory (Becker, 1965, 1981). This school argues that women and men choose to allocate their time between paid work, housework and leisure, according to the balance of reward from each (see Bourke, 1993). If women have more human capital – skills, qualifications, labour market experience – then they will be paid more and thus be more likely to be in employment than in the home. If women have husbands who earn a lot this depresses the likelihood of working themselves. Thus there is a dynamic equilibrium, or balance, between women's involvement in housework and child care on the one hand and employment on the other.

The criticism of this economic approach – that markets are not so pure as to give wage rates which depend on human capital, since they are riddled with power and discriminatory practices – can be at least partially incorporated into the more sophisticated versions of this thesis by regarding it as an extra factor depressing women's wages (e.g. Jones and Makepeace, 1996). This literature addresses the question of the extent to which varying amounts of human capital explain the wages gap between women and men (Jones and Makepeace, 1996; Mincer, 1962; Mincer and Polachek, 1974; Treiman and Hartmann, 1981; Wright and Ermisch, 1991), changes in women's employment (Mincer, 1962, 1966) or fertility rates (Bongaarts, 1993; Ermisch, 1981, 1983; Kravdal, 1994). In some studies the question of the impact of state policies on these processes is a major focus, including analysis of the impact of state benefits (Ermisch and Ogawo, 1994), and family planning programmes (Berelson, 1975; Bongaarts, 1993).

The more sociological and institutional strand has focused on the constraints within which women make their choices, including occupational segregation by sex (Bagguley, 1991; Hartmann, 1976; Reskin and Hartmann, 1986; Reskin and Roos, 1990; *Social Europe*, 1993; Witz, 1992); industrial relations and collective bargaining practices (Danielli, 1994); the division between full-time and part-time work (Hutton, 1994; Robinson, 1988); sexual practices (Adkins, 1995) – including sexual harassment (Stanko, 1988) and grounded cultural resistance by men (Cockburn, 1983, 1991) – racism (Brah and Shaw, 1992; Dex, 1983); transnational corporations (Mitter, 1986); lack of effective implementation of equal opportunities laws (Gregory, 1987); and lack of equal training opportunities (Rees, 1992).

In the more sophisticated versions of both approaches the focus on the relationship between two major elements – housework and paid work – is always in the context of wider social factors. The specification of these contexts becomes crucial to the analysis. Under what circumstances in a Western economy does employment have what kind of impact on which women?

Rather than seeing the rational choice type theory of Becker's human capital approach as irredeemably opposed to that of analysis of structural and institutional constraints, I view them as complementary but partial angles on the same question. Women make choices, but not under conditions of their own making. Women choose the best option that they can see, rationally, though usually with imperfect knowledge, but only within the range of options open to them. The decision as to whether to spend more time on the home or more time on paid work is a rational choice. But those choices cannot be understood outside of an understanding of the development of the institutions and structures which construct those options. For instance, if there is a marriage bar, then married women cannot choose to work, and rational choice theory is not very helpful in explaining the existence of a marriage bar. At this point we need to turn to more institutional and structural types of analysis. Likewise, if there is an institutional pattern of sex segregation in employment, then 'choices' will be constrained. Further, if women wish to work part-time in order to have time for activities in the home, then they are faced with a set of jobs which are on average paid less, and more restricted in occupational range than full-time jobs. But to explain the low pay of the part-time worker as a result of the

25

choice of the individual woman misses the point that the structure of job opportunities within which the woman makes a choice is also explained at an institutional and structural level.

The focus in this chapter is on the nature of the changes in the structure of job opportunities available for women. I shall argue that there have been major increases in women's employment and that these are significant for some women in reducing the gender gap in earnings and other rewards, but that these changes have occurred very variably among different groups of women. There has been a restructuring of the forms of work available in ways which are specifically gendered, such as the division between full-time and part-time work and sex segregation in occupations and industries. There are major changes in the relationship between household commitments and employment, with child care and other domestic tasks having less impact on women's participation rates than previously. There have also been changes in men's patterns of economic activity, with significantly declining rates of economic activity especially among older men.

There is considerable diversity by age, class, region, household position and ethnicity. Some women live their lives within a more private gender regime, others more public. First, there are major differences in the extent and level of economic activity according to educational qualifications. These qualifications are increasingly obtained by younger people and especially by girls and young women. Second, there are significant age differences in that it is largely younger women who have gained educational qualifications, who are entering higher level jobs, while older women are typically confined to the less remunerated and less secure part-time jobs. Third, it is women in the higher socio-economic groups who have most increased their rate of economic activity. Fourth, women's employment is unevenly distributed across localities and regions, often in ways connected with occupational and industrial segregation. Fifth, women in certain household positions, lone mothers and women married to unemployed men, have low employment rates as a result of complex interactions between household structures and the income support system, and others, such as women without children, have higher rates. Sixth, there is considerable diversity and inequality between ethnic groups. Thus statements about changes in the lives of 'women' almost always need to be qualified by reference to specific groups of women. It is women who are highly educated, in higher socio-economic groups, and are either single and child free or cohabit with an employed man, who have moved most rapidly away from a domestic gender regime towards a more public form of gender regime. Gender relations interact in complex ways with other forms of social differentiation and inequality, especially age, class, and ethnicity. There is in the UK today, as in most Western countries, the coexistence of gender regimes which vary significantly in the extent to which they are domestic or public.

GROWTH OF WOMEN'S PAID EMPLOYMENT

There has been a massive growth in the proportion of women who are in formal waged employment since the Second World War. There are now nearly as many women as men who are employees in employment – 49.6 per cent were women in 1995 – see Table 2.1. Since the 1950s women have moved from being around one-third to one-half of employees – see Table 2.1. Since 1966 there has been a simultaneous fall in the number of such men – see Table 2.1.

Table 2.1 Employees in employment, 1959–95

	1959	1966	1971	1981	1991	1995
Total	20983	22787	21648	21386	21719	21355
All male	13824	14551	13424	12278	11253	10777
All female	7159	8236	8224	9108	10467	10584
% female	34.1	36.1	38.0	42.6	48.2	49.6

Sources: Employment Gazette, Historical Supplement, Feb 1987: Table 1.1; August 1987: Table 1.1; March 1995: Table 1.1. 1991; *Labour Market Trends*, April 1996, Table 1.1. 1995. These are June, GB, and seasonally unadjusted. These statistics are based on the quarterly Employment Department survey of employers. They do not include the self-employed, those on government training programmes or in the armed forces. Unlike the EU Labour Force Survey, they are based on a count of jobs, not persons.

The changes are most marked among married women, whose economic activity rate has risen from 26 per cent in 1951 to 71 per cent in 1991. This is now little different from that of non-married women.

The longer run picture for the last century and a half is of a plateau in adult women's economic activity rates in the mid-nineteenth century of 42–3 per cent between 1851 and 1871, followed by a fall to a new plateau of 32 per cent between 1881 and 1921, thereafter rising to 53 per cent in 1991. If the focus is narrowed to women of working age, then the figures show a plateau of activity rates of 38 per cent during 1901–31, rising after the Second World War to 71 per cent in 1991, that is a steeper rise in recent years as a result of excluding women over working age. See Figure 2.1 and Table 2.2. This is a tremendous change in gender relations in paid employment. It suggests the possibility of rapid and substantial changes in the typical life experiences of women in this period. However, there are a series of caveats which place some qualifications on this picture including: the implications of the particular definition of work and employment used; that most of the increase is in part-time rather than full-time work; that there are significant patterns of difference and inequality between women.

The exact figure placed on women's increased participation in employment depends upon the particular definition of work and employment used. Statistics on employees in employment utilise a definition which shows

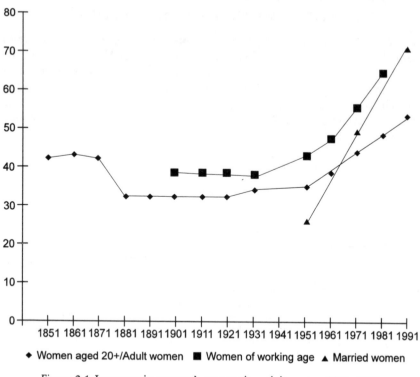

Figure 2.1 Increases in women's economic activity rates, 1851–1991

women to be closer to male rates than others, since those who are self-employed, in armed services or who are unemployed but seeking work are not included and these latter categories include disproportionately more men. For instance, while in September 1995 women were 45.8 per cent of the workforce in employment, they were only 24 per cent of the self-employed (calculated from *Labour Market Trends*, April 1996: Table 1.1). The figures for the economic activity rates also show a slightly lower proportion of women than for 'employees in employment', since these use a broad concept, for instance, including the unemployed who are actively seeking work. The economic activity rates of women of working age, 16–59, have risen from 51 per cent in 1975 to 73 per cent in 1993.

CHANGES IN MEN'S EMPLOYMENT

Convergence between the employment rates of women and men is further enhanced by the decline in men's rates of employment and economic activity. Men's economic activity rates (for men aged 16–64) have fallen from 93 per cent in 1973 to 86 per cent in 1993 (*General Household Survey*, 1993: 57). This is a significant decline over the last 20 years, especially in the

Table 2.2 Women's economic activity rates, 1851–1991

	Women aged 20+	Women of working age 15/16–59	Married women
1851	[42]		
1861	43		
1871	42		
1881	32		
1891	32		
	Adult women		
1901	32	[38]	
1911	32	38	
1921	32	38	
1931	34	38	
1941	–	–	
1951	35	43	[26]
1961	38	47	
1971	44	55	49
1981	48	64	
1991	53	71	71

Source: Derived from Hakim, 1993a: 99, 100, 102.
The data is largely derived from the Census for Great Britain for England and Wales. 1941–51 the figures are for those 'occupied'; since 1961 for those 'economically active'. Figures for 1851–71 exclude those whose sole occupation was unpaid housework, to ensure comparability.
Age to be adult:
1901, 1911 = 10+; 1921 = 12+; 1931 = 14+; 1951, 1961, 1971 = 15+; 1981, 1991 = 16+.

older age groups, over 50. Among older men non-employment is typically recorded as economic inactivity, rather than as unemployment – see Table 2.3 below. Rates of employment have also declined significantly in younger age groups under 24, partly due to increased numbers of students, and partly due to higher levels of unemployment.

These reductions in men's economic activity might mean that their lives become more similar to those of women. However, lack of employment typically has different consequences for men than for women. Among younger men unemployment is a factor which leads to greater criminal activity and the generation of aggressive and violent practices at odds with mainstream culture. While young women's crime rates are rising, they are very significantly lower than those for men. Men who are unemployed are less likely to marry and more likely to divorce than employed men.

Men's unemployment and economic activity has implications for women's rates of economic activity, often reducing these levels (OPCS, 1996b: Table 7.12). This is partly a result of the interaction with income support systems, since if and when the unemployed husband moves, after six months' unemployment, from the individual-based insurance benefit of job seekers' allowance to the household-based means-tested income

Table 2.3 Economic activity of men, by age, 1975–94

Age and economic activity	1975 %	1985 %	1994 %
16–17			
Working	62	56	46
Unemployed	7	13	15
Inactive	31	31	39
18–24			
Working	85	73	69
Unemployed	6	18	16
Inactive	9	9	16
25–34			
Working	95	88	84
Unemployed	3	10	9
Inactive	1	3	6
35–49			
Working	94	89	85
Unemployed	4	8	8
Inactive	2	3	6
50–59			
Working	93	77	73
Unemployed	3	9	7
Inactive	4	14	20
60–64			
Working	81	49	43
Unemployed	3	4	5
Inactive	16	47	51
Total 16+			
Working	79	68	64
Unemployed	3	8	8
Inactive	18	24	28

Source: OPCS, 1996b: Table 7.3a.

support, it is rarely worthwhile for the woman to work since she typically does not earn enough to match the benefit by herself. This pattern may also be partly due to preferred gender norms (Davies, Elias and Penn, 1994; Morris, 1990, 1994).

WAGE INEQUALITY

There has been a significant reduction in the wages gap between men and women working full-time between 1970 and 1995. The proportion of men's hourly wages earned by women rose from 63 per cent in 1970 to 80 per cent in 1995 (see Table 2.4). The inequality in weekly earnings has also reduced, however the gap is significantly wider here since weekly wages include the effect of men's longer working hours and various premia such as overtime.

Table 2.4 Women's and men's hourly earnings (full-time only), 1970–95

	1970	1974	1977	1981	1986	1991	1995
Full-time men	13.3	108	181	332	489	755	891
Full-time women	8.4	71	134	242	363	591	715
Full-time women as %							
of Full-time men	63	66	74	73	74	78	80

Source: calculated from *New Earnings Survey*, 1970, 1974, 1977, 1981, 1986, 1991, 1995.
Figures for adult workers including overtime, for those whose pay was not affected by absence.
Decimalisation of the currency occurred between 1970 and 1974.

Much of this narrowing of the gap can be attributed to the implementation of the Equal Pay Act, passed in 1970 but with a five-year implementation period, accounting for the fact that most of the narrowing (11 percentage points) took place in the seven years between 1970 and 1977, narrowing by only a further 6 percentage points in the following 18 years. The slow but steady improvement during the 1980s and 1990s is partly a result of further equal opportunities policies such as the tightening of the equal pay provisions, such as the Equal Value Amendment in 1984, and partly due to the rise in women's human capital consequent upon improvements in educational qualifications.

However, inequality of earnings between women and men remains as a significant feature of contemporary gender inequality. In particular, this narrowing of the wages gap is largely restricted to full-time workers.

PART-TIME WORK

Much of the narrowing of the differences and inequalities between women and men in employment has taken place among full-time workers only. There are very significant inequalities and differences between full-time and part-time work. For instance, part-time work is on average paid significantly less than full-time work, and typically has fewer fringe benefits. Since almost all the growth in women's employment in the post-war period has been in part-time work, this acts as a serious qualification to any picture of the improvement in the position of women as a result of changes in employment. The increase in women's full-time employment since 1971 has been very small (see Table 2.5 below).

The increase in full-time women workers from 1971 to 1995 is less than 200,000, a rise of only 3 per cent. During the same period the number of women working part-time has increased by over 2 million, that is 75 per cent, and as a percentage for total employment has risen from 13 per cent to

Table 2.5 Employees in employment, 1971–95 (thousands)

	1971	1981	1991	1995
Female	8224	9108	10467	10584
Full-time female	5467	5290	5764	5645
Part-time female	2757	3818	4703	4939
% Full-time female of all (M+F)	25	25	27	26
% Part-time female of female	34	42	45	47
% Part-time female of all	13	18	22	23

Sources: *Employment Gazette*, Historical Supplement, Feb 1987: Table 1.1; August 1987: Table 1.1; March 1995: Table 1.1. *Labour Force Trends*, April 1996: Table 1.1. 1991, 1994 are June, GB and seasonally unadjusted.

These statistics are based on the quarterly Employment Department survey of employers. They do not include the self-employed, those on government training programmes or in the armed forces. They are based on a count of jobs, not persons.

23 per cent. Women are now almost as likely to be working part-time as full-time, that is, 47 per cent.

Male part-time employment has been growing, but not on the same scale, rising to 11 per cent of male workers in 1994. Most of this is concentrated among young people, often students, and among older workers, while that among women is more widely spread among various age groups (Naylor, 1994).

The wages gap between women's part-time hourly rates and men's full-time hourly rates remains very large – see Table 2.6. Part-time women earned only 60 per cent of men's full-time hourly rates in 1995, and even this is an overestimate of part-time women's wages since the New Earnings Survey does not include the earnings of those beneath the PAYE tax threshold, which are estimated to involve around one-fifth of part-time workers (*New Earnings Survey*).

The gap between part-time women's earnings and the earnings of full-time men has not narrowed in the same way as that for full-time workers.

Table 2.6 Hourly earnings of full-time men and full-time and part-time women

	1974	1977	1981	1986	1991	1995
Full-time women as % of						
Full-time men	66	74	73	74	78	80
Part-time women as % of						
Full-time men	54	60	58	57	58	60
Part-time women as % of						
Full-time women	82	81	79	76	75	75

Source: calculated from the *New Earnings Survey* 1974, 1977, 1981, 1991, 1995. All hourly rates for adult workers whose pay was not affected by absence.

After a rise between 1974 and 1977 it has since then fluctuated between 57 per cent and 60 per cent. Perhaps more significantly, the hourly wage rate of part-time women workers has fallen as a proportion of full-time women's rates, that is, the average condition of full-time and part-time women workers with regard to pay has been diverging.

Part-time workers have been disadvantaged as compared with full-time workers on a variety of fringe benefits and employment rights. For instance, women who work part-time are significantly less likely to have a pension than full-time workers. Among men over 16 who worked full-time in 1993, 89 per cent were in a pension scheme (60 per cent occupational, 29 per cent personal), as compared with 77 per cent of women who worked full-time (54 per cent occupational, 22 per cent personal) and 32 per cent of women who worked part-time (19 per cent occupational, 12 per cent personal) (*General Household Survey*, 1993: 172).

Until February 1995, following a judgment by the House of Lords in the light of European rules, those who worked less than eight hours and those who worked between eight and sixteen hours who had not completed five years' service for their employer, were not eligible for a variety of employment protection rights available to full-time workers, including the right to complain of unfair dismissal, maternity leave, notice on dismissal, statutory redundancy pay (*Employment Gazette*, February 1995: 43).

The extent of part-time working among women means that the proportion of total working hours performed by women as compared with men has not risen as rapidly as the proportion of women holding jobs. If we were to have measured women's employment not in terms of jobs, but rather the percentage of total hours worked by men and women, then the picture of growth would significantly reduce. Indeed Hakim has argued on this basis that there has been no significant growth in women's employment (Hakim, 1993a, 1995), going so far as to suggest that 'Perhaps the most pervasive myth is the notion that there has been a substantial increase in female employment throughout this century, particularly since World War Two and among married women. ... The thesis is demonstrably untrue' (Hakim 1995: 430). Hakim (1993a) argues that the key question is not whether women are more likely to be in employment, but rather whether a higher proportion of the total hours worked are performed by women. Since most of the expansion of women's employment has been in part-time jobs the rise in hours worked by women as a whole is small and recent, unlike the rise in the total number of women in some form of employment. She argues that part-time working is unlike full-time employment, largely because such workers are less 'committed' to work and appear to be more similar to housewives in attitudes than full-time women workers. Hence her provocative notion that the rise in women's employment is a 'myth' – a notion based on her novel redefinition of employment in relation to part-time working.

However, there is a genuine question as to whether it is the proportion of total hours worked or the experience of some form of employment which is more important. For the purposes of understanding changing gender relations in people's lives and experiences, it is more important to focus on the experience of having a job. Part-time work should not be dismissed as something done by 'grateful slaves' who have little commitment to work (Hakim, 1991), but recognised as a distinctive form of employment with its own significance for the position of women in society and for the restructuring of employment relations for both women and men (see also Ginn *et al.*, 1996).

The division between part-time and full-time work is an important and growing form of segregation by sex in employment (Robinson, 1988). Not only is it regarded as an important form of flexibility by employers (NEDO, 1986), but most women part-time workers when asked, say that they prefer to work part-time rather than full-time, often to accommodate domestic commitments (Naylor, 1994). It is extremely important in differentiating the conditions and pay of different groups of women, with the pay and conditions of full-time workers being significantly better. Its growth has implications for the structuring of employment as a whole.

SEGREGATION

The segregation of women from men in employment is another factor which potentially limits the significance of the increase in women's employment for gender equity. Women are concentrated in a limited number of occupational and industrial classifications, relatively separate from those in which men are employed (Cockburn, 1983; Hartmann, 1976; Reskin and Hartmann, 1986; Reskin and Roos, 1990; *Social Europe*, 1993; Treiman and Hartmann, 1981; Walby, 1986a, 1988). In so far as these areas of work are less well remunerated, then women are additionally disadvantaged.

There has been a decline in certain dimensions of occupational segregation by sex between 1975 and 1994, especially between 1981 and 1991, as can be seen in Tables 2.7–2.9 below. This is primarily a result of both the disproportionate move of women into the expanding higher level occupations and the decline in several of the lower level occupational groups where men were the overwhelming majority. These are discussed below, while further details of changes at a locality level and using industrial as well as occupational classifications for the period 1971–81 can be found in Chapter 5.

There has been a decline in the extent to which top jobs in the upper socio-economic levels were monopolised by men during the period 1975 to 1994. Women have increasingly entered top positions, especially those managerial, administrative and professional jobs for which University degrees are the effective entry qualifications, during a period in which

Table 2.7 Socio-economic group by sex, 1975–94

Socio-economic group	1975	1985	1994
Men			
Professional	5	6	7
Employer/manager	15	19	21
Intermediate and junior non-manual	17	17	17
Skilled manual, own a/c non-prof	41	37	35
Semi-skilled manual, personal service[1]	17	16	14
Unskilled manual	5	5	5
Base = 100%	10902	8787	7948
Women			
Professional	1	1	2
Employer/manager	4	7	11
Intermediate and junior non-manual	46	48	48
Skilled manual, own a/c non-prof	9	9	8
Semi-skilled manual, personal service[1]	31	27	22
Unskilled manual	9	7	9
Base = 100%	11799	9439	8698

Source: OPCS, 1996b: Table 7.4.
All persons aged 16 and over
Note: 1 Skilled manual and own account non-professional.

these posts increased as a proportion of all jobs. These jobs employ an increasing proportion of women workers. Between 1975 and 1994 the percentage of economically active women who were in the upper SEGs of professionals, employers and managers increased significantly, from 5 per cent to 13 per cent. This compares with a parallel male shift from 20 per cent to 28 per cent in the same period (OPCS, 1996b: 195); see Table 2.7 above.

There has been a very significant change in the distribution of women across the occupational orders between 1981 and 1991, as is shown in census derived data presented in Tables 2.8 and 2.9. These show a similar pattern of a decrease in segregation by sex between the occupational orders and a rise in the proportion of women in the upper levels. These changes represent a significant restructuring of gender relations in employment. While most occupations still show that they are staffed predominantly by one sex or the other, indeed seven occupational orders are still over 80 per cent male in 1991 (though there are none which are 80 per cent female), there has been a marked reduction in the extent of segregation. In particular women have increased their participation in the upper occupational orders and reduced them in the lower ones – the higher the order the more likely an increase in both the absolute and relative numbers of women. The largest proportionate increase in women is in the top occupational order, 'professional and related supporting management; senior national and local government managers', where the number of women has increased by 155 per cent as compared with 33 per cent among men, shifting the gender

Table 2.8 Occupational orders for women and men, 1981–91 (tens)

	1981			1991			% increase in women
	Men	Women	% women	Men	Women	% women	
1	77,823	20,137	21	103,181	51,310	33	155
2	66,774	126,468	65	68,654	154,120	69	22
3	15,987	8,821	36	17,835	13,609	43	54
4	92,993	9,042	9	96,266	15,517	14	72
5	180,783	53,118	23	196,993	85,782	30	61
6	104,006	298,636	74	84,159	304,719	78	2
7	60,040	85,941	59	54,704	91,126	62	6
8	50,086	5,601	10	44,160	5,962	12	6
9	56,371	203,660	78	56,499	200,840	78	−1
10	32,396	5,571	15	24,501	5,768	19	4
11	123,059	57,034	32	98,704	41,358	30	−27
12	281,394	16,050	5	194,791	11,142	5	−31
13	58,425	41,708	42	44,036	30,743	41	−26
14	93,608	597	1	74,562	856	1	43
15	155,653	9,521	6	120,311	8,633	7	−9
16	48,516	4,924	9	19,161	2,690	12	−45
17	54,757	41,059	43	13,984	8,547	38	−79
Total	1,552,671	987,888	39	1,312,501	1,032,722	44	5

composition from only 21 per cent women to 30 per cent. All the top five occupational orders show significant increases in the number and proportion of women. In the lower occupations orders, largely manual jobs, where there have been some significant overall reductions in employment, the reduction in women is largely in absolute numbers and their relative proportions have remained largely stable, except for construction and mining which employs relatively small numbers of women and where the number of women has risen. Middle occupational orders – clerical, selling, security and farming – show a picture of small increases in women alongside declines in male employment. Overall then we see significant increases in women's employment at the upper levels, as compared to those of men, among the expanding higher level jobs, and comparatively equal proportionate declines at the lower level, leading to a reduction in overall segregation in a manner advantageous to women. These changes have proceeded in parallel and in related ways with a rise in the size of the upper order and a decline of the lower ones. However, there still remains a high significant amount of sex segregation in employment.

SUMMARY OF CHANGES

During the post-war period and especially in the last decade there have been very significant changes in the position of women in employment. Women

Table 2.9 Gender changes in occupational orders, 1981–91

	% increase in men	% increase in women
1 Professional and related supporting management; senior national and local government managers	33	155
2 Professional and related in education, welfare and health	3	22
3 Literary, artistic and sports	12	54
4 Professional and related in science, engineering, technology and similar fields	4	72
5 Managerial	9	61
6 Clerical and related	−19	2
7 Selling	−9	6
8 Security and protective services	−12	6
9 Catering, cleaning, hair-dressing and other personal services	0	−1
10 Farming, fishing and related	−24	4
11 Materials processing; making and repairing (excluding metal and electrical)	−20	−27
12 Processing, making, repairing and related (metal and electrical)	−31	−31
13 Painting, repetitive assembling, product inspecting, packaging and related	−25	−26
14 Construction, mining and related not identified elsewhere	−20	43
15 Transport operating, materials moving and storing and related	−23	−9
16 Miscellaneous (general labourers and foremen)	−61	−45
17 Inadequately described and not stated	−74	−79
Total	−15	5

Source: data calculated from 1981 Census and 1991 Census, 10 per cent sample, coded using 1980 occupational classification.

are almost as likely as men to be employed; but almost all this increase is in part-time work. There has been a significant narrowing of the wages gap between women and men who work full-time, but this does not extend to women who work part-time. There has been a major increase in the proportion of women in top jobs, but significant sex segregation in employment still remains.

CAUSES OF CHANGES

These changes in employment relations are part of a general change in the form of gender regime. In the long run they are the ultimate consequence of the working through of the shift in gender regime brought about by the success of first-wave feminism in winning political citizenship and the increase in demand for labour with economic development. In the recent period these changes have been further accelerated by: changes in state policy towards equal opportunities in employment and education; changes in trade union policies towards equal opportunities for women; changes in family practices; and the massive increase in women in education at all levels.

Legal and organisational changes

There have been a number of significant recent changes in both the polity and the social partners of employers and trade unions which have influenced these changes in women's position in employment. Many discriminatory barriers to women in employment and education have been removed since the 1970s.

These changes have been underpinned by a legal framework for equal opportunities introduced in the 1970s and 1980s. The Equal Pay legislation, passed in 1970 and implemented in 1975, was important in the narrowing of the wages gap between women and men from 63 per cent of men's hourly earnings in 1970 to 74 per cent in 1977. The legislation has since been regularly strengthened, with the Sex Discrimination Act of 1975, the 1984 Equal Value Amendment which legislated for equal pay for work of equal value, not merely similar work, and in 1994 the extension of many full-time rights to part-time workers.

The passage of this sex equality legislation was due to a number of political factors both domestic and international, including: pressure from organised women trade unionists; a campaign by five trade unions – the National Association of Local Government Officers, The National Union of Teachers, the Civil Service Clerical Association, the Institute of Professional Civil Servants and the Society of Civil Servants (only one of which – the CSCA – was affiliated to the TUC); pressure to ratify the 1951 International Labour Organisation Convention 100 on equal pay; the support of a woman Minister of State, Barbara Castle; and the requirements of the intended membership of the Common Market (now EU) because Article 119 of the Treaty of Rome demanded the equal treatment of women and men in employment-related matters. By the late 1960s and early 1970s when legislation was being considered by the UK Parliament there were no major institutional forces ranged against it. Organised women, the Trades Union Congress, the Confederation of British Industry, the Labour Party and the Conservative Party were all in support of some such legislation.

Further improvements to the legislation were the result of pressure from the European Commission, which took enforcement procedures against the UK Government in the European Court of Justice – for instance to expand the notion of equal pay to cover work of equal value not merely similar work, resulting in the Equal Value Amendment Act in 1984. The UK Government was also forced to provide the same rights to part-time workers as to full-timers as a result of the defeat of the UK Government's position in the House of Lords due to the primacy of EU law over UK law in the matter of equal opportunities in employment. Thus in order to understand the legal framework for equal opportunity in employment we need to recognise the importance of not only the UK state, but also the European Union and in particular its Commission. The political forces are a major factor in altering the legal and industrial relations contexts within which gender relations in the labour market are regulated. See Chapters 10 and 11 for further discussions of these issues.

Equal opportunities policies have been introduced in many companies and many trade unions since the 1970s. Policies in companies are encouraged both by the need to prevent charges of discrimination arising from their employees, and new forms of management theory which emphasise the business case for equal opportunities and diversity management. Most companies now have some kind of policy, though with varying forms of machinery for implementation. They have been encouraged since the 1970s by the CBI, the Equal Opportunities Commission, (especially through its 'Equality Exchange'), business-led campaigns such as Opportunity 2000, as well as organised women workers. Companies have innovated with 'family friendly' policies, such as the career break schemes introduced by banks (among other employers) to facilitate women combining careers with raising children (Marcus, 1996); special equal opportunities committees (Halford and Duncan, 1991; Stone, 1988); and forms of 'diversity management' integrated into wider personnel policies (Rutherford, 1996).

Most trade unions have also introduced equal opportunities policies and women's committees since the 1970s. The TUC had supported the principle of equal pay since 1888, but until the 1970s it did so without putting many resources into winning this demand in either legislation or collective bargaining. Indeed the extent to which trade unions have changed in recent years can be seen from this extract from the 1945 TUC annual report:

> The trade unions have been compelled not only to uphold, but to promote, a clear demarcation between men's and women's work – where such demarcation was possible – in order to protect the men's and thus indirectly the women's rates of pay.... There can be no question that where industries are well organised such demarcation is strongly upheld both by custom and to some extent by specific agreement between the employers and the trade unions.
>
> (TUC annual report, 1945: 467)

There has historically been considerable diversity in trade union practices towards women workers, some seeking to exclude women from their trades altogether, others accepting women but in segregated jobs, and others arguing for equal treatment (Drake, 1984; Ellis, 1991; EOC, 1983; Lewenhak, 1977; Soldon, 1978; Walby, 1986b). Some indication of the changes over the 1960s and 1970s can be gleaned from the fall in the number of unions affiliated to the TUC which had no women members from 44 out of 117 in 1967 to 17 in 1978 (WTUC 1978: 32). By the 1970s most trade unions had made a very significant change in policy towards women workers, from one endorsing unequal treatment to one in favour of equal opportunities. During the 1980s many trade unions established new organisational forms to facilitate the articulation of the views of their women members, such as women's committees and women's officers. There are several reasons for this, ranging from the increasing presence of women as workers to the increased vocalisation of women's various political, social and economic interests. First, the growth in the number of women workers and the decline in the number of male workers has led to their increased significance as potential members of trade unions, both in terms of their subscriptions and their voting power. Second, there has been a significant growth in the number and proportion of women in trade unions. The percentage of women members in unions affiliated to the TUC rose from 15 per cent in 1950 to 29 per cent in 1978 (WTUC annual report, 1978: 40). This has partly been due to the special recruitment of women workers, especially in non-traditional areas, such as part-time work. Since the 1980s there has been an overall decline in union membership, which has been much more pronounced among men than among women. This phenomenon is related to the demise of the heavily male areas of employment in manual work in manufacturing. This can be seen over even the short-time span of 1989 to 1992 when unions reported that male membership declined from 6,405,000 to 5,472,000 while female membership dipped only slightly from 3,753,000 to 3,577,000 (Bird and Corcoran, 1994: 192). There is a convergence in the gendered rates of union density as reported to the Labour Force Survey between 1989 and 1993 from 44 per cent to 38 per cent of men, and from 33 per cent to 31 per cent for women. Much of the gender difference is in fact made up of the difference between part-time and full-time workers with density rates of 39 per cent for full-timers and 21 per cent for part-timers in 1993, suggesting that density rates for full-time men and full-time women are quite close (Bird and Corcoran, 1994: 193). Third, there has been a stronger articulation of women's political interests at diverse levels of society and polity from autonomous women's groups and sections in political parties, to professional associations and women's magazines. At the official national level, all major unions are now strong supporters of equal opportunities policies for women and men workers, although there is some variation at local level. Equal opportunities has become a 'normal' discourse; it has moved from being a feminist issue to one which has entered the mainstream.

However, current discriminatory practices are not the only reason for gender inequality. Many older women built their lives around a set of opportunities in education and employment which were much more restrictive than those of today. Examples of these include: the marriage bar which operated effectively in many occupations, especially white-collar jobs, until the Second World War; the quotas for places in professional training, such as those for some University medical schools, which were not removed until the Sex Discrimination Act of 1975; the re-weighting of 11+ results so as to ensure that more girls than boys did not go to Grammar school even if on 'merit' they should have done so; discrimination against women's access to apprenticeships, especially before 1975 (see Walby, 1986b). Since early decisions on education and employment influence later possibilities, it is only younger women who are able to make many of the major work and life decisions in a context of legally enforceable equal opportunities. Age is thus crucial in new forms of differences and inequalities between women.

Education changes

One of the most important reasons for the changes in employment has been the increased educational qualifications gained by young women. Girls now achieve more educational qualifications than boys at school. The better qualified a woman is, the more likely she is to be in employment, that is, there is a clear relationship between level of education and propensity to paid work (see Table 2.10 below). This relationship holds for both men and women, but more acutely for women (OPCS, 1996b: 226, 227).

Women are much more likely to be in paid employment if they have received higher levels of education. This relationship is particularly acute among the younger age groups, but holds for all ages. In 1994, among women aged 20–29 with higher educational qualifications, 89 per cent are working and only 4 per cent economically inactive, while among the same age group with no qualifications only 33 per cent are working and 56 per cent are economically inactive.

Knowledge is increasingly important in economic development and social change (Drucker, 1993). It is a tool which levers social change and economic development. The processes of the communication and transformation of knowledge, including information technology, are becoming increasingly sophisticated. Not only do the knowledge industries underpin current forms of employment growth, in that the areas which are growing most rapidly require higher levels of skills and qualifications, but they are the key to the future shape of society. Education as practised within dedicated education institutions of schools, colleges and universities is one important part of this and has expanded in the UK, as in other industrialised countries, since industrialisation and especially over the last couple of decades.

Gender relations within education are being rapidly transformed, with women beginning to out-perform men. The greater success of men than women in achieving educational credentials is now a phenomenon of the

41

Table 2.10 Education and employment: Women, 1994

Age and economic activity status	Highest qualification level attained				
	Higher education	GCE A level or equivalent	Other qualifications	No qualifications	Total
	%	%	%	%	%
16–19					
Working	–	[68]	70	[41]	64
Unemployed	–	[19]	13	[27]	17
Inactive	–	[14]	17	[32]	19
	%	%	%	%	%
20–29					
Working	89	77	65	33	67
Unemployed	7	10	8	11	9
Inactive	4	13	26	56	25
	%	%	%	%	%
30–39					
Working	81	77	70	54	70
Unemployed	3	5	5	5	4
Inactive	16	19	25	41	26
	%	%	%	%	%
40–49					
Working	83	78	78	66	74
Unemployed	3	5	3	4	4
Inactive	14	17	19	30	22
	%	%	%	%	%
50–59					
Working	72	[78]	68	55	62
Unemployed	1	[0]	3	2	2
Inactive	27	[22]	29	43	36
	%	%	%	%	%
16–59					
Working	82	76	70	56	69
Unemployed	3	8	6	5	5
Inactive	14	16	24	39	26
Base=100%	*1031*	*597*	*2665*	*1778*	*6071*

Source: Derived from OPCS, 1996b: Table 10.6.

past. Young women are now better than or equal to young men in most levels of current educational achievement, though there are still some exceptions.

There are, however, some remaining exceptions to this picture of female advancement. First, gender specialisation in forms of knowledge obtained, with men being more concentrated in the area around technology and women in languages and similar subjects, is tenacious, but even these forms of segregation are declining. Second, this picture of the erosion of the gender gap affects younger people, not older ones. Since formal education typically takes place largely in the early stages of a person's life, the direct benefits of the changes in the education gender gap are experienced by younger women rather than older women. Thus in order to understand gender relations in education and in the obtaining of formal qualifications the question of age is crucial. The younger the age at which qualifications are obtained, the better women do as compared to men. Third, while there is currently a strong relationship between educational qualifications and employment there is no guarantee that this will be sufficient for women to reach the highest levels of employment.

In short, with some exceptions, education is a success story for women in the 1990s. Women have equalled or surpassed men in many areas of educational achievement, and remaining areas of male superiority are being eroded. Educational qualifications correlate highly with levels of economic activity both in absolute levels of participation and the levels of achievement (as shown in Table 2.10 above). They are key to increased access of women to the public sphere, and in particular, to paid employment.

The younger the age at which educational qualifications are taken, the better are girls and women doing. The gap in favour of girls is wider at the age of 16 or so when GCSEs are being taken and slightly less wide at the A level stage and smaller again in higher education.

Girls gain significantly more GCSE passes than boys now, as is shown in Table 2.11. In 1993–94 girls made up 54 per cent of those with five or more GCSE passes at the higher grades, despite being only 48 per cent of the population of 16-year olds.

Table 2.11 School qualifications by sex, 1993–94 (thousands)

	Boys	Girls	% female
GCSE			
5 or more higher grades	133	155	54
A level			
2 or more passes	93	105	53
No graded results	30	30	50

Source: calculated from *Education Statistics for the United Kingdom 1995* (DFEE, 1996): Table 28.In 1994 at age 17 there were 350,000 boys and 329,000 girls, so the above figures understate the girls' proportionate success.

Girls also gain a slight majority of A levels. In 1993–94 they made up 53 per cent of the pupils with two or more A level passes. See Table 2.11 above.

The better achievement of girls in school examinations as compared with boys is a recent development. Only ten years ago the gender gap in qualifications was the other way round. This can be clearly seen in the case of the rising number of young women gaining A levels. The proportion of girls gaining three or more A levels has risen from 9 per cent of 17-year-old girls in 1985–96 to 16 per cent in 1993–94, while in the same period that of boys has risen from 10 per cent to 14 per cent (see Table 2.12).

Table 2.12 A levels by sex, 1985–94 (percentage of those aged 17)

	1985–86	1990–91	1993–94
Male	10	14	14
Female	9	14	16

Source: *Education Statistics for the United Kingdom 1995*: Table 31. School pupils gaining three or more A-levels by sex 1985–94, England, Wales and Northern Ireland

This educational success story is not confined to schools. Women are more likely to participate in further education than men; see Table 2.13 below. In 1994–95 they constituted 62 per cent of the further education enrolments (*Education Statistics for the United Kingdom 1995*: Table C).

It might be argued that this rise in school qualifications is merely the ephemeral result of changes in school examination practices, such as the increase in the use of coursework at the expense of unseen examinations. However, these changes are found in other parts of the educational system where such changes in examination procedures are not found, as will be

Table 2.13 Participation rates in further education by sex and age, 1980/1–1994–5

	16–18		19–20		21–24	
	Males	*Females*	*Males*	*Females*	*Males*	*Females*
Full-time						
1980–81	7.2	11.1	1.4	1.3	0.5	0.5
1994–95	24.9	27.3	4.2	3.8	1.4	1.4
Part-time						
1980–81	26.7	17.0	14.2	11.2	8.5	14.9
1994–95	12.6	11.5	9.3	12.5	8.4	16.6

Source: calculated from *Education Statistics for the United Kingdom 1995*: Table 20. Percentages of the population age group.

described below. Further, the improved educational success of girls and young women is common to most Western industrialised countries. Indeed at tertiary level women constituted more than half the enrolment in Norway, Sweden, Finland and France and half the enrolments in Spain and Denmark, before the UK (UNDP, 1992: 186). Thus it is improbable that these changes in the UK are merely the result of changes in examination procedures.

Women were slightly more likely than men to be receiving job-related training in 1993–94 – 15 per cent rather than 14 per cent, according to the Winter 1993–94 and Spring 1994 Labour Force Survey. Women were both more likely than men to be in grades in which training was more likely and also more likely than men to be undergoing training in these grades. These were the higher occupational grades – managers, professionals, associate professionals and clerical workers. In all the manual grades and also the clerical grade there was both less training and women were less likely than men to be undergoing it. When full-time workers are compared with each other the gap between women and men widens to 18 per cent for women and 14 per cent for men, since part-timers are less likely to be undergoing training (*Employment Gazette*, November 1994: 391). But even here there appears to be some closing of the skill gap, since according to Gallie's data between 1986 and 1992 there was a reduction of the skill gap between part-timers and full-timers (Gallie and White, 1993).

There has also been a significant increase in the number of women who have gained professional qualifications. Between 1980 and 1987 the percentage of women members of the Chartered Institute of Accountants grew from 5 per cent to 10 per cent, that of the Institute of Chartered Accountants from 4 per cent to 8 per cent, of the Institute of Bankers from 13 per cent to 18 per cent, of the Royal Town Planning Institute from 7 per cent to 16 per cent, and of the British Medical Association from 21.5 per cent to 25 per cent (EOC, 1986: 57).

In higher education there is a similar picture of the closing and reversal of the gender gap, with recent cohorts of women doing better than earlier ones. Women are around half the student body. They were the slight majority, at 50.8 per cent, of home undergraduate students in 1993–94, see Table 2.14. There are some variations in the proportions of women depending on whether study is full- or part-time, whether the course is degree level or leads to other qualifications (women are the clear majority in the non-degree part-time sector), and whether overseas students are included (overseas students are more likely to be male than home students). Women were 50 per cent of full-time first degree home students in 1993–94, see Table 2.14.

The increase in the proportion of women in higher education has occurred rapidly since 1975–76. The number of women (home and overseas) enrolled in undergraduate courses in British higher education

Table 2.14 Higher education, enrolments, 1993–94, home students (thousands)

	First degree FT	First degree PT	Other UG FT	Other UG PT	PG FT	Total FT	Total PT	Total
Males	365.3	81.5	77.6	126.2	43.0	485.9	269.0	754.9
Females	364.6	82.3	67.9	175.2	36.4	468.8	311.7	780.5
% Female	50.0	50.2	46.7	58.1	45.8	49.1	53.7	50.8

Source: calculated from *Education Statistics for the United Kingdom 1995*: Table 21a.
Notes: FT: full-time
PT: part-time
UG: undergraduate, including first degree and others e.g. nursing
PG: postgraduate

Table 2.15 Higher education full-time enrolment, 1975–95
(home and overseas, thousands)

	Undergraduate			Postgraduate		
	Male	Female	% female	Male	Female	% female
1975–76	141	77	35	37	13	25
1980–81	157	101	39	34	15	31
1985–86	148	108	42	37	17	31
1990–91	167	138	45	41	24	37
1991–92	178	150	46	46	28	38
1992–93	191	166	46	48	31	40
1993–94	398	355	47	62	43	41
1994–95	422	390	48	68	49	42

Source: calculated from *Education Statistics for the United Kingdom 1995*: Table 25.
Note: The figures from 1993–94 onwards are larger because of the exclusion of the former polytechnic sector from this statistical series ceases on their acquisition of University status.

increased from 35 per cent in 1975–76 to 48 per cent in 1994–95. Among postgraduates they have increased from 25 per cent to 42 per cent in the same period; see Table 2.15.

It is not that women are substituting for men, rather both men and women's enrolment has increased, but that of women has increased more rapidly. The number of women undergraduates increased by over 115 per cent between 1975–76 and 1992–93, while that of men has risen by 35 per cent. The percentage increase in female postgraduates in this period was even greater at 138 per cent, while that of men was only 30 per cent (calculated from *Education Statistics for the United Kingdom 1994*: Table 25). This has been a period of expansion for both men and women in higher education in Britain, but especially for women.

The recent nature of the increase means that younger women are more likely to have formal educational qualifications than are older women. There is little difference in the educational qualifications of young men

Table 2.16 Highest selected qualifications by age and sex
(percentage of population)

	Degree	A level	GCSE or O level	No qualification
16–24				
Men	5	25	36	20
Women	4	20	39	19
25–29				
Men	15	20	29	16
Women	12	13	32	17
30–39				
Men	18	21	26	18
Women	13	10	26	26
40–49				
Men	17	19	22	25
Women	9	7	19	38
50–59				
Men	13	18	21	33
Women	5	5	13	54

Source: adapted from *Education Statistics for the United Kingdom 1994*: Table 37.

and women, but a considerable difference among older people. Table 2.16 shows qualifications by age and sex.

In the youngest age group 16–24, men and women have similar levels of qualifications. In the oldest age group, 50–59, there are considerable differences, with women being significantly less likely to hold a formal educational qualification and indeed 54 per cent of such women, as compared with 33 per cent of men, have no qualifications at all.

Thus we have age-specific patterns of gender inequality. There can be no sweeping statement about women catching up with men. This is generationally specific. The pattern of very significant gender inequality in qualifications among people over 40 is not affected by the changes discussed for younger people. The gender revolution in education hardly touches these women, except for those who have struggled to re-enter education as mature students. We see a new form of inequality – that between women of different age cohorts. We have an important age specificity of patterns of gender relations.

The picture of success among younger women is partially tempered by some remaining gender segregation in subjects of study. While the traditional pattern of young women obtaining fewer qualifications than men is over, there is still an issue about the range of subjects that they choose to do. There remains a certain degree of gender specialisation, despite very significant increases in the number of girls and women making 'non-traditional' choices; see Table 2.17. This occurs in schools, as well as in further and higher education.

Table 2.17 GCSE/SCE (S grade) attempts and achievements in schools, by sex, 1993–94 (thousands)

Selected subject group	No. of attempts			% grade A-C	
	Males	Females	% female	Males	Females
Biology	33.7	34.8	51	73	72
Chemistry	37.9	26.4	41	78	81
Physics	42.1	20.7	33	80	82
Single science	52.2	55.4	51	36	41
Double science	213.7	212.0	50	49	49
Maths	315.0	311.7	50	46	45
Computing	44.3	25.4	36	49	55
Craft, design & technology	162.4	49.1	23	38	52
Home Economics	15.2	88.1	85	21	44
Social studies	11.3	21.5	66	37	51
English	306.4	296.5	49	49	66
English literature	200.6	219.3	52	54	67
Modern languages	265.9	315.5	54	43	57

Source: calculated from *Education Statistics for the United Kingdom 1995*: Table 29.

Girls are less likely to attempt GCSE in traditionally male vocational subjects such as 'craft, design and technology' (23 per cent) and 'computer studies' (36 per cent) as well as in some sciences, 'physics' (33 per cent) and 'chemistry' (41 per cent). Boys are less likely to attempt 'home economics' (15 per cent). However, this picture should be qualified by some new gender symmetry, in that roughly even proportions of boys and girls take the traditionally masculine 'mathematics', 'science single award', 'science double award' as well as the traditionally feminine 'English', 'English literature' and 'modern languages'; see Table 2.17. This reduction in gender differentiation in subjects taken may be partially an effect of the reduction of choice of subjects with the new national curriculum. However, when these subjects are taken, girls tend to get higher grades than boys, whether the subject is traditionally masculine or feminine; see Table 2.17. That is, there is some degree of gender specialisation in some school subjects, but it is not very great, is concentrated in a few areas, and is on the decrease.

In higher education the degree of gender specialisation in different subjects is slightly greater, but here also it has declined significantly. As in the case of schools, it is some of the more vocationally oriented subjects which remain most gender segregated: engineering for men; teacher training and subjects allied to medicine for women; see Table 2.18.

Education is a female success story, with significant improvements in their absolute and relative educational achievements. The gender gap in school qualifications is now running in the favour of girls not boys. The gender gap in students (but not lecturers) in higher education is now almost

Table 2.18 Higher education selected subjects by sex, home students, 1993–94 (thousands)

Selected subjects	PG FT		First degree FT		Other UG PT	
	No.	% female	No.	% female	No.	% female
ITT & INSETT	10.9	66	45.6	80	15.6	74
Medicine	2.2	55	22.7	50	–	–
Allied medicine	2.5	64	27.7	75	98.1	86
Biology	4.9	49	36.7	59	1.0	70
Physics	7.5	25	43.1	34	2.8	39
Maths	5.2	21	43.7	25	8.5	29
Engineering	7.4	15	68.4	15	37.5	6
Social studies	9.9	53	85.2	54	11.7	74
Business	5.2	38	72.1	48	84.2	54
Languages	2.6	54	49.0	70	4.8	63
Humanities	2.6	42	28.3	51	0.7	57
All subjects	79.4	46	729.9	50	301.4	58

Source: calculated from *Education Statistics for the United Kingdom 1995*: Table 21a.
Notes: PG: postgraduate; UG: undergraduate; FT: full-time; PT: part-time; ITT & INSETT: initial and in service teacher training

closed. There remains a degree of gender specialisation in subjects, especially the more vocational areas, but this is also eroding.

Age is significant in differentiating those women who have been able to take advantage of these new social relations in education. Younger women have benefited from the changes; older women have not. Since formal education is usually completed early in life the transformation of women's educational opportunities has passed older women by. This creates two gendered patterns of inequality. First, there is a gap between younger women and older women in qualifications. This has implications for the employment opportunities, opening a gap in this as well as other arenas. Second, it means that there are different patterns of gender relations and gender inequality among younger and older people. Older women face much greater inequality in their dealings with their male peers than do younger women as a result of these different educational opportunities and achievements.

The significance of these changes depends on the significance of educational qualifications for access to social and economic opportunities. If employment chances are primarily structured by qualifications, then these changes in education will have dramatic consequences for gender relations in employment. If, however, employment chances are determined by other factors than this type of merit, then the consequences will be less important. Other intervening variables include: structures of sex segregation; work commitment; discrimination. The correlation between educational qualifications and employment cited earlier makes it clear that, whatever the remaining structures of disadvantage or differences in work commitment, educational changes are making a significant impact on gender relations in employment, at least for younger women.

It is relevant here that the areas of education which are most sex segregated are among those which are most vocational. In the case of further and higher education this was the case especially in engineering and technology for men, and teaching and occupations allied to medicine for women. That is, there is a significant remaining link between sex-segregated education and sex-segregated employment.

Nonetheless, there is a very significant link between educational qualifications and other social and economic opportunities, even if there is not a direct correlation. Insofar as the UK moves in the direction of a knowledge-based economy and society, then the dramatic improvement in young women's educational achievements will produce quite different gender relations in that society than before. However, these changes have necessarily not impacted on older cohorts. This has two implications. First, patterns of gender relations among older and younger people are diverging. Different patterns of gender relations coexist. Second, while it is older people who hold most of the decision making positions in society, the influence of the older patterns of gender relations is likely to remain dominant in the political and policy spheres.

The reducing impact of the domestic on women's paid employment

Marriage, child birth and child care reduce women's economic activity significantly less today than in previous decades. Indeed, married women are now more likely to be in paid employment than non-married women. Once children reach the age of 10 mothers are as likely to be in employment as women with no children. Despite some potentially countervailing changes, in particular the increased significance of caring for the elderly by women in their middle years and, oddly, that the increasing numbers of lone mothers are less likely to be in employment than married mothers, there has been an overall massive decline in the impact of domestic responsibilities on the propensity of women to be in paid employment over the last 20 years.

The period of time that women take as a break from the labour market following child birth has significantly declined in recent years. The economic activity rate of women with dependent children has risen from 49 per cent in 1973 to 65 per cent in 1994 (dependent children being those aged under 16, or 16–18 and in full-time education, in the family unit and living in the household). Women with a pre-school age child (aged 0–4) have almost doubled their economic activity rates from 27 per cent in 1973 to 52 per cent in 1994, so that over half the mothers with pre-school children are economically active today. Women with children over 10 are now as likely as women without dependent children to be economically active, an increase to 79 per cent in 1994 from 68 per cent in 1973, albeit with a higher propensity to work part-time (OPCS, 1996b: Table 7.7); see Table 2.19 below.

Table 2.19 Economic activity of women of working age, 1973–94, by age of youngest dependent child (women aged 16–59)

Age of youngest dependent child and economic activity	Year									
	1973	1979	1981	1983	1985	1987	1989	1991	1993	1994
					%					
Youngest child aged 0–4										
Working full-time	7	6	6	5	8	11	12	13	14	16
Working part-time	18	22	18	18	22	24	29	29	32	30
All working	25}27	28}31	25}30	24}29	30}36	35}42	41}46	43}50	46}53	47}52
Unemployed	2	3	5	5	6	7	5	6	7	5
Youngest child aged 5–9										
Working full-time	18	16	13	13	14	14	19	22	17	22
Working part-time	42	44	43	40	46	48	49	44	44	41
All working	61}63	61}64	57}62	54}60	60}63	62}66	69}72	67}74	61}69	64}69
Unemployed	2	3	5	6	3	4	3	7	8	5
Youngest child aged 10 or over										
Working full-time	30	26	26	25	28	29	31	35	33	32
Working part-time	37	45	43	42	42	45	43	40	42	44
All working	67}68	72}73	69}73	66}70	70}73	74}77	75}78	76}81	75}79	76}79
Unemployed	1	1	4	4	3	3	3	5	4	3
All with dependent children										
Working full-time	17	16	15	14	17	18	20	22	21	23
Working part-time	30	36	34	32	35	37	39	36	38	37
All working	47}49	52}54	49}53	46}51	51}55	54}59	59}63	59}65	59}66	60}65
Unemployed	2	2	4	5	4	5	4	6	7	5
No dependent children										
Working full-time	52	51	48	46	47	50	51	48	46	48
Working part-time	17	18	18	18	21	22	22	23	23	22
All working	69}71	69}72	66}73	65}73	67}74	72}78	75}79	72}78	71}77	71}77
Unemployed	2	3	7	8	7	6	4	6	6	6
Total										
Working full-time	34	34	33	31	33	36	37	37	35	36
Working part-time	23	26	25	25	27	28	29	29	30	29
All working	58}60	61}64	58}64	56}62	60}66	64}69	68}72	67}73	65}71	66}71
Unemployed	2	3	6	6	6	5	4	6	6	5
Base = 100per cent	8956	8611	9164	7397	7317	7636	7329	7090	6824	6755

Source: Derived from OPCS, 1996b: Table 7.7.

The higher the woman's level of education and the higher her occupational level the more likely she is to be in paid employment while looking after young children. In 1994, among women who are in the professional, employer or manager group with pre-school children 64 per cent are economically active, 33 per cent with full-time employment, as compared with 50 per cent among the unskilled manual group, where only 2 per cent are working full-time; see Table 2.25. Possible reasons for this difference between professional and unskilled manual workers could include: that the cost of child care is more within the reach of professionals than unskilled manual workers; the relative balance of attractiveness of the activities of paid work and homework is different between these groups.

The lessening impact of marriage, child birth and child care on employment rates is related to a number of changes, some within the workplace, some legal, and others within the household itself.

While there are major changes in the nature of household tasks, and household systems of financial management, the implications of these for equity in the household and women's employment are contested.

The presence of domestic production goods, or consumer durables has significantly increased in households in recent years – see Table 2.20. While there is controversy over the impact of such goods on the amount of time spent on housework (Bose, 1979; Cowan, 1983; Gershuny, 1983; Gershuny, Godwin and Jones, 1994), nevertheless they do create a potential for reduced time on certain household chores, even if the time spent on domestic tasks overall may increase for other reasons, such as more time spent accompanying children to school and in obtaining higher standards in the home.

There has been a decline in the proportion of households where men earn the majority of the household income when the wife works full-time from 83 per cent in 1973 to 55 per cent in 1993, along with an increase in the proportion of such households where earnings are roughly equal from 14 per cent to 30 per cent and where the wife is earnings dominant from 3 per cent to 15 per cent (Irwin, 1995a). However, this data only applies to that half of households where the wife is in full-time employment.

Table 2.20 Domestic production goods, 1979–94

Percentage of households with:	1979	1987	1994
Washing machine	74	83	89
Tumble drier	19	39	50
Deep freezer	40	74	88
Microwave oven	–	30	67
Dishwasher	3	8	19
Central heating	55	73	85

Source: Derived from OPCS, 1996b: Table 2.6.

There is a small balance of evidence that there has been a small decrease in inequality in the household and of divisions of tasks and power within the household over time, which is associated with the rise of women's paid employment (Gershuny, Godwin and Jones, 1994; Irwin, 1995a; Vogler, 1994), although this is a contested view, some arguing that there has been no significant change (Arber and Ginn, 1995; Bose, 1979; Cowan, 1983; Delphy and Leonard, 1992; Vanek, 1980), and others that there is insufficient evidence to be conclusive (Warde and Hetherington, 1993).

Women who are in full-time employment do less housework than those who are non-employed or work part-time according to time budget studies where people have been asked to fill in detailed accounts of how they spend their time (Gershuny et al., 1994). The case that paid employment enhances women's position in the household is further supported by comparative analysis of time budget studies, which show that the proportion of housework done by men has increased over time, and particularly so in the case of the partners of full-time employed women. These figures hold for a series of national studies as well as in the UK, the latter comparing 1975 and 1987 (Gershuny et al., 1994). However, the contrary case, that paid work is merely an additional burden to women, is supported by cross-sectional evidence from time budget studies which suggests that married women who have full-time employment do more hours of work (housework plus paid work) than do women who do solely housework, with women who do part-time paid work and housework being in between. Gershuny et al. (1994) suggest that this is evidence of a process of lagged change.

Household income is unlikely to be shared equally (Brannen and Wilson, 1987; Davies and Joshi, 1994). There have been changes in the systems used to allocate household finances (Pahl, 1989; Vogler, 1994; Wilson, 1987). There has been a decline in the system of men keeping hold of the wage and giving the wife a housekeeping allowance, and an increase in female participation in the management of household finance (Vogler, 1994). Among the growing forms there appears to be a polarisation between households with a joint pool systems which indicates equal sharing of household income, and on the other, the growth of female managed systems. This appears to indicate greater female financial decision making. However, Vogler is cautious about interpreting the latter as an increase in female power on the grounds that this system is associated with poverty and elsewhere in a review of the literature on the organisation of money in marriage, Vogler and Pahl (1993) conclude that there has been no significant change.

There is one important area of social and demographic change which creates more work in the household, and decreases the propensity of women to take employment – that of the increasing number of elderly people who need care as a result of the population ageing as people live longer (Arber and Ginn, 1991 Ungerson, 1990). While not all people over 65 are in need of special assistance from others, nonetheless there has been a significant increase in the amount of care given to elderly people. Recent policy developments have prioritised the care of people in their own homes wherever possible, with the informal assistance of family and friends as well as that provided by organised agencies.

Significant proportions of the population now provide care informally. This is disproportionately provided by women, but not to the same extent as child care. People who were sick, elderly or disabled either inside or outside the household were reported to be looked after or given special help by 17 per cent of women and 12 per cent of men in the adult population in 1991, according to the British Household Panel Survey. The women who provide this care are disproportionatly aged between 45 and 64, while the most typical age of men carers is over 75. At the older ages the care receiver is most likely to be a spouse, with others more likely to be cared for at younger ages. Among people of working age 45–64, slightly more than 20 per cent of women are engaged in care outside the home and a further 6 per cent or so are co-resident carers; while around 14 per cent of men of this age give care outside the home and around 5 per cent inside (*Employment Gazette*, March 1995: 103). Such increases in care giving reduce the capacity for paid employment, especially full-time employment, especially among mid-life women in their 40s and 50s (Brannen *et al.*, 1994; Evandrou and Winter, 1994; Ginn and Arber, 1995).

Women who are lone parents are less likely to be in paid employment than married mothers, so as the rate of lone motherhood rises there is a consequent fall in the propensity of women to be in employment; see Table 2.21 below.

Table 2.21 Working women by marital status and presence of children, 1977–94 (single mothers, lone mothers and married women with dependent children: percentages working full-time and part-time by marital status)

	1977–79	1992–94
All lone mothers		
Working full-time	22	16
Working part-time	24	23
All working	47	40
Single mothers		
Working full-time	25	13
Working part-time	11	16
All working	36	29
Married women with dependent children		
Working full-time	15	22
Working part-time	37	42
All working	52	64

Source: Derived from *General Household Survey*, 1993: Table 5.9.
Note: dependent children are persons under 16, or aged 16–18 and in full-time education, in the family unit and living in the household.

Lone mothers in the UK have significantly lower rates of employment than do married mothers, and comparable groups in the EU (EUROSTAT, 1993). There are a number of possible reasons for this. First, lone mothers are caught in a benefits trap because of the need to earn very considerable amounts in order to able to pay for the child care in order to work, and to beat the benefit level. Second, there is no one with whom to share child care arrangements. This has occurred despite the fact that women who live in households without men are likely to be poor, with significantly less household income than married couple households.

This group is of increasing significance. The proportion of families headed by a lone parent increased from 8 per cent in 1971 to 23 per cent in 1994. The 'traditional' family of a married or cohabiting couple with dependent children fell as a proportion of all households from 32 per cent in the early 1980s to 25 per cent in 1994 (*General Household Survey*, 1994: 15, 17). The rise in lone parenting has paralleled the decline in the extent to which all women (whether mothers or not) spend their lives married. Between 1979 and 1994 the proportion of women aged 18–49 who were married declined from 74 per cent to 57 per cent. The proportion of women aged 18–49 who were single rose from 18 per cent in 1979 to 29 per cent in 1994. The proportion of women who were divorced rose from 4 per cent to 9 per cent between 1979 and 1994 (OPCS, 1996b: 34). The rate of divorce rose from 4.7 in 1,000 of married persons in 1970 to 13.5 in 1991 (*General Household Survey*, 1993: 26). There is a pattern of later marriage and family formation, so that those women and men who do marry do so at later ages (Irwin, 1995b). However, between 1979 and 1994 there was an increase in the proportion of non-married women who were cohabiting from 11 per cent to 23 per cent, which reduces the significance of these changes in marital status to some extent (*General Household Survey*, 1994: 34).

Domestic activities reduce the level of women's employment less than previously, but there are a number of contrary changes, especially the growth in caring for the elderly by women in their middle years, and the growth in the numbers of lone mothers who are less frequently employed.

AGE

Age is a major differentiator of women's employment patterns. Younger women have gained access to education and employment much more than older women. Younger women are much more likely to be in managerial and professional jobs than older women and to work full-time rather than part-time.

The traditional impact of life cycle events on women's employment rates has ceased. This is a dramatic and sudden change over the last decade or so. There is no longer a dip in economic activity rates in the early years of women's working lives associated with early child care. In 1975 and 1985

Table 2.22 Economic activity of women,
1975, 1985, 1994

Age	1975	1985	1994
16–17	66	65	63
18–24	71	75	72
25–34	55	61	72
35–49	68	72	77
50–59	60	56	64
60–64	29	18	26

Source: Derived from OPCS, 1996b: 194.
Note: all women over 16.

there were decreases in activity rates between the ages of 18–24 and of 25–34 of 16 and 14 percentage points respectively, while in 1994 there was no decrease between these ages. Domestic activities no longer stop younger women being active in the labour market in the way that they used to do; see Table 2.22.

Younger women are more likely to be in higher level jobs than older women. Among higher level occupations women are younger than average, while in lower level occupations women are older than average (see Table 2.23). Thus among 'managers and administrators' women are 49 per cent of workers aged 21–24, but only 31 per cent of the whole; among legal professionals 54 per cent of 21–24 year olds, but only 40 per cent of the whole; among engineers and technologists 12 per cent of 21–24 year olds but only 5 per cent of the whole; among health professionals 59 per cent of those 21–24, but only 39 per cent of the whole and among teachers 77 per cent of the 21–24 year olds as compared with 62 per cent of the whole.

Among the lower level occupations the reverse holds, thus among 'other occupations in sales and services' (largely cleaners and to a lesser extent catering assistants) women are 65 per cent of those aged 21–24 as compared with 83 per cent of the whole, and among 'sales assistants and check-out operators' 73 per cent of 21–24 year olds as compared with 83 per cent of the whole.

Among 'managers and administrators' women are almost 50 per cent of those aged 21–24, but are present in ever smaller proportion in each older age group. Overall in this occupation only 14 per cent of the women work part-time, and these are predominantly in the older age groups. Among the younger age groups where women are almost as common as men part-time working is rare – 3 per cent for 21–24 year olds, and 6 per cent for 25–29 year olds. This is an occupation undergoing a rapid change in its gender composition.

Among many professional groups a similar pattern can be seen as for managers and administrators. Among health professionals women now form the majority of workers aged 21–24, while the proportion of women falls steadily with age. A similar pattern emerges among legal professionals, where women are just the majority among the younger group of 21–24, a proportion which falls steeply with age.

Even among engineers and technologists a similar shift in the gender composition by age can be found where women can be found in the younger age groups, though hardly any in older groups, but the pattern has a much lower overall proportion of women.

Among teaching professionals women have long been the majority. The picture is now one in which the younger ages are significantly more female than the older ones. However, the figures for professionals as a whole do not carry through this picture of significantly more women entering at the lower ages. This is because of the smaller numbers in the lower age groups of the large group of teaching professionals. The reductions here produce an overall picture among the professionals of little aggregate change, despite a similar direction of movement in each one.

In the lower occupational grades there is a reverse pattern of age and gender to that in the higher ones. Women are older in these areas of employment than in the higher level occupations. They are also much more likely to be working part-time. Two leading examples of this are first, 'other occupations in sales and services' which are largely 'cleaners, domestics', together with some 'counterhands, catering assistants' and other smaller, but similar categories; and second, 'sales assistants and check-out operators', that is, shop assistants. Each is very large, accounting for around a million workers each. Cleaning and its associated occupations is overwhelmingly an occupation done by older women working part-time. Over 80 per cent of workers are women, over 80 per cent work part-time and over half (51 per cent) are 45 or over. Shop assistants are likewise predominantly older women working part-time, but not quite to the same extent. This occupation is over 80 per cent female, almost 70 per cent of whom work part-time, and 31 per cent are 45 or over, 44 per cent 40 or over.

The relationship between age and level of occupation is compounded by the propensity to work part-time. Young women in high-level jobs very rarely work part-time; while older women in less-skilled work are very likely to work part-time. Overall younger women are more likely to be working full-time than older women, the percentage of part-time working rising from 13 per cent of 21–24 years olds in 1991 to 52 per cent of 55–59 year olds. Since part-time work is associated with less skilled occupations, lesser pay, and poorer fringe benefits, this is another sign of the relative disadvantage of older women. Older women are not only more likely to be found in the lower level occupations, but they are disproportionately in part-time employment. The large lower level occupations in which women are disproportionately found, for instance cleaning and shop work, have high levels of older women working part-time as compared with the higher

Table 2.23 Gender composition of selected occupations of employees in employment, 1991 (percentage female)

Age	Managers and administrators	Legal professionals	Engineers and technologists	Health professionals	Teaching professionals	Sales assistants and check-out operators	Other occupations in sales and services (largely cleaners)
21–24	49	54	12	59	77	73	65
25–29	43	49	10	48	69	81	77
30–34	33	42	6	39	64	88	86
35–39	28	42	5	39	64	91	90
40–44	28	29	3	31	62	94	91
45–54	26	21	2	33	60	94	90
55–59	22	16	1	27	56	90	86
60–64	18	14	0	25	46	83	77
All 16+	31	40	5	39	62	83	83
Total	284830	4287	38752	9223	81085	109725	110308

Source: calculated from 1991 Census Table 5 occupation and age, 10 per cent sample.

Table 2.24 Percentage of women employees who work part-time,
by age, 1991 (tens)

Age	Managers and administrators	Teaching professionals	Sales assistants and check-out operators	Other occupations in sales and services (largely cleaners)	All women employees in employ-ment
21–24	3	13	34	58	13
25–29	6	13	61	79	25
30–34	14	29	78	87	43
35–39	19	33	78	85	49
40–44	17	29	76	82	47
45–54	17	25	77	80	47
55–59	22	30	80	82	52
60–64	37	53	87	87	
All 16+	14	28	69	81	39

Source: calculated from 1991 Census Table 5 occupation and age, 10% sample.

level occupations where young women are more likely to be working; see
Table 2.24.

It is age which shows the increasing polarisation in the experiences of
women most starkly. Those young women who have high levels of education are more likely to gain entry to good jobs and work full-time. Older
women who missed out on the acquisition of educational qualifications are
much more likely to be working part-time in less-skilled and less well-paid
occupations. There are exceptions, such as some young women who did not
gain educational qualifications and became mothers rather than workers,
and some older women who successfully gained educational qualifications
as 'mature' students. Nevertheless, the overall picture remains one of
immense differentiation between the lives of younger and older women,
between those, usually younger women, who are fully and successfully
engaged in the public domains of education and employment and those,
largely older women, who early on in their lives made their choices within
the opportunity structures of a private gender regime, and are not so
engaged in the public domain today.

CLASS

Women are located in widely dispersed class locations as a result of their
different positions in the sexual division of labour. As was seen in Table 2.7
(p. 35), women are more polarised than men by socio-economic group. This
polarisation has a strong age element with younger women being more
likely to be in the upper socio-economic groups and older women in the
lower groups. Thus these age-specific engagements with different types of
employment have a class dimension. The higher the socio-economic group

Table 2.25 Economic activity by socio-economic group 1992–94
(women aged 16–59)

Age of youngest dependent child and economic activity	Socio-economic group					
	Professional or employer/ manager	Intermediate and junior non-manual	Skilled manual and own account non-professional	Semi-skilled manual and personal service	Unskilled manual	Total
	Percentages					
Youngest child aged 0–4						
Working full-time	33	16	15	6	2	15
Working part-time	28	34	40	27	44	33
All working	61⎫65	51⎫58	55⎫61	33⎫41	46⎫51	48⎫55
Unemployed	4⎭	7⎭	6⎭	8⎭	5⎭	7⎭
Youngest child aged 5–9						
Working full-time	53	22	28	10	3	21
Working part-time	27	47	39	44	61	45
All working	81⎫86	69⎫75	69⎫77	54⎫63	64⎫71	66⎫73
Unemployed	5⎭	6⎭	8⎭	9⎭	8⎭	7⎭
Youngest child aged 10 or over						
Working full-time	61	33	40	22	6	32
Working part-time	23	47	37	46	67	45
All working	85⎫90	80⎫83	77⎫81	68⎫72	73⎫79	77⎫81
Unemployed	5⎭	3⎭	4⎭	4⎭	6⎭	4⎭
All with dependent children						
Working full-time	47	23	27	12	3	22
Working part-time	26	41	39	37	57	40
All working	74⎫78	65⎫70	66⎫72	49⎫56	60⎫66	62⎫68
Unemployed	4⎭	5⎭	6⎭	7⎭	6⎭	6⎭
No dependent childre						
Working full-time	77	57	49	40	11	53
Working part-time	10	21	24	24	50	22
All working	87⎫90	79⎫84	74⎫79	66⎫75	62⎫71	76⎫82
Unemployed	3⎭	5⎭	5⎭	9⎭	9⎭	6⎭
Total						
Working full-time	65	41	38	26	7	38
Working part-time	16	30	31	30	53	30
All working	82⎫85	73⎫78	70⎫75	58⎫66	61⎫69	70⎫76
Unemployed	3⎭	5⎭	5⎭	8⎭	8⎭	6⎭
Base = 100%	2334	9658	1453	3901	1408	18754

Source: Derived from OPCS, 1996b: Table 7.11.

of the woman the more likely she is to be in employment and the more likely that employment is to be full- rather than part-time. The notion of the 'bourgeois family' model where women stay at home is empirically ✗ incorrect. The class which could most afford for women to stay at home is the one in which women do so least. Among professional and managerial women 85 per cent are economically active, 65 per cent full-time, while only 68 per cent of unskilled manual workers are economically active, 7 per cent full-time (OPCS, 1996b: Table 7.11).

These differences are compounded when women have children, as was indicated in the earlier section on the changing impact of children on women's employment pattern. It would appear that professional and managerial women are able to buy forms of child care to enable them to maintain full-time employment in a way not possible for women earning less in the semi- and unskilled workforce, and that such women avail themselves of this option. Further, that when there are effective choices between paid employment and domestic activity women with the opportunity of top jobs take them.

ETHNICITIES

Employment levels vary very considerably by ethnicity for women, although they do not vary as much for men (see Table 2.26 below). The women with the highest economic activity rate are White, closely followed by Black and Indian, with a much lower rate recorded for the Pakistani/Bangladeshi community. Unemployment is much more concentrated in ethnic minority communities. Part-time employment is more common among White women. Such ethnic differences in employment patterns result from a number of factors including racial discrimination, different age structures of the ethnic communities, and ethnically specific patterns of gender regime.

Table 2.26 Economic activity by ethnic group, 1993

	Men			Women		
	Total 16–64	Economic activity rate	ILO un-employment	Total 16–59	Economic activity rate	ILO un-employment
White	16800	86	12	15320	72	7
Black	270	80	34	270	66	20
Indian	320	81	14	300	61	11
Pakistani/ Bangladeshi	200	72	31	210	25	29
Mixed/other origins	210	76	17	200	59	17

Source: *Employment Gazette*, May 1994: Table 2.
Note: Black includes 'Black Caribbean', 'Black African' and 'Black other', but not 'Black mixed'.

First, there is direct discrimination against ethnic minorities in employment, of which there are many accounts (Brah and Shaw, 1992; Dex, 1983; Phizacklea, 1990). This is particularly pertinent in the explanation of the unemployment rates for both men and women of the Black and Pakistani/Bangladeshi groups, which are more than double the rate for the White community. This is also indicated in the extent of occupational and industrial segregation by ethnicity as well as gender shown in statistical summaries (*Employment Gazette*, 1994: 152) and much case study research (Brah and Shaw, 1992; Phizacklea, 1990; Westwood and Bhachu, 1989).

Second there are different age structures, such that there are fewer women aged 45–64 among the ethnic minorities than among the White population. This may contribute towards an explanation of the differential rate of part-time working among different ethnic groups, since such working is more common among older women. Among employees in employment 46 per cent of White women were working part-time as compared with 33 per cent of Black women, 31 per cent of Indian women, and 43 per cent of Pakistani/Bangladeshi women (*Employment Gazette*, 1994: 477). This may also contribute towards an explanation of the pattern that among the economically inactive women the highest proportion of students was found in the ethnic minorities, especially the Black population (25 per cent), as compared with a 15 per cent average for all ethnic groups (*Employment Gazette*, 1994: 151).

Third, there are ethnically specific forms of gender regime. The highest proportion of women looking after the family/home was among the Pakistani/Bangladeshi group (among the economically inactive they were 76 per cent as compared with a 56 per cent average) (*Employment Gazette*, May 1994). Further, higher proportions of lone mothers are to be found among the White and Black communities. Thus we see indications that the Pakistani/Bangladeshi community has a more domestic form of gender regime while the other groups have a more public gender regime.

There is some evidence of very rapid changes in the gender relations in some of the ethnic minority communities (Bhopal, 1996; Brah, 1993). These involve important issues of changes in ethnic identities and boundaries (see Anthias and Yuval-Davies, 1992). This appears to be especially the case among the Pakistani/Bangladeshi community. Here the highest rate of economic activity is found among those aged 16–24, 32 per cent, falling to 23 per cent for those aged 25–44. While it might be argued that this is simply indicative of a settled pattern of pre-marital employment which ceases or is reduced on marriage and child birth, it is also open to the interpretation that it indicates rapid change among younger South Asian women towards a more public gender regime. This latter interpretation is supported by the work of Bhopal (1996), on the basis of both interview data and analysis of unpublished Labour Force Survey data. She argues strongly that access to education for young South Asian women in Britain is transforming their ability to gain employment and independence. However, as both Brah (1993) and Bhavnani (1993) comment, tensions between identities articulated through both Islam, modernity and locality mean that such processes are likely to be contested. New hybridised identities may well result.

SPATIAL UNEVENNESS

Women and men are not evenly distributed through the economy. Chapters 3 and 4 and Appendix 1 explore the significance of variations between localities which are identifiable labour markets. The implications are that the lived experience of gender relations in employment is very variable and the national average is merely an average.

CONCLUSIONS

Gender relations are being transformed by the latest round of restructuring. This builds on previous restructuring which brought women into the public sphere especially in polity, education and employment. It particularly affects younger women who are currently making choices about education, employment and children, rather than older women who have typically already made many of these life-determining decisions. Current features of the restructuring are the expansion of education in which young women are seizing the opportunities more rapidly than younger men, the expansion of upper levels of employment, which younger women are reaching into to an extent unknown in the past, a reduction in the impact of home life on women's employment, and a decline in the extent to which women live with life-long partners.

These opportunities for women are a result of a number of factors; in particular, they rest on the new forms of politics and state regulation of employment. Since women gained the vote the state has stopped being an instrument of closure against women, ceasing to uphold legislation to exclude women from employment (Walby, 1986b), but only very recently, since 1970, have there been significant overt policies to enhance gender equity in employment and elsewhere. These recent initiatives are partly a result of changes in notions of equity and justice relating to women in the UK, partly a result of pressure by women in the UK, but the timing and effectiveness is partly a result of the increasing impact of European integration, in particular the slow but steady enforcement of Article 119 of the Treaty of Rome, the founding treaty of the European Union, which laid down that there should be equal treatment of women and men in employment-related issues. These legal measures for women have underpinned the development of equal opportunities policies by employers and trade unions. They are also part of a wider cultural change in which equal opportunities have become part of mainstream policy discourse, rather than a specifically feminist issue, albeit with minimal resources for implementation.

Step by step women are increasingly participating in the public institutions of education, employment and political decision making. However, the coexistence of women who have built their lives around a domestic gender regime and those who have built them around a more public regime leads to new forms of differences and new forms of inequality.

The massive changes which are taking place in women's employment and education are transforming gender relations. Some younger women are taking up the educational opportunities offered and then using them to gain good jobs. Domestic tasks are less frequently acting as an obstacle to this strategy, in that women are returning to work more rapidly after child birth, and women are less likely to be married. These changes in education and employment are the leading edge of the change from the private gender regime to the public one.

But these changes do not involve all women. They particularly miss those women who, for reasons including generation, ethnicity, and pregnancy, have not gained educational qualifications. For example, many older women missed the recent expansion of educational opportunities and are much less likely to have qualifications and good jobs (although there are exceptions). Their current choices are constrained by choices made earlier in their lives when private patriarchal relations were more prevalent. Older women are taking up disproportionately the newly restructured lower skilled occupations, especially in services. These are disproportionately part-time, poorly paid forms of employment. This exerts downwards pressure on the availability and conditions of employment for men as well. Further, women in different ethnic communities have different priorities and opportunities which generate different sexual divisions of labour, but recognisable as either of more public or more private form of gender regime. The complex interventions of the state as provider of minimal benefits interact with some household structures so as to discourage some women's employment. Not all young women are doing well, for instance lone parents without employment are likely to be very poor, and women from ethnic minorities are more likely to be unemployed.

Women who are not participating in paid employment with the benefit of educational qualifications are likely to be poor and disadvantaged. We are seeing new forms of polarisation between women. These are based less on the class of their husband and much more on their own education and employment. In practice because of the speed of the changes the more advantaged women are among younger women, the more disadvantaged among the older.

These changes for women interact with changes for men. Men are much less likely to be economically active than 20 years ago, young ones with high rates of unemployment, older ones as economically inactive. The conditions of part-time work have assisted in driving down the conditions of employment for men as well as for women, given the context of deregulation and globalisation. In this way, gender affects class relations. This reverses previous suggestions as to the relationship between gender and class – that class shapes gender – for instance, that women workers were a reserve army of labour for employers, or that the class position of the husband determined that of the wife. Rather now, it is at least as much that gender shapes class. The change in the form of gender regime, in the context of globalisation and deregulation alters the nature of employment and thus of class relations.

Changes in the economy as a whole cannot be understood outside of an understanding of the transformations in the structures of gender relations, the change from a private gender regime or private patriarchy, to a more public gender regime, or public patriarchy. These changes in the form of gender regime are proceeding rapidly, giving rise to new forms of opportunity and inequality.

3

FLEXIBILITY AND THE CHANGING SEXUAL DIVISION OF LABOUR

INTRODUCTION

Women's employment has often been considered secondary or marginal in social and economic theory. This has included conceptions of women as a reserve of labour; as secondary workers; and, more recently, as 'numerically flexible' workers. Further, women are seen to inhabit only the secondary, and less skilled, part of the labour force. However, the changes in women's employment described in the last chapter cast doubt on the extent to which women's employment as a whole is secondary or marginal.

That women constitute a labour reserve has been the focus of debate in a considerable body of literature. Women have been considered to be pulled into employment when there is a boom in the economy and returned to the family when there is a recession, according to both socialist feminists (Beechey, 1977, 1978; Bruegel, 1979; Milkman, 1976), and neoclassical economists (Mincer, 1962, 1966). However, women have not been expelled from the workforce in the many recessions in twentieth-century Britain, rather there have been steady increases in women's employment in Britain over the last 25 years, as Table 3.1 below shows. Rather it is male employment which has been in decline since a peak in the mid–1960s, a decline exacerbated in each subsequent recession. Women are not a short-term reserve army of labour.

Table 3.1 Employment trends, 1959–95

Employees in employment	1959	1966	1971	1976	1981	1986	1991	1995
All persons	20983	22787	21648	22048	21386	21105	21719	21355
All male	13824	14551	13424	13097	12278	11643	11253	10777
All female	7159	8236	8224	8951	9108	9462	10467	10584
% female	34.1	36.1	38.0	40.6	42.6	44.8	48.2	49.6

Source: calculated from *Employment Gazette, Historical Supplement*, Feb 1987: Table 1.1 for 1959–83; August 1987: Table 1.1 for 1986; *Labour Force Trends*, April 1996: Table 1.1.

A slightly different version of the thesis that women are a reserve is that of Braverman (1974), who saw women as a reserve of labour pulled into employment over a much longer period of time, not cyclical fluctuations of the economy. He suggested that women increasingly entered paid work as time spent on housework was reduced as a result of domestic labour entering capitalist production, for instance, that people bought bread and clothes, rather than women making them at home. He considered that women would be employed in the less-skilled areas of employment as part of the overall dynamic of monopoly capitalism in which there was a general process of deskilling of work as a result of a standard Taylorist inspired managerial strategy to reduce jobs to their simplest components in order to increase managerial control (Beechey, 1982; Wood, 1982). There is a considerable debate as to whether there is such a process of deskilling in the UK, or whether rather there has been a net increase in employment requiring skills and qualifications as employers seek to use the full range of human capacity and initiative (Elger, 1928; Gallie and White, 1983; Gallie *et al.*, 1994; Piore and Sabel, 1984). Further, it is not clear that the empirical evidence supports the contention that women's employment in particular has grown most in the less-skilled areas of employment, as will be discussed below and in the following chapter.

A more recent account of the development of marginality among workers is that of Atkinson's (NEDO, 1986) version of the flexibility thesis. While some versions of the flexibility thesis suggest that these processes, in a move from Fordist to post-Fordist production regimes, enrich skills and provide variety of forms of employment (Piore and Sabel, 1984), that of Atkinson is more pessimistic in that he sees only a core of workers enhancing their skills, while those workers in the periphery are subject to flexibility in terms of whether they have work or not.

Can this more sophisticated theory of marginality and flexibility help our understanding of the transformation in the gender composition of the work-force? Is the account by Atkinson and others of changes in the workforce in terms of a developing differentiation between core and peripheral workers of use for explaining the major changes in the gender composition of the work-force? Hakim (1987b) shows that, if the workforce is divided into two – permanent, full-time on the one hand and 'flexible', either part-time or temporary on the other – then the 'flexible' portion of the workforce rose from 30 per cent in 1981 to 34 per cent in 1986. While one-quarter of men were among the 'flexibles', one-half of women workers were to be found there. Part-time women workers are the largest single category of non-permanent workers. In 1985 they made up 16.6 per cent of the workforce, while temporary workers (female and male) made up only 5.5 per cent, despite their big increase over 1981 (calculated from *Employment Gazette*, Historical Supplement, Feb 1987, Table 1.1, and Hakim, 1987b: 93). Since then the proportion of women who work part-time has increased even further to 23 per cent of the workforce in 1995, while the proportion of temporary workers fluctuates around 5–6 per cent (*Labour Force Trends*, April 1996).

Does this mean that flexibility is gendered? Is the 'core' masculine and the 'periphery' feminine? Whose flexibility is it? Does part-time work simultaneously meet the needs of women, employers and husbands or merely one of these groups? Is 'flexibilisation' 'feminisation', given the increase in a 'flexible' part-time female workforce? Can recent changes in women's employment be understood in terms of increases in flexibility?

This chapter will draw out the implications of flexibility theses for gender relations. I will focus on the work of Atkinson (NEDO, 1986) because he and his colleagues have produced one of the most developed models of flexibility. While Atkinson does not addresses the issue of changes in gender relations as part of his account of flexibility, it is my contention that the model they construct is gendered.

ATKINSON'S MODEL

Atkinson constructs a model of the flexible firm and asks whether there have been significant moves towards it over the last decade. He identifies four main types of flexibility: numerical flexibility, functional flexibility, distancing (especially subcontracting) and pay flexibility (the first two being the most important). In numerical flexibility employers are able to vary the amount of labour they employ at short notice; in functional flexibility, workers are able to take on a wider range of tasks, which is considered to increase efficiency by, for example, enabling them to perform the work of absent colleagues.

Atkinson constructs a model of the flexible firm in terms of a division between core and peripheral workers, the division being theoretically one of degree, but in practice being effectively treated as dichotomous. Peripheral workers are those who are semi-skilled or unskilled and numerically flexible, as a result of short-term contracts, agency hiring and being employed by subcontractors, and those who are part-time or job sharing. Core workers are likely to be skilled and have secure contracts of employment and be employed by particular firms for a long period, unlike the peripheral ones. Atkinson states that the distinction between these two types of employment has grown since 1980 among the 72 firms in which he interviewed. As a consequence he suggests that the labour market has become more segmented over this period.

He suggests that there has been a significant change in management conduct towards workers over the last few years, which has accelerated the move to the flexible firm. He suggests the following as causes:

1 the recession, especially in so far as it weakens union power and increases the labour supply (it might, therefore, be a temporary effect);

2 technical change;

3 legislative change, although this has had only a limited effect;

4 changing business objectives, especially changes in the environment demanding faster responsiveness, decentralisation and headcount reduction.

The 'permissive factors' encouraging these are summarised as reduced 'union power and slack external labour markets'.

Evidence consistent with these IMS claims about the increase in flexibility is widespread (Cross, 1985; Curson, 1986; Hakim, 1987b; Incomes Data Services, 1982, 1983, 1984), though some writers emphasise national variations in its form (Lash and Bagguley, 1987). Others such as Pollert (1987), are, however, sceptical about its newness in Britain on grounds, for instance, of its similarity to struggles over 'productivity'.

Atkinson's model and gender

How gendered is Atkinson's model of the flexible firm? Does it capture accurately the nature and implications of the different positions of women and men in the labour market? Atkinson (NEDO, 1986) makes little reference to gendered processes in his account, but he does consistently note in passing that the part-time workers and 'distanced homeworkers' who make up a significant part of the numerically flexible workforce are usually female. However, this is noted empirically, rather than the significance of the gender of these flexible workers being integrated into his analysis of these changes. Do these processes, which have gendered effects, have gendered social forces as their causes? I shall examine this in stages. First, by asking whether the division between core and periphery is essentially one between male and female workers. Second, by questioning whether the changed environment is critically one in which gender relations have altered, especially in relation to equal opportunity and job protection legislation which differentially affects women and men workers, and in terms of household structure and domestic labour which have resulted in women spending a smaller proportion of their lives as full-time housewives. Third, by discussing the theoretical arguments underlying his model, as to the underlying structural processes. Finally I shall present an alternative view of these rounds of gender restructuring.

Core/periphery

There is a tendency for core workers to be equated with male workers and peripheral workers with female workers, although there are countervailing factors. I shall explore first the reasons which support the notion that these dichotomies are coterminous, and second, those which do not.

It is commonplace to argue that women, on average, hold jobs which are designated as less skilled, lower paid, more insecure and with fewer promotion prospects than those of men. Taken at the level of the labour market as a whole the typical women's jobs do appear to conform to this model, in that women earn significantly less than men, gain fewer pension rights, and are less frequently found in the higher occupational grades (see Chapter 2). The existence of occupational and industrial segregation by sex means that women are confined to a narrow range of occupations. For instance, while men are evenly spread between services and the production sector, with 56 per cent in services, in 1986 81 per cent of women and 91 per cent of part-time women were in this sector (*Employment Gazette*, Feb 1987, Historical Supplement, Table 1.1) (see Chapter 2 for further details). Women's work is typically designated as less skilled than men's even when the amount of learning time is considerable. Part-time women workers, especially, appear to fit the model of peripheral workers, particularly in their lack of rights to permanent employment. Until 1995, in Britain, employees must have worked at least 16 hours a week with the same employer for two years in order to qualify for most of the state-backed employment rights, such as protection from unfair dismissal, maternity rights, and redundancy pay. Those who work between eight and sixteen hours must have been with an employer for five years to qualify. A significant proportion of women fell outside the provisions of the legislation protecting them from dismissal because they work too few hours to qualify for security of employment. While these forms of differentiation were declared illegal under EU law in 1995, nonetheless, much of the development of part-time work in the 1970s, 1980s and early 1990s took place in this context (see Chapter 2).

In 1995 47 per cent of women workers were part-time as compared with 11 per cent of men (*Labour Force Trends*, 1996; Naylor, 1994). On average, they earn considerably less than full-time women workers, as well as men. In 1995 the hourly earnings of part-time women were 75 per cent of those of full-time women and 60 per cent of full-time men's (calculated from *New Earnings Survey*, 1995). Most of this difference is due to part-time workers performing different, or differently categorised, work from full-timers, since there is no evidence that the same employer pays the same job at different rates for full- and part-time workers. Typically part-time work is among less-skilled areas of employment (see Chapter 2). As a proportion of the workforce part-time women workers are growing, from 13 per cent in 1971 to 23 per cent in 1995, while the proportion of full-time women in the workforce has been nearly constant over the same period, rising from 25.3 per cent in 1971 to only 26.4 per cent in 1995 (calculated from *Employment Gazette*, Feb 1987, Historical Supplement, Table 1.1; *Labour Force Trends*,

1996). Part-time workers are less likely than full-time workers to be on the relevant promotion ladder or to achieve the seniority necessary for attaining the status of core worker.

Homeworkers, as women on low rates of pay, working for a few hours a week outside the protection of much of the employment legislation, might be considered the quintessential peripheral workforce. Hakim (1987a) shows that while these women exist, especially among manufacturing homework, they do not constitute all home-based workers. In particular, they need to be carefully distinguished from workers, often male, who merely use their home as a base, and who have high earnings and greater continuity of employer. Hakim (1987b) suggests that the full-time, part-time division is the most important in differentiating the conditions and pay of these workers.

Against

On the other hand there are factors which might mitigate against such an equation of men in the core and women in the periphery. In particular, a case against such a core–periphery dualism can be made if the employment of women is disaggregated, especially if clerical work, which employs so many women, is examined.

In a more disaggregated picture the labour market is revealed as highly segregated and with major differences between forms of women's employment which contradict simple generalisations about women's work. Vastly differing proportions of men and women in the 17 socio-economic groups (SEGs) demonstrate the complexity of the picture, as is shown in Chapter 5. While women are much less well represented in the upper echelons of the SEGs, the pattern is, nonetheless, not simply one of all the men at the top and all the women at the bottom. There are small, but significant, numbers of women in professional jobs such as teaching and nursing, and increasing numbers of women who are gaining qualifications in, for example, accounting and law. And it is the nature and scale of women's employment in clerical work which most significantly challenges the over-simplistic picture. Of all women in employment, 39 per cent were in the junior non-manual category, which typically means clerical work; women made up 71 per cent of this SEG. This work, while at the bottom of any hierarchical classification of non-manual work, cannot be placed beneath the SEGs for manual workers in a simple way. It is better in terms of pay and conditions of service than women's manual work; it is worse in terms of pay than most male skilled and semi-skilled work, but better than the male unskilled. But is it worse in conditions of service than these male workers? In terms of responsibility, control over the labour process in clerical work is varied. There is in fact considerable controversy as to the place of clerical workers in the stratification system (Abercrombie and Urry, 1983; Braverman, 1974;

Crompton and Jones, 1984; Goldthorpe, 1980; Klingender, 1935; Stanworth, 1984; Stewart *et al.*, 1980, West, 1978). Some of this controversy reflects the wide range of situations within clerical work.

This debate has especially focused upon women's skill level, responsibility and control over the labour process of themselves and other workers, and their likelihood of promotion, all of which are generally believed to be low for women clerical workers. Their conditions of service and rates of pay have received less attention in the more theoretical literature, although these have been addressed in some of the empirical studies (e.g. McNally, 1979; Vinnicombe, 1980). It would appear that because of their conditions of service, security of tenure and technical levels of skill a significant proportion of them should be considered to be part of the core, as well as some in the periphery.

Clerical workers often receive 'staff' conditions of service, rather than those accorded to 'production' workers in relation to payment method, length of working week, regulation of working hours (e.g., no clocking in, more generous sick leave, pension arrangements), clothing, pleasantness of working conditions, etc. Many, although not all, clerical workers have stable employment of the kind usually associated with primary jobs (although this is partly a consequence of the fact that clerical work is disproportionately located in those industrial sectors which are normally most buoyant).

In the strict Bravermanian sense of control over the labour process, it is now common to consider that such clerical workers are not skilled (Braverman, 1974; Crompton and Jones, 1984). However, many of these workers have levels of technical skill which require better than average schooling, certainly higher than average levels of literacy, and often skills such as typing which require six months' training to reach full proficiency, even if these skills are not recognised as socially significant.

This argument is reinforced by Dex (1987), who argues that clerical work constitutes a discrete cluster of jobs within which women experience job movement, and that it is separate from other jobs such as semi-skilled factory work, shop work and personal service work. That is, there is a barrier to mobility for women between clerical work and these other jobs. Dex argues that clerical work is a woman's primary labour market. A significant proportion of clerical work is part of a primary, not secondary labour market, and part of the core not periphery.

Women workers are too highly differentiated in employment conditions for women as a whole to be seen as numerically flexible workers. While some, especially part-timers do fit this model, others such as many clerical workers, and also the growing numbers of professional women, do not.

So far the analysis has focused upon women, in order to argue that a simple correlation between women and periphery cannot be made. Men, too, do not fit neatly on one side of this divide, although the majority do.

One-quarter of men do not fall into the permanent full-time category (Hakim, 1987b). Thus, while the majority of the core workers may be male and the periphery female, there are some significant exceptions to this which preclude a simple equation of the two

Environmental change

Atkinson (NEDO, 1986) makes reference to changes in the wider environment as being a factor in the concern for more flexibility within management's strategies. I am going to assess whether these changes are significantly gendered, in particular whether gender is a causal factor in the changing structure of employment. Atkinson's main concern is with changes in the business environment, especially changes in the product market and international competition. He suggests that legislative changes have had little impact and implies that the main changes are ungendered.

If, however, we take a broader definition of the environment, we might observe major changes in both the immediate business context regarding the use of female labour and in the wider environment, which have significantly affected the supply of female labour. The changes in the business context include: the dropping of the marriage bar after the Second World War (i.e. only five decades ago); the significant lessening of male trade union opposition to women in paid work; equal opportunity legislation which undercuts barriers to women in paid work; employment protection legislation which protects full-time, but few part-time workers (Walby, 1986b: 202–42).

Other relevant changes in the business environment include the increased access of women to education, as detailed in the previous chapter, with young women gaining at least as many educational qualifications as young men. The increased rate of divorce also acts as an encouragement to female career development. The rate of divorce rose from 4.7 in 1,000 of married persons in 1970 to 13.5 in 1991 (*General Household Survey*, 1993: 26). Women in employment spend less time on housework, even though the extent and effect of this reduction is controversial (Cowan, 1983; Gershuny, 1983; Vanek, 1980). The fertility rate continues to fall. Further details of related changes can be found in Chapter 2.

In short, the gender environment is very significantly different from what it was even 20 years ago, both within the business context (with greater rights and protections given to male workers, and to a lesser extent full-time, but not part-time, women workers), and in the wider business environment (in the increased supply of women workers because of changed domestic conditions and gendered educational changes).

While the extent of the impact of the equal opportunity legislation is the subject of some controversy (Dex and Shaw, 1986; Hakim, 1981; McIntosh and Weir, 1982; Snell, 1979; Snell *et al.*, 1981), few would doubt that it reduces the legitimacy of directly discriminatory practices against women. The implication of the employment protection legislation for the gendering of the terrain of industrial relations is less well explored. It would appear to have been important in differentiating the conditions of work of men from those of part-time women. A male-dominated labour movement won legislation which secured protection from arbitrary dismissal of the occupants of the types of jobs which were more often held by men than by women. These were the full-time jobs, and jobs of people who had already been in employment with one employer for some time. Part-time employment, typically held by women, was much less protected.

On this new terrain there is then greater differentiation of job security of the average male and a significant minority of female workers, since that of the typical male has been improved to a greater extent than that of the part-time female. There has been a divergence in the conditions of employment of men and part-time women as a consequence of this gendered legislation. A consequence of this one-sided improvement in the job security of male workers is that part-time women workers are more exposed when there is an employer offensive on job security. This is not to suggest, however, that men, even in the 'core', have not been made redundant.

Further differences in the conditions of employment of full-time and part-time workers resulted from state insurance and welfare policy (Hakim, 1987b; Manley and Sawbridge, 1980). Part-timers became more attractive to employers because of state policy relating to the level of the threshold for the payment of national insurance, and, before 1995, differential maternity rights and differential eligibility for redundancy pay. During the period of growth of part-time work in the 1970s, 1980s and early 1990s in the UK, this differentiation of the conditions of full- and part-time workers was higher than in many other countries. Britain has consistently had one of the highest proportions of women working part-time among the Member States of the European Union – in 1994, second only to the Netherlands (*Labour Force Survey*). These differences have historic roots in the particular British experience of the mobilisation of women workers in the Second World War (Summerfield, 1984; Walby, 1986b).

We should, however, be wary of leaping to the conclusion, as did some of the early theorists on women as a reserve army of labour, that lack of employment protection means that women are less likely to be employed as a consequence of employers shedding such workers. Rather the reverse is the case. Less-protected workers are more attractive workers to employers, precisely because they have less job security. If employers are indeed seeking greater numerical flexibility, then they are more likely to create categories of employment which are more likely to be filled by part-time women. This is indeed what we see. The strategy of numerical flexibility, whether it be old or new, is one which provides employment opportunities to women, albeit under worse conditions of service.

When asked, most women who work part-time say that they do so out of choice, and that they are not actively seeking full-time work; in 1994 80 per cent of women asked by the Labour Force Survey why they worked part-time said that they did not want a full-time job (Naylor, 1994). Part-time working permits many women to balance existing commitments to employment and to home life more effectively than full-time working, under current arrangements. The positive response to this question does not mean, of course, that women prefer to work for lower wages, to be less likely to gain a pension, to have fewer employment rights than full-timers, or to have no access to publicly funded child care, merely that, under current structural constraints they see this pattern of working as their best option.

CONTRADICTIONS BETWEEN DIFFERENT FORMS OF FLEXIBILITY

Numerical flexibility is only one form of flexibility; the other major kind being functional flexibility. It is on this latter kind that the more optimistic of the post-Fordist writers have concentrated (see e.g. Piore and Sabel, 1984), seeing in it a source of job enrichment and the possibility of a simultaneous increase in both worker satisfaction and productivity. An example of an attempt to increase functional flexibility has been in the health professions, where some nurses have been encouraged to take on a wider range of tasks alongside an attempt by some nurses to develop a professionalisation strategy based upon a willingness to increase their range of responsible decision making (see Walby and Greenwell et al., 1994). A problem arises when functional flexibility is introduced in an era of cost-cutting or cost-containment, and workers refuse to implement new functionally flexible forms of working arrangements as part of a resistance to cuts. This has been an aspect of recent health service restructuring. For instance there has been some resistance among some nurses to taking on some extra tasks, when these can be interpreted as being merely 'dumped' on them by doctors restricting their own hours, or as part of a general strategy of cost containment (Walby and Greenwell et al., 1994).

One of the motivations of management in seeking to introduce functionally flexible working patterns is the removal of labour market rigidities which impede the efficient utilisation of labour. Neoclassical economic theory has long held that a perfectly competitive labour market helps towards an efficiently functioning economy and that any form of labour market rigidity impedes this goal. One significant aspect of labour market rigidity is that of occupational segregation by sex (Equal Opportunities Commission, 1985a; Hakim, 1979, 1981; Treiman and Hartmann, 1981). Yet, sex segregation among the part-time workforce is more pronounced than in the full-time workforce, since these part-timers are focused in a very few areas of very high female concentration (see Chapter 2). In this way numerical and functional flexibility appear to be contradictory as currently practised, in that the increase of numerical flexibility (the development of part-time work) is at the expense of functional flexibility (the increased labour market rigidities of greater sex segregation).

ROUNDS OF GENDER RESTRUCTURING

Some of the key divisions in the workforce that the flexibility literature addresses are essentially gendered. The most important and sizeable change in the composition and structure of the labour force over the last couple of decades has been the dramatic increase in the number of part-time women workers. Part-time women workers are the largest single category of flexible workers. However, as argued above, we should hesitate before stereotyping core workers as male and female workers as peripheral. While part-time women workers do tend to fit the model of peripheral workers, many full-time women workers, who made up 53 per cent of the female workforce in 1995, do not.

Women are entering waged labour in larger proportions. Yet women are not simply at the bottom of the pile, nor are they a disposable reserve. There are more of them, at various positions in the vertical hierarchy of paid employment, and they are often segregated from men.

It is because of the erosion of some forms of patriarchal practices in paid work that women have a different place in the new rounds of restructuring than in the old. The attempt to subordinate women in the labour market is not new, but part of a continuing dynamic in the interrelationship of gender, class and ethnic structures and practices. It is partly in response to the successes that women have won in terms of entry to the labour market and elsewhere that this new round of restructuring is taking the form that it is. Part-time work for women fits the desire of many women for paid work which is compatible with their existing domestic responsibilities and of employers for cheap flexible labour.

The employment protection legislation, won under the pressure of the labour movement, gave protection from dismissal to those workers with a period of full-time employment in one firm. Other legislation gave national insurance benefits to employees who worked more than a certain number of hours, and charged employers for this. The new flexibility offensive is at least partly a response to that round of labour movement activity. It does not so much contest the advantages given to those workers by legislation, but rather seeks to side-step these issues by both increasingly employing workers on contracts which do not qualify for this state-backed protection, and enforcing lesser job security on those workers who fall outside the protection of the legislation. (It is on the terrain of functional flexibility that the employers are directly taking on entrenched labour movement positions.)

The notions of rounds of struggle, each setting the conditions for the next, as introduced by Edwards (1979), and rounds of accumulation as introduced by Massey (1984) are useful here. We may fruitfully extend these concepts and apply them to the situation which has been developing in Britain in the 1980s and 1990s. The essence of Edwards' notion is that employers and employees do not engage in simple pendulum-type struggles over the same issues, but rather the terrain of struggle is transformed by each round of struggle, and new issues and forms of struggle.

In the context of full-time female and male workers having won greater legislative protection than part-timers, it is to be expected that where possible, the next round of jobs created by employers would not be full-time. Further, the forms of resistance that male workers have historically used against the entry of women workers have been undercut by the successful struggles of women against these forms of patriarchal closure. The equal opportunity legislation and changes in trade unions' policies under pressure from their recently enlarged female membership prevent some of the forms of closure that previously occurred, while not guaranteeing women equal access to the better jobs with men.

In Britain then, the growth of peripheral part-time work for women, as an integral and permanent part of the workforce, is a result of a new round of capital restructuring in the context of the new balance of gender and class forces. This particular balance of forces is not a historical inevitability within capitalism. Indeed Britain is unusual in the Western industrialised world in the extent to which the workforce is composed of part-time women (the Netherlands is the only country in the EU with a higher rate in 1994, *Labour Force Survey*, 1994)(see Table 3.2).

Because this pattern of part-time labour varies between countries, an explanation in terms of the technical requirements of industry (National Economic Development Office, 1986: 22–3; Robinson, 1988; Robinson and Wallace, 1984) is insufficient. Table 3.2 also shows that Britain has the second highest rate of part-time women, and one of the highest rates of female participation, in the European Union. It is the only country in the European Union in which the rate of unemployment among women is lower than that among men. This is at least partly because part-time women workers are uniquely open to low pay and flexible employment

Table 3.2 Rates of female economic activity, part-time working and gender unemployment ratios in the European Union

	Bel	Dk	D	Gr	Sp	Fr	Irl	It	Lx	Ne	Pt	UK
F activity rate	40	58	48	35	35	48	40	34	38	48	50	53
% F p-t	28	34	33	8	15	28	22	12	20	66	12	44
F/M unemp	1.6	1.3	1.4	2.3	1.6	1.3	1.0	1.8	1.4	1.3	1.3	0.6

Source: calculated from *Labour Force Survey*, 1994: Tables 001, 050.

conditions in Britain, making their labour especially attractive to employers seeking such labour. The table also shows a general tendency for countries with low levels of part-time work among women to have a higher proportion of unemployment amongst women. Further it is countries with the lowest levels of female 'economic' activity which tend to show the highest ratios of female to male employment.

The form of gender regime and the relationship between gender, class and ethnic structures varies between nations, localities and industries. The widespread entry of women into labour market participation is not new to the post-Second World War period. Historically, men were a minority in the workforce of the first factory employment in the world, cotton textiles in Lancashire. Resistance to women working in these mills, though organised, was too weak to prevent their continuance. At the same time, women were barred from not dissimilar work in engineering by the much more strongly organised male unions. In clerical work, men also lost their battle to exclude women, though they were able to maintain strict segregation, retaining the better jobs. The regional distribution of these forms of employment gave rise to regionally specific female participation rates, which were considerable before the Second World War (Walby, 1986b).

CONCLUSION

The influx of women into employment in the post-war period is not a temporary expedient of employers seeking 'reserves' of labour to use in a crisis, either of an overtight labour market, or an overslack one (cf. Beechey, 1977, 1978; Mincer, 1962). It is, rather, a long-term restructuring of the gender composition of the workforce. It can occur because there have been long-term changes in gender relations both within and outside employment. The removal of many overt and covert forms of patriarchal closure in the labour market is a major structural change. Changes in gender relations outside employment, such as greater access to education, changes in patterns of marriage and divorce, in political citizenship and in household structure, improve women's access to paid work on a long-term basis. Further, many of these changes, such as the educational qualifications attained by young women today, may continue to have a positive impact on women's employment prospects for decades to come. The continuing entry of women into paid employment is part of the change in the form of gender regime from a private to a more public form.

Women's employment is polarised to a considerable extent between the professional, managerial and white-collar work of younger women, and the less-skilled manual work of older women. As was discussed both here and the previous chapter the former tends to be full-time and the latter part-time. The different types of flexibility strategy engage with the quite different parts of this polarised female workforce. Part-time women workers are more often subject to the numerical flexibility strategy. More skilled workers, such as public sector professionals, especially nurses, are subject to twin pressures to both be more functionally flexible, yet at the same time to cut costs.

The majority of the numerically flexible workforce is female, and in this way flexibility is gendered. The growth of flexibility has been dependent upon the availability of women as part-time workers. This is bound up with women's increased paid employment, but the part-time form which has so expanded leaves women vulnerable to poor wages and conditions. The development of this type of flexibility in Britain has been dependent upon the change in the form of the gender regime from domestic to public, which has facilitated the increased availability of women as cheap and flexible workers.

4

LOCALITIES AND GENDER RESTRUCTURING

INTRODUCTION

Gender relations vary significantly across space, not only by nation, but also by region and locality. Spatial differences are an important source of diversity in gender relations. Restructuring theory has made some very important contributions to our understanding of economic change, especially in its spatially and temporally sensitive account of the relation between capital and labour. This chapter will consider the extent to which such theories have enabled us to address the question of different patterns of gender relations in employment in different localities. While gender divisions within labour have been infrequently addressed as an overt and central issue in this theory (with some exceptions), yet there are necessarily implicit theses about gender in these accounts. This chapter is an attempt to develop restructuring theory by drawing out these implicit theses, testing them against empirical data, and suggesting a revised way in which restructuring theory and theories of gender relations can be synthesised. Many of the writers considered here did not set out to produce a full theory of gender and restructuring; the intention here is to develop this theory.

Within restructuring theory we can find three implicit theses regarding women's employment and space: that woman are a spatial reserve army of labour; that rigid sex-typing means that changes in female employment are contingent upon the expansion and decline of specific sectors; and that there is a feminisation of the new peripheral regions which is related to deskilling. We shall show how these theses are embedded in some of the more developed of the restructuring writings.

Where gender divisions in employment have been examined in depth, it has been unusual to find a spatial dimension, for instance, in theories of women as a reserve army of labour (Beechey, 1977, 1978; Braverman, 1974) and in accounts of occupational segregation (Cockburn, 1983; Hakim, 1979; Oppenheimer, 1970). This has resulted in some over-general accounts in which local, regional, and even national differences are glossed over, if noticed at all. Yet the regional data clearly shows that there have been massive regional differences in female employment rates, which are now disappearing (Walby, 1985).

Massey (1984) and Massey and Meegan (1982) are unusual in the literature on the spatial division of labour in devoting much attention to this issue (other exceptions include Townsend, 1986; Women and Geography, 1986). Massey (1984) and Massey and Meegan (1982) argue that women, especially married women, are a spatially specific reserve army of semi-skilled and unskilled labour. There are three stages to this argument: first, the differentiation of three main types of labour; second, the argument as to why and how male and female labour is to be distinguished; and third, the evidence of the changing spatial employment of women (and men).

They divide labour into three categories: 'best staff' doing research and development work, usually graduate and male; skilled and manual craft workers, usually male; semi-skilled and unskilled workers, typically female. These forms of labour are unevenly spatially distributed: the research and development staff being concentrated in the South-east, with some outlets in areas such as Chester; skilled manual workers are to be found in the old manufacturing heartlands in the North and Midlands; and semi-skilled and unskilled female labour in many areas, albeit historically utilised at different rates in different localities. These forms of labour are factors in the relocation of manufacturing industries.

Although the distinction between these three types of labour is given by the intersection of technology with the capital labour relation, Massey and Meegan suggest three different types of factors which differentiate male and female labour. These include: ideological factors, including belief about women's capabilities (which may often be untrue), and beliefs about the level of skill of the work done by women (which may be seriously under-estimated) (Massey, 1984: 25, 35, 140, 141); the sexual division of labour outside the workplace, especially the greater responsibility of women for domestic work, with its implications, of restrictions on both married women's time and daily mobility (pp. 95, 97, 144, 162); and less assistance from unions than is given to male workers (p.141).

Massey suggests that women are newly entering into capitalist wage relations, and are expanding the workforce. Married women were once a latent reserve army, now they are joining the ranks of the workforce (page 212). This, she suggests, results in the working class becoming 'more internally differentiated' (1984: 210). Massey argues that this female labour reserve is unevenly spatially distributed:

There are therefore locational advantages, so far as access to this kind of labour is concerned, where there are reserves of new workers coming onto the labour market for the first time. A number of areas of the country have such reserves, in particular of female labour.

(1984: 144)

81

These female labour reserves also take different forms. She compares South Wales and Cornwall, each of which have low, but rising, female economic activity rates. In these cases, the different historical development of the regions gave rise to different relations between capital, the state, and the labour movement, which affect contemporary changes in female employment. Massey suggests that these reserves of female labour are attractive to capital, though in the case of Cornwall there is a division of interests between local capital and national capital over its exploitation. In Wales, she suggests, there is a conflict within the working class over the creation by capital of jobs which were sex-typed for women.

There is also a subtheme in these accounts which relates to the significance of occupational segregation by sex. Massey and Meegan (1982) suggest that changes in women's employment are closely related to changes in those jobs which have been sex-typed as female. While noting that this is a social rather than technical construction, they nonetheless treat sex-typing as a constant in their analysis. Thus increases in the overall size of industries which have 'traditionally' employed women are seen to constitute an explanation of increases in female employment in that industry. This inappropriately treats sex-typing as not in need of explanation.

How may Massey's account of the changing spatial structure of women's employment be assessed? First, how does it compare with other accounts of women as a reserve army of labour? Massey's account of the increasing use of female labour by capital has many parallels with that of Braverman (1974), albeit one which takes full cognisance of the spatial dimension which Braverman does not. Like Braverman she conceptualises women workers as a reserve army of labour, albeit one which is spatially variable. Again like Braverman, she considers women to be in jobs which are neither skilled nor managerial.

A further aspect of reserve army theory as it has often been applied to women, for instance by Beechey (1977, 1978), is that in times of economic recession women are the first to leave the labour market. Curiously this issue is not discussed, not even in the book by Massey and Meegan on job loss (Massey and Meegan, 1982). Rather, Massey presents an image of the continually expanding employment of women. This leaves Massey with a distinctive version of reserve army theory.

Indeed Massey and Meegan (1982) could be interpreted as an implicit critique of reserve army theory (of the ungendered type originally discussed by Marx) in that here they argue that there is no simple relationship between employment level, job loss, and economic growth or decline. Rather, they construct a complex model of the relationship between production change and employment, which differentiates between intensification, investment and technical change, and rationalisation, each of which has different employment effects. So why is reserve army theory, of any type, introduced for women?

Another curious and related silence in the text is that concerning why there should be changes in the gender composition of the workforce at all. If there are these reserves of female labour, why were they not utilised before? What is new about the post-Second World War period? Why was there once a very significant spatial differentiation in the female participation rate? Massey's writings do not significantly address these issues. In the discussion of the very low female activity rates in the South Wales coal field she suggests that it was a result of the nature of the work done by men (in particular it demanded large inputs of domestic labour, and was often shift-work) (Massey, 1984: 198–9). However, in fact women did work underground in the mines until this was prevented by the 1842 Mines Act.

Massey only refers to women doing work which is semi-skilled or unskilled manual work. Curiously, clerical work, which employs nearly half of the total women workers, is totally absent from these accounts. This work is not manual, though there are debates as to whether it should be regarded as skilled (Braverman, 1974; Crompton and Jones, 1984; Goldthorpe, 1980; Vinnicombe, 1980), but it is an important part of women's work and has a different spatial distribution from semi-skilled and unskilled manual work, which is in need of consideration.

In short, there are problems with the argument that women's patterns of employment can be explained using the concept of 'reserve', even the more sophisticated notion of spatial reserve. These stem from overemphasis on the significance of capital in the explanation of women's patterns of employment, a taken-for-granted approach to sexual segregation in employment, neglect of the better forms of women's work, and neglect of examination of changes in patriarchal structures.

A related theme in restructuring theory and gender, raised by Massey but developed more fully by Cooke (1983b), is that of the 'feminisation' of the peripheral regions. This is an argument that while the skilled manual work of men in traditional industrial regions is contracting, that of semi-skilled work for women is increasing and was popular in regional policy debates in the 1970s and 1980s:

> the question of the *type* of job may be at least as important, for many new jobs in Development Areas have involved semi-skilled work for women at a time when the pressing social need was for fresh male employment.
>
> (Hudson, 1978: 361)

> Ray Hudson expresses certain doubts about the effects of regional policy, notably ... the permanence of the jobs created, and their bias towards semi-skilled female workers. I share his concern over the last point, given all the evidence that new jobs have been disproportionately oriented towards low-level production tasks and to female workers.
>
> (Keeble, 1978: 363).

This argument is related to Braverman's argument about the tendency for work to be deskilled in advanced capitalist economies, except that it is spatially sensitive in a way in which Braverman's analysis is not.

> New and more highly differentiated local labour markets come into existence because of the ways in which the production process in large corporate organisations is decomposed or fragmented in ways that take advantage of the size, skills and levels of unionization of local labour markets ... most importantly, it expresses an increase in the expulsion of male working class members from waged work, especially in 'traditional' heavy industry areas ... and the corresponding insertion of women in both the new, decentralised production units and in service industry, both state and private sector.
>
> (Cooke, 1983a: 222)

Indeed Cooke (1982: 221) suggests that those areas of Britain in receipt of regional aid have seen women take a 'disproportionate' share of new employment.

Thus we see in the new restructuring theory three implicit theses regarding women's employment and space: that women are a spatial reserve army of labour; that rigid sex-typing means that changes in female employment are contingent upon the expansion and decline of specific sectors; and that there is a feminisation of the new peripheral regions which is related to deskilling.

These theses will be evaluated primarily by way of a comparative analysis of five local labour markets during the period 1971–81. This was a crucial decade, in which aspects of gender relations in employment were undergoing major change and the basis for these later changes was laid. As can be seen from Chapter 2, these changes have gathered pace during the 1980s and 1990s. Spatial differences in patterns of gender relations are undergoing further rounds of restructuring.

FIVE LOCALITIES

The five local labour markets considered in this chapter were among the localities chosen for study by the ESRC Changing Urban and Rural System (CURS) initiative. Two of the original seven CURS localities are not discussed here as they did not constitute self-contained labour markets, but are rather part of larger metropolitan areas. The localities studied under the ESRC's Changing Urban and Regional Systems (CURS) Initiative were not chosen at random. The five considered here – Cheltenham, Swindon, Lancaster, Thanet and Teesside – stand out as relatively self-contained freestanding local labour markets (the other two localities – Southwest Birmingham and Kirkby/Speke – form part of larger metropolitan areas which made obtaining official data for them almost impossible). Cheltenham and

Swindon were selected for their location in the affluent 'sunbelt' of South-east England, and this is reflected in the growth of employment between 1971 and 1981 of 33 per cent in Cheltenham and 10 per cent in Swindon. Lancaster was chosen to represent possibilities of affluence in the North of the country, having deindustrialised early in 1960s and developed large public sector services and nuclear power and natural gas extraction sectors. In Lancaster total employment between 1971 and 1981 grew by a modest 3 per cent, whilst national employment declined by 2 per cent. Thanet and Teesside were selected as contrasting declining localities with total employment falling by 5 per cent and 9 per cent respectively between 1971 and 1981. Thanet, consisting of the East Kent towns of Broadstairs, Margate and Ramsgate, exemplifies the run-down seaside resorts of the Southeast. Teesside represents the more familiar stereotype of the Northern rapidly deindustrialising city of the 1980s. We have, then, localities which crudely represent stereotypes of North and South, decline and growth, manufacturing and services based (Cooke, 1989).

The five have been defined, where possible, in terms of travel-to-work areas, as the issue of interest is that of the operation of local labour markets, using a date of definition of 1978. The main source of data for this chapter was the Census of Employment gathered by the then Department of Employment. This yields data on employment in terms of industrial structure down to minimum list heading level for 1971 and 1981. Data on socio-economic groups is available for 1981 but not for 1971 travel-to-work areas, so this data, taken from the population census, was based on 1974 district authority areas.

The five local labour markets have very different employment trajectories over the decade from 1971 to 1981 (see Table 4.1). Cheltenham experienced the greatest growth, with employment increasing by 33 per cent, whereas Teesside had the greatest contraction, with employment falling by 9 per cent. These compare with an aggregate national reduction of 2 per cent. The production sector slumped in all localities with the exception of Cheltenham, as in Britain overall. All localities, except Thanet, saw growth in service employment, again in line with the national picture. Thus even on such crude measures as employment growth and decline, and a division between production and services, there are large differences between the five local labour markets.

Variations in gender composition

The gender composition of the labour markets varies significantly between localities, as can be seen in Figure 4.1. The local labour market with the highest participation of female workers in 1981 was Thanet, followed by Lancaster, Swindon, Cheltenham, and last, Teesside. In all cases this was higher than for 1971.

Table 4.1   Change in employment by sector, sex, and women's part-time employment for all localities and Britain, 1971–81.

Locality	Production	Services	Total employment
Cheltenham			
Men	12.39	31.17	26.65
Women	35.85	30.95	42.90
(part-time)	(68.06)	(40.42)	(67.87)
Total	16.99	31.05	33.02
Swindon			
Men	−24.82	29.51	−1.06
Women	−36.41	37.40	27.80
(part-time)	(−58.64)	(47.76)	(50.74)
Total	−27.55	33.91	9.75
Lancaster			
Men	−4.32	−4.11	−4.11
Women	−26.11	17.86	12.45
(part-time)	(−11.80)	(30.48)	(39.42)
Total	−9.33	7.96	2.54
Teesside			
Men	−31.33	7.42	−19.79
Women	−29.42	21.99	13.37
(part-time)	(−5.20)	(42.31)	(61.46)
Total	−31.04	16.10	−8.89
Thanet			
Men	−11.95	−5.51	−8.43
Women	−10.20	4.36	0.18
(part-time)	(26.00)	(15.96)	(20.11)
Total	−11.37	−0.20	−4.64
Britain			
Men	−19.84	5.38	−8.94
Women	−21.20	20.05	10.46
(part-time)	(−11.64)	(33.02)	(37.14)
Total	−20.18	13.26	−1.57

Sources: NOMIS, 1971, Census of Employment; NOMIS, 1981, Census of Employment.

There were significant differences between the localities in the rate of growth of female employment, as can be seen in Figure 4.1. This follows the general post–1945 trend towards the reduction in the regional variations in women's employment rates (see Walby, 1985). That is, the localities with the lowest rates of female labour in 1971 experienced the highest growth of women's employment over the decade (see Table 4.2). The closing of the gap between the proportion of women in each local labour market might appear to support the thesis of spatial reserves of labour. However, as Table 4.1 shows, the localities with overall declines in employment, Teesside and Thanet, and all four with declines in male employment, Swindon, Lancaster,

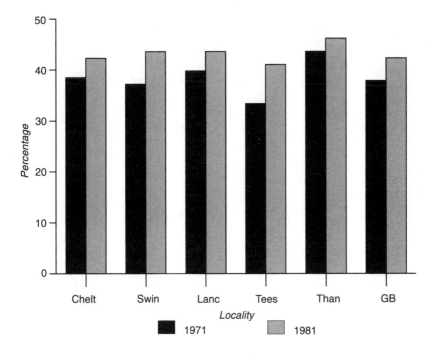

Figure 4.1 Women as percentage of all employees for 1971 and 1981

Teesside and Thanet, saw increases in women's employment. This is not then, the using of a reserve in the sense in which it is usually meant – the utilisation of secondary capacity because the usual capacity is already fully used. The reduction in male employment meant that there was unemployed male labour available. It is inappropriate to consider the employment of women here as the utilisation of a reserve.

CHANGES 1981–91

Uneven spatial patterns in the gender composition of local labour markets have continued through the 1980s into the 1990s. In 1991 in Britain one-third of local labour markets had a majority of women as employees in employment. This compares with the fact that women were overall 48 per cent of such employees. These local labour markets with such a female majority are listed in the Appendix.

Among the five labour markets under scrutiny here, two had gained a female majority by 1991 – Lancaster and Thanet, with 52 per cent and 55 per cent respectively. Both had proportions of female part-time workers above the national average, both at 28 per cent as compared with the national picture of 22 per cent.

Table 4.2 Employment for five localities and Britain, 1971 and 1981, by sex and by women's part-time employment

Locality	1971			1981			1971–81
	Number	*%*	*LQ*	*Number*	*%*	*LQ*	*Change (%)*
Cheltenham							
Men	33 866	60.8	0.98	42 890	57.9	1.01	26.6
Women	21 860	39.2	1.03	31 273	42.2	0.99	43.1
(part-time)	(8 393)	(15.1)	(1.18)	(14 089)	(19.0)	(1.07)	(67.9)
Total	55 726	100.0		74 127	100.0		33.0
Swindon							
Men	44 519	62.5	1.01	44 048	56.4	0.98	1.1
Women	26 656	37.5	0.99	34 067	43.6	1.02	27.8
(part-time)	(10 325)	(14.5)	(1.14)	(15 564)	(19.9)	(1.12)	(50.7)
Total	71 175	100.0		78 115	100.0		9.8
Lancaster							
Men	25 479	59.8	0.96	24 431	55.9	0.97	4.1
Women	17 125	40.2	1.06	19 257	44.1	1.03	12.4
(part-time)	(6 501)	(15.3)	(1.20)	(9 064)	(20.7)	(1.17)	(39.4)
Total	42 604	100.0		43 688	100.0		2.5
Teesside							
Men	131 142	67.1	1.08	105 189	59.1	1.03	−19.8
Women	64 194	32.9	0.87	72 776	40.9	0.96	13.4
(part-time)	(21 090)	(10.8)	(0.85)	(34 052)	(19.1)	(1.08)	(61.5)
Total	195 336	100.0		177 965	100.0		− 8.9
Thanet							
Men	26 200	56.0	0.90	23 992	53.8	0.94	−8.4
Women	20 572	44.0	1.16	20 609	46.2	1.08	0.2
(part-time)	(7 324)	(15.7)	(1.23)	(8 797)	(19.7)	(1.11)	(20.1)
Total	46 772	100.0		44 601	100.00		− 4.6
Britain (1000s)							
Men	13 424	62.0	1.00	12 224	57.4	1.00	− 8.9
Women	8 224	38.0	1.00	9 084	42.6	1.00	10.5
(part-time)	(2 757)	(12.7)	(1.00)	(3 781)	(17.7)	(1.00)	(37.1)
Total	21 648	100.0		21 308	100.0		− 1.6

Sources: NOMIS, 1971; 1981.
Note: LQ location quotation.

Women's part-time employment

Differences between local labour markets emerge even more clearly when the data is disaggregated. This appears when we distinguish between part-time and full-time women workers, between production and service sector employment, and between industrial orders. As the growth of most of women's employment has been in part-time work, it is appropriate to consider in some detail women's part-time employment in these five local labour markets.

The growth of part-time employment is a marked feature of all these local labour markets; indeed by 1981 all of our localities are above the British average in terms of the percentage of their local labour-force which was made up of women part-time workers. This makes these five localities a particularly 'acid' test of the 'spatial reserve army of labour' thesis, because if this thesis is valid they should all have other common labour market characteristics relating to the utilisation of women as a labour reserve. However, as we shall see, the data does not support that thesis.

Although all the labour markets show an increase in the extent of part-time working, there are, nevertheless, some differences between these localities, especially in changes over the decade 1971–81 (see Tables 4.1 and 4.2). In 1971 four of our localities had very similar rates of part-time employment, either 15 per cent or 16 per cent; only Teesside was distinctive with a figure of 11 per cent (the national average was 13 per cent). During the decade all the areas showed considerable increases in the extent of women's part-time working, the national average of a 37 per cent increase being surpassed by all localities except Thanet. Most interestingly, Teesside, which had the lowest rate of part-time working in 1971 showed the highest rate of growth in this work over the decade, a staggering 62 per cent increase. This brought it into the 'middle' of our localities with a rate of 19 per cent within a locality range of 19 per cent to 21 per cent, as compared with a national average of 18 per cent. This massive increase in part-time working by women in Teesside runs counter to the spatial reserve army theory, as Teesside – which was simultaneously having the largest reduction in the male workforce, of any of our localities, a shuddering 20 per cent decline in male employment over the decade – might have been considered to have sufficient 'primary' labour available not to need to draw upon 'secondary' female labour. It cannot be argued that women's labour was being used as a secondary reserve when so many men were available on the labour market as a consequence of the dramatic decline in men's employment.

Although all localities showed significant rates of growth in part-time work, the lowest being 20 per cent in Thanet, there were two exceptionally high rates of growth, Teesside (as already mentioned) and also Cheltenham with a 68 per cent increase. These massive increases do not correlate simply either with growth or with decline, as in one instance it took place in the economy with the largest decline, Teesside, and in the other, in the economy with the largest growth, Cheltenham. Rather, they took place in the economies with the greatest amount of change (either expansion or contraction); in contrast the economy with least overall change in employment level, Thanet, experienced the lowest rate of growth in women part-time workers. We conclude that the introduction of women part-time workers is associated with restructuring and change, but not exclusively with either a

89

shortage or a surplus of labour. In this context notions of reserve do not help the explanation of these patterns of labour market change.

Socio-economic groups

The analysis so far has focused on the extent to which women are employed in localities, whether this is full-time or part-time, and whether this correlates with changing aggregate employment levels and changing industrial structure. Access to paid work is one indicator of women's position in a stratified division of labour. Analysis by socio-economic group (SEG) enables us to locate this work more finely in a hierarchy. Figure 4.2 is a comparison of the distribution of employed women by SEG across locality, in 1971 and 1981.

The graphs in Figure 4.2 present the location quotients of each group of SEGs for each of the five local labour markets, comparing 1971 and 1981. This quotient is the percentage of women's part-time employment in a locality expressed as a ratio of the corresponding percentage for Britain. This ratio is 1.00 if the proportion is the same in the locality as in Britain, greater than 1.00 if the proportion in the locality is greater, and less than 1.00 if the proportion in the locality is less than in Britain. This ratio automatically controls for changes in proportion nationally when comparing the local with the national percentages. Hence, if the national percentage declines but the local percentage remains constant, then the locality's quotient would *increase*. The national percentage may increase and the local percentage may increase even more again, resulting in an overall increase in the location quotient. Thus we note that Cheltenham has a profile close to the national one, with a slight tendency to be overrepresented in the middle SEGs. Swindon has a marked absence of professional women and presence of supervisory non-manual workers. Lancaster has an absent middle, representing absence of clerical workers, and high extremes, representing high presence of women in the professions on the one side and personal service and skilled manual on the other. Thanet's profile reveals a very marked absence of professional women, and also of unskilled women workers. Teesside's profile shows low female employment which is heavily weighted to jobs at the lower end of the scale.

The comparison with 1971 reveals that: in Cheltenham in 1981 women were less represented in the middle SEGs and more in the lower ones than in 1971, as compared with the national average; in Swindon the pattern moved closer to the national average and the distinctiveness of the underrepresentation in the top SEGs and overrepresentation in the bottom ones was somewhat mitigated; in Lancaster, the distinctive pattern of overrepresentation in professionals and underrepresentation in junior non-manual was exacerbated over the decade; in Thanet the significant overrepresenta-

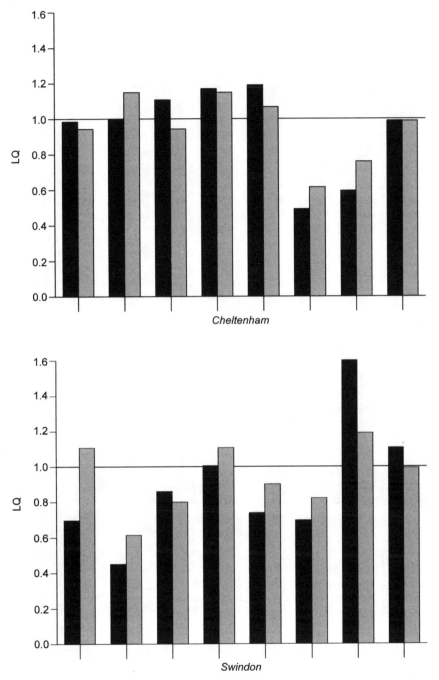

Figure 4.2 Location quotients of grouped socio-economic groups for women in the five localities for 1971 and 1981

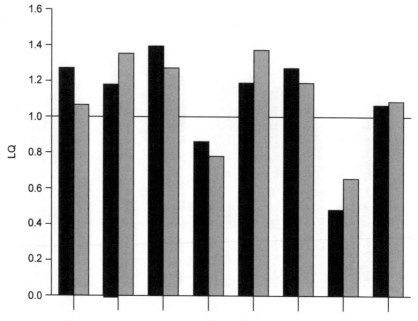

Lancaster

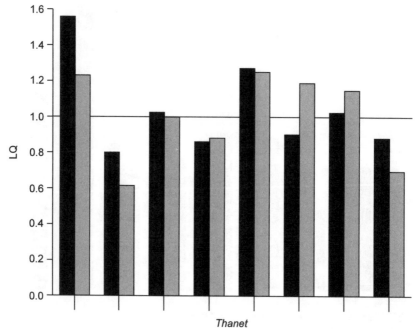

Thanet

Figure 4.2 cont

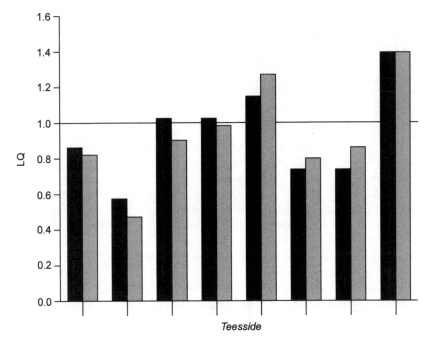

Figure 4.2 cont

Notes:

Socio-economic groups and socio-economic classes:
SEG 1 Employers and managers in central and local
       government, industry, commerce, etc. – large
       establishments
SEG 2 Employers and managers in industry, commerce,
       etc. – small establishments
SEG 3 Professional workers – self-employed
SEG 4 Professional workers – employees
SEG 5 Intermediate non-manual workers
SEG 6 Junior non-manual workers
SEG 7 Personal service workers
SEG 8 Foremen and supervisors – manual
SEG 9 Skilled manual workers
SEG 10 Semi-skilled manual workers
SEG 11 Unskilled manual workers
SEG 12 Own account workers (other than professionals)
SEG 13 Farmers – employers and managers
SEG 14 Farmers – own account
SEG 15 Agricultural workers
SEG 16 Members of armed forces
SEG 17 Inadequately described occupations

Grouped SEGs
1 Employers and managers
2 Professional
3 Intermediate non-manual
4 Junior non-manual
5 Personal service workers
6 Skilled manual workers
7 Semi-skilled manual
8 Unskilled manual

tion in managerial positions was somewhat reduced and the underrepresentation in professional ones exacerbated; in Teesside the underrepresentation
in top SEGs and overrepresentation in the bottom ones increased between
1971 and 1981.

The bar charts enable us to see the range in the positioning of women in the vertical hierarchy between the different towns. The comparison with Figure 4.1, which shows the extent of women's employment in the localities, demonstrates that although there is some correlation between the extent of employment with position in employment, this is only partial.

Industrial sectors

There are marked differences between the localities in the industrial composition of their economies. Even when a simple dichotomy between production and service sector is considered, there are significant variations between the localities, as Table 4.3 shows. For the production sector location quotients range from 0.71 for Lancaster to 1.18 for Teesside in 1971, and from 0.78 for Lancaster to 1.10 for Teesside in 1981. That is, Teesside had a much higher proportion of the production sector in its local economy than the national average, whereas Lancaster's proportion was much less than the national average.

It is now well known that the production and service sectors have different proportions of male and female workers at the national level, men taking the majority of jobs in production and women the majority in services. Interestingly, our localities show significant divergences from the national average in the proportion of men and women in each of these sectors. That is, the sex-typing of these sectors is spatially variable, not uniform across the country. These divergences from the national picture are even greater when the figures for women part-time workers are examined. These location quotients range from 0.39 for women's part-time employment in production in Lancaster in 1981, to 1.28 for Thanet in the same year. That is, Lancaster had a much smaller proportion of its workforce who were female part-time workers in production than was the national average, whereas Thanet had a higher proportion.

There were significant changes in the gender composition of the local labour forces between 1971 and 1981, as Table 4.3 shows. Can the changes in the gender composition of local labour markets be accounted for in terms of the changing industrial structure of the localities? Can the gender composition of a particular local labour force be accounted for as a consequence of changes in the relevant balance of industrial sectors, while the composition of each sector stays constant? Bowers (1970) suggested that this was the cause in 1961 and also for changes during the decade 1954–64. However, this data was at a regional level and for an earlier period. It is also implied by Massey and Meegan (1982). Does the thesis apply to our later time period and at a local level of disaggregation? When this is investigated at the sectoral level of production and service sector a slight relationship is present, but it is quite tenuous (see Table 4.3) in that the percentage changes by gender in any sector are significantly different from that of the sector as

Table 4.3 The composition of employment by sector, sex, and women's part-time employment

| Locality | Location quotient | | | | Sectoral composition of employment (%)[a] | | | | Percentage of total employment | | | | | |
| | Production | | Services | | Production | | Services | | Production | | Services | | Total | |
	1971	1981	1971	1981	1971	1981	1971	1981	1971	1981	1971	1981	1971	1981
Cheltenham														
Men	0.99	1.00	1.01	1.00	56.57	50.29	43.33	49.71	34.4	29.1	26.3	28.8	60.8	57.9
Women	0.68	0.90	1.15	1.03	21.42	20.37	78.58	79.63	8.4	8.6	30.8	33.6	39.2	42.1
(part-time)	(0.63)	(0.97)	(1.09)	(1.00)	(12.50)	(12.51)	(87.50)	(87.49)	(1.9)	(2.4)	(13.2)	(16.6)	(15.1)	(19.0)
Total	0.90	0.98	1.09	1.01	42.84	37.68	57.16	62.32	42.8	37.7	57.2	62.3	100.0	100.0
Swindon														
Men	1.12	0.97	0.83	1.03	64.37	48.91	35.63	51.09	40.3	27.6	22.3	28.8	62.5	56.4
Women	1.05	0.73	0.98	1.08	33.22	16.53	66.78	83.47	12.4	7.2	25.0	36.4	37.5	43.6
(part-time)	(1.36)	(0.58)	(0.91)	(1.06)	(27.12)	(7.44)	(72.88)	(92.56)	(3.9)	(1.5)	(10.6)	(18.4)	(14.5)	(19.9)
Total	1.11	0.90	0.90	1.06	52.70	34.79	47.30	65.21	52.7	34.8	47.3	65.2	100.0	100.0
Lancaster														
Men	0.76	0.87	1.32	1.14	43.75	43.66	56.25	56.34	26.2	24.4	33.6	31.5	59.8	55.9
Women	0.61	0.57	1.18	1.13	19.42	12.76	80.58	87.24	7.8	5.6	32.4	38.5	40.2	44.1
(part-time)	(0.40)	(0.39)	(1.15)	(1.09)	(7.95)	(5.03)	(92.05)	(94.97)	(1.2)	(1.0)	(14.0)	(19.7)	(15.3)	(20.7)
Total	0.71	0.78	1.26	1.14	33.97	30.04	66.03	69.96	34.0	30.0	66.0	70.0	100.0	100.0
Teesside														
Men	1.23	1.20	0.69	0.80	70.68	60.51	29.32	39.49	47.5	35.8	19.7	23.3	67.1	59.1
Women	0.81	0.71	1.09	1.08	25.73	16.02	74.27	83.98	8.5	6.6	24.4	34.3	32.9	40.9
(part-time)	(0.76)	(0.69)	(1.06)	(1.05)	(15.13)	(8.88)	(84.87)	(91.12)	(1.6)	(1.7)	(9.2)	(17.4)	(10.8)	(19.1)
Total	1.18	1.10	0.84	0.94	55.91	42.32	44.09	57.68	55.9	42.3	44.1	57.7	100.0	100.0
Thanet														
Men	0.83	0.91	1.23	1.09	47.62	45.79	52.38	54.21	26.7	24.6	29.3	29.2	56.0	53.8
Women	0.94	1.18	1.03	0.95	29.70	26.62	70.30	73.28	13.1	12.3	30.9	33.9	44.0	46.2
(part-time)	(0.79)	(1.28)	(1.05)	(0.96)	(15.70)	(16.47)	(84.30)	(83.53)	(2.5)	(3.2)	(13.2)	(16.5)	(15.7)	(19.7)
Total	0.84	0.96	1.15	1.03	39.74	36.93	60.26	63.07	39.7	36.9	60.3	63.1	100.0	100.0
Britain														
Men	1	1	1	1	57.29	50.43	42.71	49.57	35.5	28.9	26.5	28.4	62.0	57.4
Women	1	1	1	1	31.60	22.55	68.40	77.45	12.0	9.6	26.0	33.0	38.0	42.6
(part-time)	(1)	(1)	(1)	(1)	(19.95)	(12.85)	(80.05)	(87.15)	(2.5)	(2.3)	(10.2)	(15.5)	(12.7)	(17.7)
Total	1	1	1	1	47.53	38.54	52.47	61.46	47.5	38.5	52.5	61.5	100.0	100.0

Sources: NOMIS, 1971; 1981.
Note: a production employment plus services employment is equal to 100 per cent (total employment) for both 1971 and 1981 in all categories.

a whole, although they follow it in general direction. That is, sectoral composition and sectoral changes explain a portion, but only a portion, of the gender changes, unlike Bowers' earlier findings. So, the second thesis about changes in women's employment, which suggests that they can be explained as a result of changes in rigidly sex-typed industries, is only partially consistent with the data.

Order-level analysis

On the more detailed level of analysis at the order level, with 28 types of industry, more divergences appear between the localities. Table 4.4 shows the extent to which the employment of men, full-time women workers, and part-time women workers followed the upward or downward trend of the order in that locality.

Although in most cases men's employment followed, or at least did not run counter to, the overall change in that industrial order, the same could not be said for that of women, especially those in part-time work. That is, changes in women's employment often ran counter to the overall trend. Further there were local differences in the extent to which women's and especially women's part-time pattern followed that of the order as a whole.

Table 4.4 Changes in employment at order level by sex and congruency.

Locality	Congruent change	No change	Increase while total declined	Decrease while total declined
Cheltenham				
Men	25	2	0	1
Women	20	3	2	3
Women (part-time)	18	3	6	1
Lancaster				
Men	24	1	0	3
Women	19	2	4	3
Women (part-time)	16	5	7	0
Swindon				
Men	24	4	0	0
Women	20	4	2	2
Women (part-time)	18	4	4	2
Teesside				
Men	24	1	2	1
Women	21	1	4	2
Women (part-time)	14	3	11	0
Thanet				
Men	25	3	0	0
Women	17	3	5	1
Women (part-time)	11	4	13	0

Sources: NOMIS, 1971, 1981.

Thanet had the most contradictory movements between men's and women's employment, with women part-time workers following the men's movement in less than half of the orders. However, these represented relatively small changes. Swindon and Cheltenham had less contradictory movements.

In the majority of cases where there were contrary movements between a part of the workforce and the whole, it was women's, usually women's part-time employment which rose, while that of the whole fell. That is, women's employment was increasing simultaneously with a decrease in men's. It is clear in these cases that women are not being used as a labour reserve. This raises the question of whether women were being substituted for men. However, given the high degree of segregation at the more disaggregated minimum list heading (MLH) level, this suggests that it is not the case that women are being substituted for men in any simple sense (Bagguley and Walby, 1988: 21–6). The most contrary tendencies were to be found in the two labour markets which had experienced net decline in overall employment, Teesside and Thanet.

CONCLUSION

These results show that gender is an important variable in restructuring. Indeed women's employment changes are more spatially variable than are men's. Further, women can hardly be a reserve army when the largest increase in part-time workers took place in the labour market with the largest overall employment loss. But neither can the argument be simply turned around to support a notion that women are brought in to substitute for men in areas of restructuring, because of the high degree of sex segregation at MLH level.

There are three implicit theses about changing gender relations in the writings of those social scientists who take spatial issues seriously. These are: first, the notion of women as spatial reserves of labour, which develops reserve army theory; second, the notion of a new international and regional division of labour, in which deskilling results in the greater employment of women in semi-skilled and unskilled work and a decline in skilled work by males (this has a spatial dimension which is related to the growth of the branch plants in the peripheral regions); third, that changes in women's employment are contingent upon the sex-type of the expanding and contracting sectors, which is explored in the next chapter.

The first thesis, that women constitute spatial reserves of labour, can be found in some of the leading writers on industrial restructuring (Cooke, 1982; Massey, 1984; Massey and Meegan, 1982). This was a development of earlier non-spatial forms of theorisation of women as a reserve army (Beechey, 1977; 1978; Braverman, 1974; Bruegel, 1979).

The examination of the contrasting changes in the gender composition of the workforce in the five local labour markets in this study demonstrated that women were not used as a reserve of labour to be brought into paid employment when other forms of labour were fully utilised. The most striking example which ran counter to the theory of women as spatial reserves to labour was that of Teesside, where between 1971 and 1981, women's part-time working increased by 62 per cent, whereas men's employment fell by 20 per cent. This means that those forms of the theory of restructuring which conceptualised gender relations in such a way were flawed.

The second thesis concerning changes in gender relations in employment is the deskilling thesis. This can be found especially among those restructuring writers who argue that a branch plant economy in a region is likely to increase the proportion of semi-skilled and unskilled female workers, whereas that of skilled male manual workers declines. This is clearly related to Braverman's thesis on the changing sexual division of paid work, in which he suggested that as work was deskilled by capital, women would be brought in as new unskilled labour. This would predict that women would be brought into industries as they are being deskilled and men ejected: that we would see a substitution of women for men as deskilled jobs are substituted for skilled ones. Braverman's thesis is presented in a modified form by Cooke and by Massey. It is modified by a sensitivity to geography and to the spatial discontinuities in capitalist organisation. In their view it is the new industries in new locations which employ women, especially as 'green labour'. They thus retain Braverman's emphasis on women as 'green' unskilled workers, and as a form of labour reserve, but moving a long way from suggestions of direct substitution. However, we have shown that the changes in the socio-economic composition of the localities are not consistent with this thesis.

How then are we to understand the changing gender relations in our spatially distributed local labour markets? Existing theories are badly flawed. At best there is some occasional and partial correlation between theory and evidence; at worst the evidence is directly contradictory to the theses advanced. The underlying problem with these theories is that they do not adequately address the theorisation of gender relations. These theories imply that gender relations are either a by-product of the capital or the capital-labour relation, or are contingent, that is, inexplicable.

We need rather a theory which explicitly deals with the specificity of gender relations as autonomous or relatively autonomous relations from capital, and which engages with the causal determination of these. Gender relations should be theorised as a result of the interaction of gender, class, and other relations in a spatial and temporal context. The balance of gender forces is critical to the changes in gender patterns of employment, as well as class and other forces. In this approach the historically greater proportion of men in the upper SEGs is a consequence of the closing of these occupations by men against women (see Cockburn, 1983; Hartmann, 1976; Walby,

1986b). A full application and testing of this fourth thesis is difficult with economic data only because political and organisational resources utilised by gendered forces are a key part of the thesis. These will be explored in later chapters in this book.

There are key periods of the restructuring of the gender composition of industries, and periods of stability. That is, as in the case of capital and labour, there are rounds of restructuring of gender relations in industries followed by periods of stability. New rounds of gender restructuring build upon the old. The evidence is consistent with this view since it was in those localities with maximum restructuring, entailing either large expansion or large contraction of employment, that there was most change in the gender composition of industries. For instance, this is the only thesis to make sense of the changes in part-time work in particular, that the greatest growth in female part-time work was in the local economy with the greatest expansion and the greatest contraction.

The reduction in forms of patriarchal closure against women in the decade 1971–81 dominates the period under study; women increased their access to all jobs and a disproportionate share of the best new jobs. It was the decade of the Equal Pay Act and Sex Discrimination Act, of women increasingly joining unions, of previous forms of patriarchal exclusion being undermined. It was a decade in which the wages gap between women and men working full-time started to narrow. So it was an unusual decade. The new rounds of industrial restructuring embody the newer forms of patriarchal relations of employment which are less exclusionary, allowing women greater access to employment.

5

SEX SEGREGATION IN LOCAL LABOUR MARKETS

INTRODUCTION

Labour markets are significantly structured by both sexual segregation and by locality. This chapter seeks to explore this by developing a more nuanced means of measuring sexual segregation, and applying it to specific labour markets. It seeks to refine the concept and techniques of measurement of segregation, with a view to effective comparison of segregation between localities. Previous studies of segregation in Britain have been largely at the national level (Hakim, 1979, 1981; Siltanen, 1990). Here the focus will be on localities to see whether at the level of actual local labour markets there are significant differences in patterns of segregation and to determine the implications of this.

The findings challenge several existing theses concerning changes in women's employment. First, there are changes in occupational segregation by sex. Hakim's findings are frequently interpreted as demonstrating that there has been no significant diminution in the extent of occupational segregation this century. (In fact, Hakim's work is more complex than this, allowing for small decreases in segregation.) The work here shows that there have been significant changes in segregation during the decade 1971 to 1981. Women have made significant inroads into previously nearly all-male arenas of the upper jobs, reducing this aspect of the vertical segregation of the sexes in work. It is the service class which is feminising, not the proletariat, in this decade. Yet simultaneously with this reduction in vertical segregation there has been an increase in the extent of horizontal segregation of women.

An important thesis as to the nature of changes in gender relations in employment has been the deskilling thesis. As discussed in the previous chapter, this can be found especially among those restructuring writers who argue that a branch plant economy in a region is likely to increase the proportion of semi- and unskilled female workers, while that of skilled male manual workers declines. This is related to Braverman's thesis on the changing sexual division of paid work, in which he suggested that as work was deskilled by capital, women would be brought in as new unskilled labour. This would predict that women would be brought into industries as they are being deskilled and men ejected; that we would see a substitution of women for men as deskilled jobs are substituted for skilled ones. It has been given a more sophisticated spatial dimension by Cooke (1983a), Massey (1984) and Massey and Meegan (1992) as discussed earlier.

There have been simultaneous increases and decreases in different aspects of segregation. This part of the analysis pushes Hakim's separation of the vertical and the horizontal aspects of segregation further apart so as to explore the complexities and paradoxes involved.

One explanation of changes in the gender composition of paid work is to see it as a result of contingent changes in rigidly sex-typed industries – the rigidity thesis. Bowers (1970) has argued that the regional variation in women's employment rates in 1961 and changes in regional variations 1954–64 were a consequence of changes in industrial structure. This is a spatial version of Oppenheimer's (1970) argument that changes in women's employment were contingent upon changes in industrial structure because of the rigidity of the sex-typing of employment. The evidence she used in support of this was the changes in women's employment in post-war US at a national level. She considered that the increase in women's employment in the US in that period was a result of a contingent increase in the service sector in which women are concentrated.

There is some suggestive evidence that there might be more intense segregation at the local level than revealed in nationally aggregated data. This can be seen from surveys which have asked questions about the experience of segregation at the level of the individual and of the establishment. The DE/OPCS study found that 63 per cent of women worked only with other women, while among their husbands 81 per cent worked with only other men (Martin and Roberts, 1984: 27–8), while the EOC national survey of establishments found that 45 per cent of jobs had no women and 21 per cent had no men (McIntosh, 1980). This comparison between nationally aggregated data with that at the establishment level leads us to expect that segregation at the level of the local labour market would be greater than that at the national.

Hakim's (1979, 1981) national level analysis of census data suggested that there has been a small decline in the extent of occupational segregation at the national level between 1901 and 1971 and indeed from 1971 to 1979. An international comparison of levels of segregation between Britain, Sweden, the US and West Germany showed that it was highest in Sweden and lowest in Germany (Jonung, 1983). We shall ask whether there are changes in segregation at the local level, and whether they follow Hakim's findings for Britain as a whole.

Hakim (1979) distinguishes two elements in segregation: the horizontal and the vertical:

Horizontal segregation exists when men and women are most commonly working in different types of occupation. Vertical occupational segregation exists when men are most commonly working in higher grade occupations and women are most commonly working in lower grade occupations, or vice versa. The two are logically separate.

(1979: 19)

Hakim uses occupational distinctions as indicative of horizontal segregation, and broad groupings of ranked occupations as indicative of vertical segregation. However, there are other ways of distinguishing between horizontal and vertical segregation which make the distinction more clearly than Hakim's own method.

Occupations as a measure inevitably contain both horizontal and vertical elements simultaneously. Since they are often distinguished from each other on grounds of hierarchical relation, they do not constitute an ideal measure of horizontal segregation. Further, when broad groups of occupations are used to capture vertical segregation they miss certain aspects of hierarchy which relate to supervision and control over other workers, which are not fully captured in the concept of occupation.

This study will make the following refinements. Instead of using occupations as the basic unit we would substitute MLHs (minimum list headings of the standard industrial classification) and SEGs (socio-economic groups). First, horizontal segregation is more accurately captured by using an industrial classification, which is based on separation of industries. Second, vertical segregation is more accurately captured by using SEGs, which contain more hierarchical elements.

Recent work has attempted to create a single statistical measure of segregation (e.g. Duncan and Duncan, 1955; Siltanen, 1990; Siltanen, Jarman and Blackburn, 1992; Watts, 1990). This could potentially have the advantages of enabling accurate comparisons over time and between countries. However, there are several obstacles to this, including unrealistic conceptual assumptions, and the lack of appropriate data. Siltanen (1990) and Siltanen, Jarman and Blackburn (1992) suggest that the best way to operationalise segregation is through the use of a single measure based on 'matching marginals', arguing that the measure needs to be based on an assumption of symmetry between the segregation of women and the segregation of men; that for the purposes of an indicator they should be treated the same.

The major problem with this approach derives from the fact that segregation is not a symmetrical process between women and men, but rather one centrally structured by inequalities of power. For instance, a high-level occupation being constituted by 80 per cent men and 20 per cent women is not 'symmetrical' with, or balanced by, a low level occupation being 80 per cent populated by women and 20 per cent by men. It matters that the

102

occupation which is monopolised by men is one which, typically, bestows greater power and rewards and that by women much less so. The concentration of men in, say, senior management is not symmetrical with a concentration of women among, say, cleaners. Thus a statistical indicator which makes symmetry between women and men a central assumption is inherently flawed as a guide to understanding gender relations in employment. In any analysis of segregation we need to be aware of which occupations have a concentration of which gender. A further issue, and in practice often the largest obstacle to comparisons of the degree and nature of segregation over time and between countries, is the variability in the boundaries and size of the occupational or industrial units under analysis. This is partly because the degree of segregation is sensitive to the size of the unit – greater segregation is found if the size of units is smaller. For instance, Martin and Roberts (1984) found in a survey of 'individuals and their husbands' that 81 per cent of men worked with no women and 63 per cent of women worked with no men, but this is not reflected in the larger units used in occupational analysis. Related to this is the factor that occupational terms can mean different things in different times and places. For these various reasons we cannot expect a single statistical indicator to be adequate to the task of capturing the nature of segregation and its changes over time and across countries. Hence one has not been used here.

HORIZONTAL OR INDUSTRIAL SEGREGATION

We can gain a measure of horizontal segregation by examining the distribution of women and men through the industrial structure at the level of MLH. This gives us quite a fine differentiation of employment by the product of the establishment. At the level of local labour markets (LLMAs), MLHs may contain several establishments or none. The disadvantage of this measure is that it is likely to understate the degree of segregation since it refers to employment in units of an establishment. Essentially we have an index of industrial segregation here.

In order to compare localities it is necessary to reduce the complexity of the data. However, as I argued in Chapter 2, it is inappropriate to seek to conflate all the dimensions of segregation into one numeric measure. We have chosen to compare the extent to which people are to be found working in industries, here operationalised as MLHs, which contain 100 per cent, 90 per cent, 80 per cent and 70 per cent of the same sex. These measures might be understood as *degrees* or *intensities* of segregation. This is done separately for men and for women, using data for both 1971 and 1981. The numbers of people who work in MLHs at a given degree of concentration of the same sex are then added together and expressed as a proportion of the total workforce of that sex in that locality. This method produces a complex index, which represents the extent to which people in a locality work in sex-segregated employment at the MLH level. The comparison is then between localities at the same degree or intensity of concentration.

The data for this project is taken from five of the seven local labour markets studied as part of the ESRC initiative on the Changing Urban and Regional System as described in Chapter 4.

Table 5.1 shows the segregation in both the localities and in Britain. The first feature of the table is the extreme extent of the segregation at MLH level. With only two local exceptions, in all the local labour markets in both sample years, 1971 and 1981, some men and some women work in MLHs which employ no member of the other sex whatsoever.

The second feature is that men are more likely to be working in industries with members of their own sex than women. At the level of 90 per cent, that is, that at least nine out of ten of the other people in that MLH in that locality were of the same sex, we find markedly higher proportions of men in this position than women. The greater segregation is noticeable at the 80 per cent level and in less extreme fashion at the 70 per cent level (i.e, that 80 per cent or more and 70 per cent or more people were of the

Table 5.1 Horizontal segregation by sex, 1971, 1981, five localities and Britain

	100%		90 + %		80 + %		70 + %	
	1971 %	1981 %	1971 %	1981 %	1971 %	1981 %	1971 %	1981 %
Cheltenham								
Men	0.32	0.08	15.84	1.45	38.91	30.23	70.25	61.03
Women	0.02	0.03	1.89	1.03	9.87	17.14	20.68	35.04
Swindon								
Men	0.08	0.00	34.60	20.28	53.71	43.26	64.98	53.00
Women	0.00	0.01	0.20	0.93	5.92	3.98	22.31	49.89
Lancaster								
Men	0.28	0.43	25.72	23.88	53.34	49.95	68.09	60.90
Women	0.41	0.17	3.26	1.19	7.93	4.69	23.06	46.40
Thanet								
Men	0.34	0.10	26.80	9.88	45.58	39.73	54.60	54.63
Women	0.02	0.02	3.03	1.19	6.29	10.76	33.80	28.47
Teesside								
Men	0.07	0.01	66.44	52.85	72.15	61.20	82.54	70.51
Women	0.11	0.05	5.57	1.66	15.62	24.98	65.70	68.16
Britain								
Men	0.00	0.00	20.61	7.41	42.64	35.71	60.32	54.60
Women	0.00	0.00	0.00	0.00	2.39	2.10	15.08	23.26

Source: Census of Population, 1971, 1981.

same sex). The experience of segregation is *greater* for men than for women, since men are more likely to work in areas with few members of the other sex than women, since women are more effectively excluded from certain industries than vice versa.

The third feature is that changes over time in the extent of segregation are in opposite directions for men and for women. Women's employment has generally become more horizontally segregated between 1971 and 1981 for Britain and for all localities except Teesside. Men's employment, on the contrary, has become slightly less segregated for Britain and for all localities.

Most of the increase for women is at the 70 per cent level, and its proximate causation is one-third attributable to the increase in size of female majority forms of employment, such as medical (at the national level this MLH grew from 779,233 to 1,072,270 women workers), and two-thirds due to the *increased segregation* of forms of employment such as legal services, pubs, and other services, which entered the 70 per cent level in 1981 at the GB level. (The degree of segregation for each MLH in each locality is calculated from a working table which is too long to reproduce here.) In the case of men, the decrease in segregation was overwhelmingly a result of the decline in the size of male majority MLHs, and only partly a result in the decline in the extent of segregation. The largest declines were to be found in the production rather than service sector.

Thus we find that, at the British level, declines in men's segregation between 1971 and 1981 are largely due to the changing industrial structure, while increases in women's segregation are largely due to changes internal to the organisation of an industry (MLH).

The fourth feature is the much greater extent of segregation revealed at the level of the locality as compared with that at a national level. The figure for Britain represents a high level of aggregation and hence shows the least segregation. The level of segregation in localities was, in nearly every instance, significantly above the national level in a particular year at a particular degree of segregation. The picture of segregation which uses the national level of aggregation thus significantly underestimates the level of segregation as experienced in workers in a given labour market.

The fifth feature is the substantial local variation in the extent of industrial segregation. For instance, the proportion of men working in 90 per cent male MLHs in 1971 varied between 66 per cent in Teesside and 16 per cent in Cheltenham. Is it possible to build local profiles of horizontal segregation? Teesside appears to have a significantly higher level of horizontal segregation for men and women at all levels than the other localities in both years. Thanet has the lowest levels of horizontal segregation.

The sixth feature of the comparison is the association of the overall changes in the labour market with changes in segregation. Where men's employment declined so did the extent of men's segregation; with only one exception, that of Cheltenham, where men's employment increased at the same time as the degree of men's segregation. The locality with the largest decrease in men's employment, Teesside, had the largest decrease in men's segregation. Decreases in men's employment are then positively correlated with decreases in men's segregation. Women's employment and women's segregation increased significantly in all localities except Thanet, giving us a positive correlation between the increase of women's employment and the increase in segregation.

Why is Teesside so markedly above the national average in its horizontal segregation for both men and women? For men, this is partly a result of the heavy concentration of heavy manufacturing in the locality, which generally employs largely men, but more importantly because this industry is even more segregated in Teesside than at the national level. The main reason that Teesside has such a high proportion of men in the 90 per cent segregated category – 66 per cent in 1971 and 53 per cent in 1981, as compared to 21 per cent and 7 per cent at the national level respectively – is the greater segregation of these MLHs in Teesside, rather than the greater representation of 90 per cent male national MLHs in Teesside. In relation to women, the segregation is due to both the disproportionate representation of those forms of employment which are heavily segregated, especially those in manufacturing, and the lesser representation of those forms which are less segregated, as well as the greater segregation of these forms of employment, with the latter tendency being the most important.

Lancaster had an average profile as compared with the other localities in the study, but it had levels of segregation somewhat higher than those at the national level, especially for women. Lancaster has followed the national trend of a slight decline in male segregation and an increase in female segregation. The main proximate cause of the increase in female segregation is the increased level of segregation in the medical MLH, which enters the 1981 figures at the 70 per cent level, and takes with it 21 per cent of Lancaster's female workforce. Significant increases in the size of 'other services' and 'other retail', which remain at the 70 per cent level of segregation over the decade, largely account for the remainder of the increase.

The change in the pattern of segregation among Lancaster's men is more complex. Although there is an overall fall of seven percentage points in the number of men working in 70 per cent segregated MLHs, the percentage of men in MLHs in which there has been a reduction of segregation at this level is only 3 per cent. Further there has been a significant increase in segregation in some other MLHs. The main cause of the drop in segregation is then a decrease in the size of MLHs in which there was at least 70 per cent men (most especially artificial fibres and linoleum), which together caused a drop of 14 per cent in the men in 70 per cent segregated MLHs.

Thus Lancaster follows the overall national trend in that there is an increase in the proportion of women in segregated MLHs largely because of an increase in segregation in a small number of MLHs in which many women work, while there has been a reduction in male segregation, primarily as a result of a reduction in size of MLHs which were at least 70 per cent male.

Cheltenham shows a slightly different pattern, largely as a consequence of having the only expanding male labour force in our study. Nevertheless, it still shows the same decline in male segregation across the decade, only this time it is a result not of the decline in the size of heavily male MLHs, but rather because of the expansion of non-segregated male employment. The male labour force grew by 21 per cent of its 1971 size, and of this 72 per cent were in MLHs which were not segregated to the 70 per cent level. The movement amongst the women follows the national trend in that there is an increase in their segregation at the 70 per cent level. The pattern of the increase is also consistent with the national, with a 21 per cent increase in segregation internal to MLHs, the largest being among 'other retail' and 'hotels', and only 13 per cent due to an increase in the size of MLHs already at the 70 per cent segregation level.

Thanet is a local labour market whose segregation pattern has slightly diverged from the national trend, although the overall picture is not too dissimilar, allowing for the greater segregation at local as compared to national levels. In Thanet, while male segregation declines at the 90 per cent and 80 per cent levels, in keeping with the national trend, at the 70 per cent level there is negligible change over the decade. Women's segregation at the 70 per cent level similarly defies the national trend, going down rather than up. The latter is very largely due to a reduction in the segregation of the large education MLH to below the 70 per cent level, with small movements in a variety of other directions. Thanet is unusual in our localities in not having a significant increase in the percentage of women in the paid workforce, so we might surmise that the limited amount of restructuring in this way is related to the absence of an increase in the segregation of women's employment.

Swindon follows the national pattern in having a reduction in men's segregation over the decade and an increase in women's. It has the lowest rate of male segregation among our localities (though only marginally lower than Thanet), this being even lower than the British average at the 70 per cent level (though higher at the 80 per cent and 90 per cent levels). It has a particularly steep drop in men's segregation at the 70 per cent level over the last decade. The most important element of this is the decline in the size of the MLHs in which men were more than 70 per cent of the workforce, which fell 16 per cent, especially the decline in the size of the 'motor vehicle' MLH. The increase in the segregation of women's employment is largely due to an increase in the segregation of MLHs, this amounting to 28 per cent of women's 1981 total of employment, being primarily the result of 'other retail' and 'education' becoming segregated to the 70 per cent level.

VERTICAL SEGREGATION

So far the analysis has been of horizontal segregation. We shall now turn to vertical segregation. The best measure of hierarchy within the local labour market over time would appear to be that of SEG. A brief overview of the differences in the profiles of the localities using this measure is in another paper (Bagguley and Walby, 1988). This considered the extent to which localities varied in the availability of higher level work. Only in Lancaster were women overrepresented in the higher SEGs for both 1971 and 1981. Here the focus is on differences between men and women in the vertical hierarchy. Table 5.2 shows the changing distribution of women and men across the localities by the 17 categories of the SEGs between 1971 and 1981.

The 17-fold classification is not in hierarchical order, and is complex, so to assist a reading of the comparative distribution they have been grouped in some of the tables into a nine-fold classification. Despite the grouping of

Table 5.2 Socio-economic groups by sex, five localities and Britain, changes 1971–81

		Locality					
SEG		Cheltenham	Swindon	Lancaster	Thanet	Teesside	Britain
1	Men	116.67%	77.12%	7.14%	27.62%	25.29%	41.88%
	Women	45.00%	530.77%	14.81%	−11.76%	115.00%	101.98%
2	Men	−5.77%	48.02%	13.67%	5.54%	13.54%	10.08%
	Women	16.13%	75.34%	25.27%	10.00%	23.93%	35.10%
3	Men	3.33%	41.18%	−25.81%	−28.57%	−2.44%	2.78%
	Women	100.00%	0.00%	0.00%	0.00%	−50.00%	22.99%
4	Men	11.68%	10.27%	35.04%	25.93%	1.80%	6.33%
	Women	7.14%	77.78%	31.82%	−15.38%	17.24%	12.59%
5	Men	34.81%	47.19%	7.46%	7.88%	27.27%	28.21%
	Women	6.80%	35.10%	32.89%	27.14%	31.93%	40.45%
6	Men	−29.56%	−12.94%	−22.32%	−16.91%	−22.93%	−22.28%
	Women	−1.15%	34.24%	6.69%	11.98%	19.22%	8.17%
7	Men	−31.03%	36.67%	−19.23%	1.79%	52.17%	11.49%
	Women	−17.60%	38.16%	24.23%	−1.09%	22.91%	5.19%
8	Men	15.94%	6.21%	−18.49%	8.75%	2.20%	−0.75%
	Women	50.00%	15.79%	80.00%	75.00%	62.50%	19.85%
9	Men	−14.56%	−16.13%	−7.27%	−9.38%	−4.42%	−14.34%
	Women	−17.39%	−4.72%	−37.50%	−24.19%	−15.62%	−28.58%
10	Men	13.17%	7.24%	−7.93%	12.25%	25.19%	3.63%
	Women	6.67%	−33.90%	29.57%	0.47%	9.98%	−10.21%

Locality

SEG		Cheltenham	Swindon	Lancaster	Thanet	Teesider	Britain
11	Men	−18.75%	6.86%	−15.08%	−9.71%	−22.45%	−25.87%
	Women	−12.60%	3.50%	8.90%	−24.24%	7.58%	−0.33%
12	Men	38.66%	44.58%	11.17%	28.22%	7.38%	16.93%
	Women	−13.64%	−16.13%	−10.53%	13.04%	−7.61%	2.51%
13	Men	50.00%	50.00%	32.14%	200.00%	−22.58%	−13.68%
	Women	0.00%	−100.00%	−37.50%	100.00%	−66.67%	−18.19%
14	Men	100.00%	−44.44%	−18.75%	0.00%	−64.29%	−21.04%
	Women	−100.00%	−25.00%	−33.33%	−100.00%	−16.67%	−35.23%
15	Men	−53.85%	16.67%	−6.67%	−18.92%	−29.51%	−20.26%
	Women	0.00%	−69.23%	−33.33%	−10.00%	0.00%	−12.59%
16	Men	29.41%	36.90%	0.00%	31.82%	63.16%	−1.71%
	Women	−100.00%	0.00%	0.00%	100.00%	0.00%	50.04%
17	Men	55.81%	114.71%	131.25%	101.43%	79.08%	98.21%
	Women	5.17%	11.34%	−8.89%	0.00%	2.53%	9.46%
Totals							
	Men	1.84%	7.35%	−1.59%	3.96%	1.89%	−2.34%
	Women	−1.65%	17.16%	11.63%	5.48%	17.19%	8.06%
	All	0.42%	10.96%	3.38%	4.54%	7.07%	1.46%

Source: Census of Population, 1971, 1981.
Notes: Socio-economic groups and socio-economic classes:
SEG 1 Employers and managers in central and local government, industry, commerce, etc. – large establishments
SEG 2 Employers and managers in industry, commerce, etc. – small establishments
SEG 3 Professional workers – self-employed
SEG 4 Professional workers – employees
SEG 5 Intermediate non-manual workers
SEG 6 Junior non-manual workers
SEG 7 Personal service workers
SEG 8 Foremen and supervisors – manual
SEG 9 Skilled manual workers
SEG 10 Semi-skilled manual workers
SEG 11 Unskilled manual workers
SEG 12 Own account workers (other than professionals)
SEG 13 Farmers – employers and managers
SEG 14 Farmers – own account
SEG 15 Agricultural workers
SEG 16 Members of armed forces
SEG 17 Inadequately described occupations

SEGs in this way there still remains the problem of a rigid manual/non-manual division. This introduces elements of a sectoral (production versus services) logic to the hierarchy, which is questionable. In particular the work and market situations of personal service workers are likely to be rather inferior to those of skilled manual workers. However, SEGs do at least keep these groups distinct, and if taken separately reflect the hierarchies within non-manual and manual work.

There are some further problems in using this data, making any conclusions tentative. First, using small area statistics (SAS) data, it is impossible to pull the unemployed out of the SEG data, disaggregated by SEG and sex for 1971. Hence to produce comparable categories for 1971 and 1981 the

Table 5.3 Grouped socio-economic groups by sex, changes 1971–81

			Locality			
Group	Cheltenham	Swindon	Lancaster	Thanet	Teesside	Britain
1 Men	31.33%	57.66%	12.93%	13.32%	17.11%	18.33%
Women	23.17%	133.33%	19.05%	5.88%	41.41%	49.01%
2 Men	10.18%	13.50%	22.30%	11.93%	1.25%	5.71%
Women	18.75%	63.64%	36.36%	−15.38%	2.70%	13.93%
3 Men	34.81%	47.19%	7.46%	7.88%	27.27%	28.21%
Women	6.80%	35.10%	32.89%	27.14%	31.93%	40.45%
4 Men	−29.56%	−12.94%	−22.32%	−16.91%	−22.93%	−22.28%
Women	−1.15%	34.24%	6.69%	11.98%	19.22%	8.17%
5 Men	−31.03%	36.67%	−19.23%	1.79%	52.17%	11.49%
Women	−17.60%	38.16%	24.23%	−1.09%	22.91%	5.19%
6 Men	−4.05%	−8.85%	−5.83%	−0.67%	−3.35%	−9.65%
Women	−12.00%	−5.00%	−22.87%	−1.42%	−8.64%	−18.59%
7 Men	13.17%	7.24%	−7.93%	12.25%	25.19%	3.63%
Women	6.67%	−33.90%	29.57%	0.47%	9.98%	−10.21%
8 Men	−21.66%	7.82%	−13.80%	−11.32%	−22.71%	−24.94%
Women	−7.87%	−0.94%	4.27%	−21.85%	7.48%	−1.32%
9 Men	48.33%	71.71%	110.53%	84.78%	77.19%	51.77%
Women	0.00%	9.48%	−8.89%	1.06%	2.81%	10.72%
Totals						
Men	1.84%	7.35%	−1.59%	3.96%	1.89%	−2.34%
Women	−1.65%	17.16%	11.63%	5.48%	17.19%	8.06%
All	0.42%	10.96%	3.38%	4.54%	7.07%	1.46%

Source: Census of Population, 1971, 1981.
Notes: SEGs
1 Employers and Managers SEGs 1 and 2, 13
2 Professionals SEGs 3 and 4
3 Intermediate non-manual SEG 5
4 Junior non-manual SEG 6
5 Personal service workers SEG 7
6 Skilled manual workers SEGs 8, 9, 12, 14
7 Semi-skilled manual SEG 10
8 Unskilled manual SEG 11
9 Other
(16 and 17 excluded.)

numbers in any SEG include not only those employed, but also unemployed persons who used to belong to a particular SEG. Thus as an indicator of vertical hierarchy the SEG data is compromised, since unemployment results in a major loss of economic and social rewards and status. (Some tables for SEGs also included the retired, but these non-workers are excluded from the ones presented here.)

Second, comparison with MLH data is restricted because of the different spatial unit for SEG as compared to MLH data. This is different for two reasons: (1) the geographical area for MLH data is based on the travel-to-work area, while SEG data is based on local authority district boundaries. The significance of the discrepancy varies between our five localities: the Lancaster area is the closest, Teesside the most discrepant. (2) MLH data is based on returns from the workplace, while SEG data is drawn from the 10 per cent census and thus based on a household sampling unit. The problem here is that some people who work in an establishment in a given locality (on MLH boundaries) may live outside the district boundary (for SEG data). Again the extent of the problem varies with locality, with Lancaster appearing to have the least problem. In other localities the problem is greater, for instance Cheltenham having a population for the MLH data which is 50 per cent larger than that for the SEG data, presumably because many people who work in the urban area of Cheltenham live in the rural areas outside the urban boundary. The third problem is that the SEG classification changes between 1971 and 1981, so some apparent changes are merely artefacts of classificatory change and not 'real'. Finally in 1971 the data counts 'persons present' rather than 'persons resident' in 1981 which complicates comparisons over time.

These limitations are serious for two of the tasks of this chapter. It is difficult to give a measure of hierarchy if unemployed people are placed in the same category as employed people rather than being excluded since we are concerned with those in paid employment. This makes it very difficult for us to give any index of comparison between our localities, or even of inequality between them. It also means that there are limits on the extent to which we can ask about the relationship between vertical and horizontal segregation, since we would be comparing slightly different populations for each 'locality'; further, these would be expected to vary as to their socio-economic composition precisely because of their residential location.

With such serious limits is it worth exploring the SEG data at all? The changes in the classifications between 1971 and 1981 are much less significant if the SEGs are grouped to some extent, which we have done. In this we follow Fielding and Savage (1987) who suggest that the classificatory changes are not overwhelming (although we use a slightly different grouping in order to clarify major distinctions between forms of work which are especially pertinent for gender relations). It is legitimate to make some statements about change over time using the SEG data if this is kept distinct from the MLH set. In order to cope with the different boundaries, each name (eg Lancaster) must be thought of as representing two areas: one the travel-to-work-area (TTWA); the other the district. (There is Lancaster I (TTWA) and Lancaster II (local authority district). However, comparisons between SEG and MLH data must not be made at the level of locality, only nationally. Finally, it is necessary to remember the issue of unemployment in using all the SEG data.

So, holding all these provisos, what can be said? Table 5.4 shows the degree to which men and women work in the same or different SEGs in 1971 and 1981 in the five localities and in Britain. The first striking feature of the table is the extent of the vertical segregation. Some men and women work in SEGs in which no member of the other sex is present in that locality, while in one locality in 1971, Teesside, nearly half the men were in

Table 5.4   Vertical segregation by sex, 1971 and 1981, five localities and Britain

	Level of segregation							
	100%		90 + %		80 + %		70 + %	
	1971 %	1981 %	1971 %	1981 %	1971 %	1981 %	1971 %	1981 %
Cheltenham								
Men	0.63	1.11	36.58	29.27	46.01	48.59	66.43	69.66
Women	0	0	0	12.82	15.30	12.82	15.30	55.69
Swindon								
Men	0	0.46	40.66	36.70	51.17	43.74	56.84	55.91
Women	0	0	0	0	9.21	10.86	9.21	51.81
Lancaster								
Men	1.34	0.38	5.05	24.95	54.83	40.10	71.51	71.87
Women	0	0	0	0	15.14	16.85	15.14	46.39
Thanet								
Men	1.02	0.77	32.18	29.28	35.12	37.00	56.75	57.10
Women	0	0	0	0	15.97	14.97	15.97	14.97
Teesside								
Men	0.28	0	45.23	43.15	49.10	47.41	69.58	71.63
Women	0	0	14.58	15.30	14.58	15.30	14.58	52.60
Britain								
Men	0	0	5.81	28.84	45.56	49.12	51.75	59.10
Women	0	0	0	0	09.37	12.16	09.37	49.49

Source: Census of Population, 1971, 1981.
Note: calculated on SEGs (1974) local authority districts.

SEGs which were 90 per cent male. Second, there are variations in segregation. Men are more segregated than women; some localities are much more segregated than others, especially at the 90 per cent degree. The third striking feature is the increase in hierarchical segregation over the decade, for both men and women in Britain as a whole, and in most of the localities. This is shown in Figures 5.1–5.3.

For Britain the increase in male segregation shows up most noticeably at the 90 per cent degree with an increase from 6 per cent to 29 per cent of men working in SEGs which are 90 per cent male, but is also represented at the 80 per cent degree with an increase from 40 per cent to 49 per cent and at the 70 per cent degree with an increase from 54 per cent to 59 per cent. The increase for women shows up most strikingly at the 70 per cent degree with an incredible increase from 9 per cent to 49 per cent of women working in SEGs which are at least 70 per cent female, but is also represented at the 80 per cent degree with an increase from 9 per cent to 12 per cent, as shown in Table 5.4 (p. 112). This tremendous increase for women is a result of the increasing numbers of women in junior non-manual work (SEG 6) which reaches 70 per cent female in the course of the decade. For men the large increase at the 90 per cent degree is composed primarily of the increasing 'masculinisation' of skilled manual work, as women leave this SEG in larger proportions than men.

The localities vary somewhat in the extent to which they have changes similar to the national average. Thanet is the only locality in which there has not been a dramatic increase in female segregation rate; this is the local economy with least restructuring overall. Swindon has experienced a decrease rather than increase in the rate of male segregation. Lancaster follows the national pattern more closely than most. Teesside has the highest rate of male segregation at the 90 per cent degree.

While these data are not comparable at the level of locality with the MLH data, they are comparable at the national level. Here women experienced an increase in both horizontal and vertical segregation simultaneously, while men had a decrease in horizontal segregation and increase in vertical segregation. This clearly indicates that horizontal and vertical segregation are not dependent variables, and that they measure something different.

So far SEG data has been used to examine the extent to which men and women are in different or similar positions in the hierarchy. There is also the slightly different question of the extent to which men are higher up the hierarchy as compared to women, and how this varies across locality.

The figures for Britain as a whole show that there has been an increase in the proportion of the population in the upper SEGs and a decline in those in the lower SEGs. Given that unemployment is concentrated at the lower ends of the job market, and thus that the lower SEGs will have a higher proportion of unemployed members, the hidden unemployment need not be a negative qualification on this statement. Rather, the SEG data probably

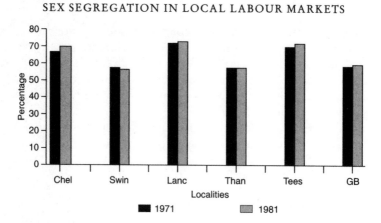

Figure 5.1 Percentage of men in socio-economic groups comprising 70 per cent or more men

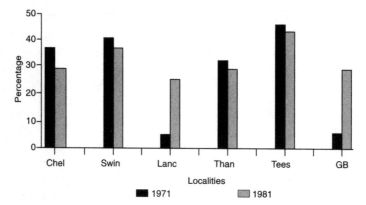

Figure 5.2 Percentage of men in socio-economic groups comprising 90 per cent of more men

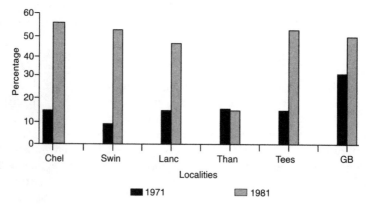

Figure 5.3 Percentage of women in socio-economic groups comprising 70 per cent or more women

114

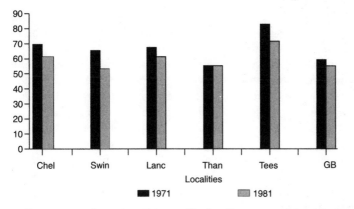

Figure 5.4 Percentage of men in minimum list headings comprising 70 per cent or more men

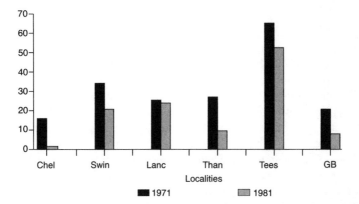

Figure 5.5 Percentage of men in minimum list headings comprising 90 per cent or more men

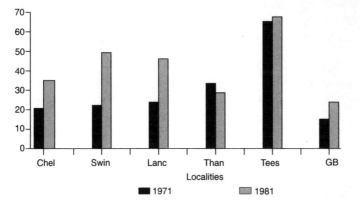

Figure 5.6 Percentage of women in minimum list headings comprising 70 per cent or more women

115

underestimates the extent of increase in employment in the higher SEGs. The biggest declines are those in the agricultural SEGs (13–15). Service class occupations continued to grow throughout the period 1971–81.

This increase in the upper SEGs is more marked among women than among men (SEGs 1 to 5). Thus we might speak of the 'feminisation' of the service class. This is true for all levels of the service class, except the agricultural sphere which is in decline. This is taking place at the same time as the increase in horizontal segregation of women at MLH levels. This might appear contradictory, since segregation is usually thought to be inconsistent with the advance of women. It should be remembered that there are two separate dimensions of segregation, the horizontal and the vertical, not segregation and hierarchy. These results show merely that horizontal and vertical segregation do not necessarily correlate. Indeed one interpretation of this might be that as women come to be the majority of the workforce in a given industry (MLH), then they are more likely, rather than less likely, to take the top positions in that industry, and thus to rise up the SEGs. Or, on the other hand women are entering the service class but in 'peripheral' functions of the occupations concerned (Spencer and Podmore, 1987). However, it could also represent changes in different sectors of the economy, for instance women rising to the top in some areas of employment, while becoming the majority of other sectors of employment which are low paid.

The picture of feminisation of the service class is in general reflected across our localities, although the extent of this varies. However, it is not to be found in Cheltenham nor Thanet, where there was a further masculinisation of the service class. It was most marked in Teesside and Swindon where the growth of women in the service class was twice the rate of growth for men (see Table 5.3).

In Britain the lowest level SEGs showed the most overall decline. This decline was more marked among men than women. Thus we might write of the demasculinisation (emasculation?) of the manual working class. The most extreme version is to be found among unskilled manual workers (SEG 11).

In skilled manual work there is a larger decrease in women's jobs than in men's jobs: SEG 9 shows a drop of 14 per cent of men and one of double that for women of 29 per cent. Further, when we look at semi-skilled manual work we find that men's employment has increased nationally by 4 per cent, while women's has fallen by 10 per cent. This contradicts the feminisation thesis which suggests that men's skilled manual jobs are destroyed and female semi-skilled work is created. On the contrary, women have lost a higher proportion of skilled work than men, and women's semi-skilled work has decreased not increased.

In the manual SEGs we find that all of our localities have changes between men and women in a direction counter to that of the national figure. That is, in each case men's decline is greater than that of women and in two instances, Lancaster and Teesside, there is actually an increase in women's jobs at this level. At a more detailed level of breakdown we can see more clearly the similarities and differences. In the case of skilled manual work (SEG 9) in every instance except Swindon the study's localities followed the national picture of a greater decline among women than men. Among skilled workers (SEG 11) the national pattern of greater decline among men and women is followed by only Cheltenham and Teesside, while in Swindon both men and women show an increase. In Lancaster, while the men decline the women increase, and in Thanet the women decline more than the men. Among semi-skilled manual workers only Swindon follows the national pattern of a decline in women and an increase in men's employment. In Cheltenham, Thanet and Teesside there is an increase in both men's and women's semi-skilled employment, as shown in Table 5.3, while in Lancaster there is a decrease for men and an increase for women.

At neither the national level, not that of the localities in the study is there any evidence to support the feminisation thesis which predicts a decrease in men's skilled manual work greater than that of women's and an increase in women's semi-skilled manual work greater than that of men's. Rather women have disproportionately lost skilled work (though the men have lost some too) everywhere bar Cheltenham, and men have disproportionately gained semi-skilled manual work everywhere bar Lancaster.

One SEG, number 6, junior non-manual, contains 39 per cent of the total of women's employment. Nationally this has seen a decline in the numbers and proportion of men in this category, and an increase in women. This is reflected in all the localities except Cheltenham which has seen a decline in the number of women as well as men, although the decrease for women is significantly lower than that for men. The national increase in the number of women in this SEG is roughly proportionate to the increase in the number of women who are economically active, an increase of 8 per cent for the SEG, as compared with 7 per cent for all women's economic activity.

Overall then women have seen a significant movement upwards in the SEGs over the period 1971 to 1981. Women's employment in middle grades around junior non-manual have increased in line with the general increase in women's employment, while the top grades have seen a very large increase, and the lower ones a decrease. From the SEG data (which includes the unemployed listed by last job) it can be seen that the numbers of men in higher SEGs has also increased but not as much as for women. Men have also experienced a considerable reduction in employment in the middle grade of junior non-manual and in the manual grades. The feminisation thesis, which suggests that there is a movement from male skilled manual jobs to female semi-skilled is not supported by these figures. This is the most important conclusion refuting a central plank of restructuring theory.

CONCLUSIONS

This chapter has shown that there have been significant changes in the sex composition of particular industries; that the sex composition of an industry can change. It is possible that the change in sex composition within industries at the MLH level may be due to the changing balance of occupations within them, especially in large MLHs such as 'medical', but the frequency and extent of these changes mean that the sex composition of the workforce is not totally dependent upon industrial structure. Rather the data on changes in women's employment in Britain 1971–81 suggests that sex segregation has been restructured independently of industrial restructuring. The rigidity thesis holds best for men, since the major reduction in segregation has come from a reduction in the areas of employment in which men are concentrated. However, a thesis which works for one sex and not the other is at best only half a theory.

There was an increase in horizontal segregation for women and a decrease in this type of segregation for men in the period 1971–81. The decrease in this segregation for men is a result not of their movement into traditionally women's jobs, but of the decrease in the number of jobs available in traditionally male areas of work. The increase in the horizontal segregation of women's jobs is not primarily a result of a parallel process, but instead due to an increase in the extent of segregation in such areas.

Existing theories are badly flawed because of an underlying problem of failing to address adequately the theorisation of gender relations. It is not the case that gender relations are either a by-product of the capital or the capital–labour relation, or are contingent, that is, inexplicable. Theorisation of sex segregation needs to deal with the specificity of gender relations as autonomous or relatively autonomous relations from capital. The sex-typing of an industry is sometimes stable and sometimes changing. There are key periods in which there are rounds of restructuring of gender relations in industries followed by periods of stability. New rounds of gender restructuring build upon the old. Thus data which shows rigidity in the sex composition and that which shows change can both be consistent with this theory, *if* we can adequately explain the periods of gender restructuring. The only way to explain why Teesside could have such degrees of male dominance in specific industries, above those typical for those industries at a national level, is by a thesis about the level of patriarchal hegemony in that area. That is, the degree of male dominance produced by the industrial structure assists a particularly high degree of male dominance in the political and social structures, including those of the labour movement, which assists the exclusion of women for paid work.

The reduction in forms of patriarchal closure against women dominates the period under study (1971–81); women increased their access to all jobs and a disproportionate share of the best new jobs. Industries and occupations which were created or expanded significantly in this period were less likely to embody forms of patriarchal closure than those industries set up in the nineteenth century. The new rounds of industrial restructuring embody the newer forms of gender relations of employment which are less exclusionary.

6

LABOUR MARKETS AND
INDUSTRIAL STRUCTURES IN
WOMEN'S WORKING LIVES

INTRODUCTION

The intersection of structural and biographical change is a crucial feature of the differentiation of women's lives. The analysis of women's position in society is often considered to be particularly affected by their stage in the life cycle. This chapter will examine that hypothesis in relation to one aspect of women's position in the labour market. On the one hand it can be argued that women are particularly affected by their stage in the life cycle because of the importance of child birth and child care in their lives. On the other, it can be argued that this overstates the significance of biological events at the expense of the significance of other factors structuring women's lives. In particular, that there is a problematic tendency to use a 'job model' to explain men's work patterns and a different one, 'a gender model', to explain women's work patterns (Feldberg and Glenn, 1979). That is, labour market and industrial structures tend to be used to explain patterns in men's work while domestic events are used to explain patterns in women's work. The greater tendency to use the life history method in the analysis of women's as opposed to men's labour force experience thus may push our understanding of women's employment in a different direction from that of men to a greater extent than is warranted.

This chapter will also discuss methodological issues in researching women's employment. In particular, the strengths and weaknesses of the life history method is the best way of gaining an understanding and explanation of patterns of women's participation in paid work.

DOMESTIC VERSUS LABOUR MARKET
EXPLANATIONS

There are three parallel debates on women's participation in paid employment which deal particularly with the question of the significance of women's life cycle, and hence the pertinence of the life history method. First, whether women's disadvantaged position in paid work is due on the

120

one hand to their possessing less human capital than men, or on the other, to discrimination against them. Second, whether it is family structures or labour market structures which underlie women's different position in paid work. Third, supply-side versus demand-side models of women's participation. These debates all bear upon the issue of whether longitudinal or cross-sectional methodologies are more appropriate for the analysis of gender relations in employment. These discussions have considerable overlap, as I shall show below.

The first debate, as to whether human capital models can explain the different positions of men and women in paid work has been subject to extensive discussion (see e.g. Amsden, 1980; England, 1982; Mincer, 1962; Mincer and Polachek, 1974; Treiman and Hartmann 1981; Walby, 1988). On the one hand human capital theorists argue that women's lower wages can be explained as a consequence of women's lesser human capital as indicated by their skill, qualifications and labour market experience. On the other, it is argued that it is discrimination which accounts for the lesser wages and lesser access to occupations of women than men. (An overview analysis by Treiman and Hartmann of tests of this model by human capital theorists suggests that while this theory is able to account for some of the wages gap between men and women, it is unable to explain more than two-fifths of this.)

In the second debate, one side argues that women's position in paid work can be understood primarily as a result of their position within the family, while the other emphasises the importance of labour market structures. Here one set of writers has suggested that it is women's role as homemaker, in particular taking care of children and a husband, which means that women have a different relationship to the labour market than a man does, whose principle role is that of breadwinner. Women typically spend less time in paid work than men as a consequence of their domestic work and have fewer skills partly as a direct consequence and partly because women's anticipation of this role means that they typically acquire fewer qualifications than men. The other side of this debate stresses instead the structuring of the labour market which leads to women's confinement to those jobs which are paid less and are considered less skilled. Here it is the role of organised men in the labour market as trade unionists or employers which is seen to structure opportunities in favour of men and away from women.

The third debate is constructed around the dichotomy of supply-side versus demand-side factors. On the one hand women's position in the labour market is considered to be a result of supply-side factors, such as the structuring of their human capital by their domestic situation. On the other, women's participation in paid employment is considered crucially to depend on what employers offer, in the context of patriarchally structured industrial relations.

As can be seen these three debates overlap. Indeed in certain circumstances they might look as if they were merely different expressions of the same debate. Thus it may be argued that women's position in paid employment is different from that of men because they have less human capital because of their position in the family and that this supply-side variable is determinant. On the other it could be argued that women's position is different from that of men because of discrimination which is rooted in the labour market and leads to different demand for women as compared to male workers. However, the three debates do not necessarily overlap, although this is often the case. For instance, some Marxist feminists have argued that it is the family which leads to women's disadvantaged position in the labour market, and this is not a human capital approach, while still focusing on the supply-side variable of the family.

The point here is that life histories are of more importance if the first side of each of these three debates is considered to be correct, and less important if the second side is taken as correct. Life histories gather data on the factors considered relevant by the first position, and rarely gather data on factors considered central by the second approach. Life histories used in the analysis of employment usually collect information on a person's education and training, periods of labour market participation and withdrawal, geographical and occupational mobility, and life events such as child bearing and rearing. They are not suited to gathering information about the nature and sources of the structuring of the labour market. This is because life histories collect information on individual characteristics.

However, this point should not be overstated, since life histories will necessarily record the effects of labour market structuring. Indeed they provide information about how an individual experiences the labour market. Cross-sectional analyses cannot tell us about how a given individual, or cohort, experiences structural change. Thus life histories provide us with information which is otherwise unobtainable about the implications of structural change for individuals or specific social groups. This is the great strength of the life history methodology for analyses of work.

This chapter will examine these issues about the life history method in relation to women's employment. The data set which is used to explore these issues is described below.

LANCASTER WOMEN'S WORK HISTORIES

The Lancaster Women's Work Histories was a data set gathered in Lancaster in 1980–81. It contains information on a sample of 300 women in the Lancaster travel-to-work-area (TTWA). The data concerned life histories, with an emphasis on employment histories, together with contemporary data on a wider range of issues including the domestic division of labour and political and social attitudes. In addition we asked for the areas in which the women had previously lived.

The most detailed information was on employment. Women were asked to recall all the jobs they had ever held. For each job each woman was asked about the occupational and industrial classification, rate of pay, amount of job-specific training and reason for leaving. These were coded using the Census and Standard Industrial Classification (SIC) distinctions, and our own 19-fold classification of reasons for leaving a job.

The sample was obtained from the electoral registers for the area, Lancaster having a near coincidence of administrative and TTWA boundaries. The wards were stratified in order to ensure a balance between the two main urban areas of Lancaster and Morecambe as well as the associated rural area, all of which are part of the TTWA. The women were interviewed by Anne Green using a structured questionnaire, some for several hours.

This is only one of several data sets on the Lancaster TTWA which are available. This local labour market was the focus of intense study by the Lancaster Regionalism Group as part of the ESRC financed initiative on the Changing Urban and Regional System, so we have separate sources of data on structural change from various survey sources, including the Department of Employment Census of Employment, and also on its political history.

Methodological issues

We encountered a number of predictable methodological problems in the collection and coding of these data. Those which are discussed here are the sample size, the recall problem, the unit of data collection and the occupational classification problem.

The typical method of data collection in Britain has been that used in the Lancaster survey – the use of a questionnaire survey conducted by interviewer using retrospective recall of information by the respondent. People's memories are fallible and they are likely to be more fallible the further back they are asked to remember. Thus the early data is likely to be less accurate than the recent data. The question of the degree to which the early data is inaccurate is unknowable, unless the respondent admits to not knowing. Where the respondent admits to not knowing we were able to disregard the question and analysis on that topic. In this study respondents were asked a variety of questions about each job. Some of the answers on detailed issues, for instance pay, were recorded as 'not known' sufficiently frequently for this data to be considered not worth analysing. It is more likely that people will remember the occupation and industry of jobs held recently for a long time, than for jobs held 30 years prior for a few months. Repeat interview panel surveys, in which respondents are asked to report on the present at regular intervals throughout their lives may overcome these problems, but at considerable expense, as in the case of the British Household Panel Study at Essex.

It is the issue of selective recall which lends support to the argument that the life history method is inevitably subjective. If we cannot collect data which have a direct correspondence to events in a person's past then should we abandon notions of scientific reliability and settle for a notion of life histories as rich ethnographic data instead? In this view life histories are not irrelevant, but they are not the kind of hard data which are appropriately analysed with statistics and computers. Instead they give us memories of the past, which are interesting precisely because they are selective. Dex (1991) in her review of research work on recall suggests that it can be reliable for certain topics, thus the claim that life histories are purely subjective goes too far.

A second methodological issue concerned the sample size. The size of the sample needs to be quite large in order to deal with the effects of different cohorts. This makes life history collection even by recall extremely expensive. The Lancaster Women's Work Histories data set is at the limit of acceptable size for the analysis performed upon it. Even so, the aggregations which had to be performed in order to achieve statistically significant results were sometimes less than desirable. Some analytic questions were not considered capable of reliable answer and hence abandoned. One way past this problem is to abandon the attempt to gather data on more than one age cohort at a time. For the Lancaster study this was considered an unacceptable limitation since the intersection with the different structural changes was a question of central interest. For other studies it might be an acceptable limitation. Another alternative is to utilise a large sample, but to ask only limited questions – the kind of questions for which a guiding interviewer is not necessary. This is the practice in the OPCS Longitudinal Survey (LS). (This is a 1 per cent sample survey from the Census. Records are linked across the decade-long gap, in order to build up a set of longitudinal data. The strengths are the size of the sample and the reliability of the sampling frame. The restrictions include the limitation of the range of questions which can be asked on the Census form, and also that data is collected only at 10-year intervals, missing many changes. A further current restriction is that only the last two censuses have been so linked.) These data were used by Dan Shapiro within the Lancaster CURS study (see Bagguley *et al.*, 1990). The issues which were analysed in the above analysis could not have been raised using data from the LS which were restricted to a few pieces of information. Indeed the Lancaster Women's Work History data set is unusual in asking questions about all job changes over a working life, rather than over a limited number of years or a limited number of points in a life time.

These strengths and weaknesses of the life history method so far discussed are common to analyses of work histories for men as well as women, although the data set utilised above concerned only women. There are other issues which especially relate to the gender aspect. In particular there is the issue of the household. While many analyses of men's working lives assume that the nature of a man's coresidents is of only marginal interest, the opposite assumption is usually made about women. An open-minded analysis would, of course, ask the household questions about men as well as women, in order to test, rather than merely assume, that the household is of significance to women's employment and not to men's.

Our data set contained some questions about household composition. However, it was not possible, given the limited time available for the interview, to ask many questions about other household members over time. While it is reasonable to ask about the occupational and financial status of current household members, there was not time to ask about this for the respondent's lifetime, nor would it have been likely to be accurate. This is partly because recall about others is less likely to be accurate, even if the respondents had once known the information. And there is a particular difficulty about asking about ex-household members, whose absence may well have been due to a traumatic event, such as death or divorce. Interviewee cooperation is likely to cease in a sufficiently large proportion of these cases to make any data collected unreliable. Thus retrospective collection of household data is particularly difficult. Our data set was based on individuals. If, however, the hypothesis that women's employment patterns are significantly determined by that of their husband and household were being adopted, then it would be logical to make the household rather than the individual the data collection unit. The amount of interviewee cooperation needed to achieve this increases significantly. This is particularly difficult over time, given the propensity of households to change membership. Retrospective questioning would have to deal with the issue of which household is under analysis, while panel interviewing would be faced with the alternate dissolution and extension of the unit under study. Given the current rates of divorce in Britain, never mind 'simple' issues such as marriage and death, longitudinal analysis of employment taking the household as the unit would be bedevilled with methodological difficulties. It should be noted however, that the current study takes the individual as the unit on theoretical grounds, not that of methodological ease.

An additional problem faced was that of the choice of occupational coding. Analysis of women's occupations is fraught with classificatory difficulties. The conventional classifications have been based upon male occupations, but the main distinctions here are different from those between types of work done by women. The heavy preponderance of clerical work and semi-skilled service-sector work among women, and the small presence of women in skilled manual work, are in sharp contrast with the balance of occupations among men. Various alternatives have been suggested (see e.g. Dex, 1987).

In this study we decided to proceed pragmatically and to see how the occupations grouped. We worked on the now standard assumption that people are more likely to move between jobs which are similar than they are between those which are dissimilar. We had the data on job changes and so could discover which jobs our 300 women moved between most frequently. We placed in the same grouping those occupations between which there was most movement, and drew distinctions from other occupational groupings between which our 300 women moved less frequently. The analysis was done with the assistance of Richard Davies, using techniques described in Goodman (1986) and Green (1989). This does have the disadvantage of not being directly comparable with the classification of men's jobs, but men were not included in this sample anyway.

This procedure produced an eight-fold classification: professional; intermediate; clerical; skilled manual; factory manual; service workers; sales; and unskilled. This was very similar to the occupational groupings classified as profiles produced using a similar method by Dex on the 5,230 women of the DE/OPCS Women and Employment Survey in 1980. This classification is different to that typically used for men in a number of ways. First, the classification splits factory and service workers (both either subsumed under semi-skilled or scattered), which reflects the distinctiveness of the service sector niche especially for part-time women workers. Second, it separated sales from clerical workers; this separation is now widely commented upon where sales workers have worse rates of pay and conditions than clerical workers, that is, have circumstances more akin to manual workers than white-collar workers.

In a separate exercise the industries in which the women worked were grouped into two: production and services, the former involving a conflation of manufacturing and the tiny extractive sectors.

DOMESTIC VERSUS LABOUR MARKET EXPLANATIONS

As I have suggested earlier, the classic divide in the literature on women's employment is that between domestic/human capital and labour market/discrimination models. I have argued that the life history methodology has an in-built imperative towards the former and away from the latter explanations. Thus the data set outlined above would often be analysed by examining correlations between domestic events and labour market events. For instance the standard questions would include:

- Does a greater number of departures from the labour market for child or husband care lead to lower labour market status and lower earnings?
- Does a longer absence from the labour force for such unpaid work lead to a similar outcome?

126

The answer to these questions is, on average, an unequivocal affirmative as a multitude of studies of similar data sets have shown. For instance, this is the clear outcome of the analysis of the nationally representative sample of women in the Women and Employment Survey (Martin and Roberts, 1984). Hence it would appear to confirm the domestic/human capital model. However, Martin and Roberts were careful to consider other elements in their analysis, asking questions, for instance, about the extent of occupational segregation.

The contrary thesis emphasises the importance of labour market structures, discrimination and the demand side of the economy. Indeed the Lancaster economy had undergone major structural change, especially over the period 1960–80. The Lancaster Women's Work History data set was gathered in the same TTWA as a range of cross-sectional data sets which point up a range of other possible hypotheses. The Lancaster TTWA underwent early deindustrialisation in the 1960s and 1970s, so that by 1980 the structure of the labour market was heavily weighted towards the service sector. The manufacturing sector, which had been based on the production of linoneum, more or less closed down during the 1970s and 1980s, apart from those firms which were able to diversify into plastic-covered wallpaper. Textile mills (not cotton but artificial fibres) similarly were closed down by multinationals which moved production abroad to cheaper sources of labour.

The period 1960–80 saw the collapse of the sector of the economy which had traditionally employed many men – manufacturing – and the growth of the sector which today employs many women – services. During this period census data show an enormous increase in the paid employment of women.

One question here is which had greater effect on women's patterns and experiences of paid employment – the life cycle, or deindustrialisation? Do we conclude that the enormous increase of women workers is due to these sectoral shifts in the economy? Or do we conclude that despite the overall increase in women's employment the life-cycle effect remains the overwhelming feature structuring women's experiences of work?

Since the answer is, obviously, that both are significant, the question becomes – can we disentangle the different implications of these developments for women? In particular, what happens at the intersection of life and work trajectories on the one hand, and industrial and labour market change on the other?

In this context I hope to have shown that the study of life history data by itself is problematic. It pushes towards certain explanatory hypotheses, even if the authors of the study are careful to add appropriate qualifications. Rather we need to utilise both longitudinal and cross-sectional data sets. The most interesting results are at the intersection of the two.

The Lancaster data set on Women's Work Histories is strongest on the issue of job changes. Changes in jobs are a routine aspect of all working lives. The point of change potentially gives us some important indication of the social and economic processes at work. We can analyse the direction of change and the various correlates of this. We can examine the nature of the changes which women made from job to job and on the point of entering and leaving the labour market. We can examine these changes by occupational group, by industrial sector, and by full-time and part-time working.

My question is whether the changes correlate better with aspects of domestic or labour market structures. Many women do take a break from paid work in order to work at home looking after children and husbands for certain periods of their lives. But how important is this break for the nature of the paid work that women take? The domestic or gender model suggests that it is the overwhelming structuring event, while the 'job' model would focus on the nature of the labour market structures.

The complexity of a data set such as this one on Lancaster is that domestic events are occurring simultaneously with changes in labour market opportunities. When women re-enter the workforce after a break they are not entering the same labour market, but rather one which has been changed by industrial restructuring. Over the period of study the nature of the Lancaster labour market was significantly changed by the deindustrialisation of the local economy. The manufacturing sector underwent significant decline, as both the product market changed and as production was moved abroad by the multinational owners, while the service sector underwent considerable expansion.

DEINDUSTRIALISATION AND THE EXPERIENCE OF THE LABOUR MARKET

This process of deindustrialisation occurred in Lancaster a little earlier than in many other British cities, but otherwise is similar to the change undergone in the rest of Britain in the early 1980s. The Lancaster economy had been dominated by a few large manufacturers, but these largely closed down in the 1960s and 1970s. These firms were part of multinational conglomerates. In the textile sector, the product was artificial fibres. This process was first run down by a failure to invest in the newer forms of technology; it then moved abroad to sources of cheaper labour. In the case of linoleum the product itself was one of the problems as the market changed and carpet became the preferred and affordable alternative. Chemicals was a further manufacturing sector to suffer serious contraction. The main types of occupations in these plants were manual, involving various levels of skill. They were jobs held predominantly, but by no means exclusively, by men.

At the same time as the manufacturing sector was collapsing the service sector was expanding. From the nineteenth century Lancaster had been a centre for health care – from its early period as the county town. Even after it lost its status as the centre for county-level government its hospitals remained. These included not only general physical hospitals, but also those for the mentally ill and mentally handicapped. This sector expanded during the 1960s and 1970s. Further, Lancaster became a centre for education, with the founding and expansion of the University from 1964, together with the development of a college of higher education. This service sector was primarily in the public rather than private sector. In addition there was the development of the retail sector as Lancaster became more of a regional shopping centre, that is, there was growth in the private-sector services. The occupations in this service sector were at all levels of skill, including a more significant professional component than those of the declining manufacturing sector. A higher proportion of these jobs were held by women than had been the case in the declining manufacturing sector. The changes in the economy of Lancaster are explored in more detail in Bagguley *et al.* (1990).

At this aggregate level the changes in industrial structure and gender composition of the workforce appear to go neatly together. But the aggregate-level data cannot tell us whether individuals themselves directly experience deindustrialisation in their own personal work lives. We do not know whether, for instance, the typical worker moves from manufacturing to service sector during the course of their lives. An alternative possibility is that it is new entrants to the workforce who take the new service jobs, while the ex-manufacturing workers become either retired or unemployed. In the former case workers experience and are able to compare both sectors. In the latter they cannot. This has important implications for people's experience and consciousness of social and economic change. Also, changes of this kind must have implications for local politics.

The work history method then adds something to the analysis of deindustrialisation which cannot be gained from the aggregate data alone. These changes have massively different implications for consciousness and action according to how individuals move through these industrial and labour market changes.

The analysis of job changes enables us to answer some questions about the way individuals experience these changes. Do people stay within the industrial sector and occupation? If they change does this have a pattern, or does it appear to be random?

An examination of the job changes of our 300 women shows that 75 per cent of job changes were within an industrial sector. A slight majority of movements between sectors was from production to services rather than from services to production. The change from production to services at the structural level of the Lancaster economy was directly experienced in terms of a direct change from a production job to a service job in only 15 per cent of job changes, as Table 6.1 illustrates.

Table 6.1 Job movement by sector for Lancaster women

	1960–80		All working life	
	No.	%	No.	%
Production to service	36	15	188	24
Service to production	25	10	121	16
Service to service	123	51	278	36
Production to production	57	24	186	24
Total	241	100	773	100

These figures show that despite the very considerable restructuring of the Lancaster economy during the period 1960–80, the number of job changes which followed the direction of change from production to service was not very great.

This initial analysis examines the impact of structural change only, following the suggestions of the 'job' rather than 'gender' model. In the second approach we would expect to analyse the impact of domestic events. We know from other sources that a period out of the labour market has a detrimental impact on women's occupational position in work. For instance the Women and Employment Survey showed that women who re-entered the labour force after such a period were likely to come back at a lower level than that at which they had left. This effect is exacerbated if women return to part-time rather than full-time work. Some women do slowly regain their original occupational level, but others never do, and few better it (Martin and Roberts, 1984).

My question here is how women negotiate this break through the changing industrial and occupational structure. The labour market is different on their return. Do they go with this change, or are the women committed to their earlier work identifications? This is a question about women's commitment to work. Are they committed to particular forms of work, or not? Is women's attachment to their occupations firm or flimsy? This question is difficult to answer directly since women's options are highly constrained. If women wish to return part-time rather than full-time, then their options are even more constrained, since part-time jobs are concentrated in the lower levels of the service sector. If domestic considerations were paramount then we might expect women re-entrants to be flexible in their industrial sector and occupation in order to maximise compatibility with domestic needs.

We divided job changes into two categories. The first, 'job-to-job', entailed a direct movement from one form of paid employment to another with no intervening break. The second, 're-entrants' involved a break in paid employment. This enabled us to compare the nature of the job changes between these two types of behaviour.

Table 6.2 Sectoral change of re-entrants compared to job-to-job changes

	Job-to-job	Re-entrant
Production to service	65	33
Service to production	64	11
Service to service	79	199
Production to production	70	116

Interestingly we found that women have a high degree of attachment to their industry and occupation. Indeed this attachment is quite striking over the duration of the break from employment. Shifts between industrial sectors are more likely to occur on job-to-job changes than they are over a break in employment. Re-entrants typically return to the industrial sector which had previously employed them. This occurs among workers in both the production and the service sectors, as Table 6.2 illustrates.

The most important change from the perspective of the deindustrialisation thesis is that from production to service. This represents the structural changes in the economy. The majority of women who make this move during the course of their working lives do so directly from one job to another without a break.

So the majority of women returners take employment in the same sector as they left. Most changes between sectors involve job-to-job moves not involving a break from employment. That is, the employment break is of little significance in understanding the shift of women from the manufacturing to the service sector.

These findings are different to those of Dex (1987) on industrial mobility over the life course. Dex's results suggested that women did experience deindustrialisation over the life course, and suggest that the sectoral shift occurs particularly frequently over the break from the labour market during child bearing. This difference may be due to sample differences, for instance, that Lancashire women are more attached to their industrial niche than women over Britain as a whole. Alternatively it may be that the analysis of the Lancaster Women's Work Histories used a different operationalisation of the employment break for child rearing. The Lancaster analysis used a very precise separation of the various job changes, according to whether it was job-to-job or whether there was a break, while the Dex analysis used a simpler operationalisation of employment profiles in terms of age and pre- or post-birth of first child. The Lancaster analysis of 'breaks' thus included those for second and any subsequent children, while these were not included by Dex, and it may be that the first break is more likely than the second or third break to lead to a shift in industrial niche.

PART-TIME, FULL-TIME AND INDUSTRIAL SECTOR

Most women who return to employment after a break for child care do so part-time rather than full-time. This might be considered to be a pattern determined by domestic factors. But even this can be shown to be significantly affected by the industrial and occupational structure. The most obvious interaction here is because part-time jobs are not randomly distributed through the industrial and occupational structures. Instead they are concentrated in the service sector and in lower level occupations. Thus the return to work might be thought to drive women towards the lower level jobs of the service sector, since this is where the part-time jobs are located.

The Lancaster data shows, as expected, that returners are more likely than job-to-job movers to move from full-time to part-time work during a job-change event. However, the extent to which the return is of this type of change from full-time to part-time is itself significantly affected by the industrial location of the former job. Women returners who stayed within the production sector were more likely to return full-time, while women returners who changed from production to service were the most likely to change from full-time to part-time. See Table 6.3 below.

Table 6.3 Full-time to part-time changes

	% full-timers in the original sector moving to part-time in the destination sector	
	Job-to-job	*Returners*
Production to service	17	48
Service to production	4	31
Service to service	8	24
Production to production	5	5

These patterns reflect the lack of availability of part-time work in the production sector in Lancaster and its presence in the service sector. They indicate the significance of the industrial and occupational structure in determining women's patterns of full-time and part-time work. The domestic model alone is insufficient.

OCCUPATIONAL CHANGE

The analysis has so far concentrated on the division between industrial sectors. This is the aspect of the employment structure which is most directly related to industrial restructuring. However, it is the change in occupational structure which is usually considered to have a more direct bearing upon a person's work experience. The work history data set has the advantage of enabling us to ask about the relationship between industrial/ occupational change and individuals' work histories, and not merely about relationships for aggregate populations. We can ask whether workers who change their industrial sector also change their occupation. In this way we can ask about the impact of deindustrialisation upon occupational experience.

The most interesting group, from the point of view of the deindustrialisation thesis, is that of people who have moved from the manufacturing to the service sector. We have already noted that returners in this category were the most likely to make the transition from full-time to part-time work. Women who were clerical workers in the manufacturing sector tended to stay within this occupational grouping after a transfer into the service sector. That is, for this group, one of the largest occupational groups for women, the change in industrial sector is likely to have made little difference to their experience of employment since they stayed within the same occupation. The skilled and unskilled factory workers who changed sector logically changed occupation. The skilled workers were more likely to experience downward than upward mobility, though a significant minority made an upward move. Sales work was the biggest recipient of these workers followed by unskilled work (often cleaning). See Table 6.4 below.

Table 6.4 Occupational changes for those moving from production to service industries

	Numbers of those making transition from production to service									
From production	P	I	C	Sk	M	Se	Sa	Usk	Ukn	Total
Professional (P)	2	2	0	0	0	0	1	0	0	5
Intermediate (I)	0	0	3	0	0	0	1	1	0	5
Clerical (C)	1	6	20	0	0	1	1	0	0	29
Skilled (Sk)	3	5	5	1	1	7	12	10	0	44
Manual (M)	8	9	11	0	1	6	23	19	0	77
Services (Se)	0	0	0	0	0	0	1	0	0	1
Sales (Sa)	1	1	1	0	0	1	2	2	0	8
Unskilled (Usk)	0	0	3	0	0	2	4	7	0	16
Unknown (Ukn)	0	0	1	0	0	1	0	1	0	3

The reverse sectoral movement, from services to production, involved fewer people. Again the large grouping of clerical workers tended to cross the sectoral divide without changing occupational category. This stability in attachment to clerical work happens again in the production-to-production changers and service-to-service.

Indeed the overall picture from the analysis of industrial and occupational change is the resilience of women's occupational attachment despite job changes even if these involve sectoral shift. We see here that the 'job' model rather than the 'domestic' model is more useful in understanding these aspects of women's employment.

THE EXPERIENCE OF DEINDUSTRIALISATION

Most of the workers in the service sector were new entrants to the labour market. The figures for those who first entered the labour market in the 1970s show that the majority entered the service rather than the production sector: 74 per cent entered services and only 26 per cent production.

This means that the direct experience of deindustrialisation by having the sectoral shift over the life time is less than one might have expected from the aggregate figures. Not so many workers make the transition from manufacturing to service work. The new service jobs are taken by new workers. Even those workers who did make that sectoral transition are unlikely to have experienced a major transformation of their work experience, since the largest group did not change their occupation during this transition.

POLITICAL AND LEGAL CHANGES

Data sets on life histories and employment necessarily contain data from the viewpoint of individuals. I have discussed the analysis of this data in interaction with data on structural changes in employment and have argued that it is this intersection of analyses which is the particularly important addition to our knowledge. However, there are other social factors which are not taken account of here. These types of analysis may well lead readers to think that industrial and occupational patterns determine employment patterns, and that the economic factors recorded in such data sets constitute a complete causal system. However, this omits such relevant changes as those in the legal and political structure. For instance the rise in the number of married women in paid employment might be attributed solely to changes in the economic system, such as the increasing demand for cheap labour. This would ignore an important change not visible in the data – that of the removal of the marriage bar. Changes in patterns of economic participation by women have also been affected by legislative changes – for instance the introduction of equal opportunity legislation, and the introduction of legislation which gave rights to full-time workers, but not part-time workers, making the latter more attractive to employers. That is political struggles have been important in the restructuring of labour market opportunities for women. Obviously, these do not appear in the data sets, so analyses of these data for correlations necessarily miss important variables. In short, the life history method has difficulty incorporating an appreciation of political struggle and legal change into its causal analysis. This is not an argument against doing life histories, merely a plea for modesty in its claims.

CONCLUSIONS

This study has shown that women have a considerable degree of continuity of employment type, despite the break that many women take in order to raise children. It has suggested that women are committed to their initially developed employment expertise, in so far as the changes in the labour market allow them to do so. Sometimes they are able to maintain continuity of occupation despite changes in industrial structure. However, the priority given to working part-time rather than full-time on returning to employment after child care can mean that discontinuity of employment type is experienced. As a result of this commitment to initial type of employment fewer women directly experienced deindustrialisation in their own working lives than might have been expected from the cross-sectional data. Rather, the expanding service sector jobs were disproportionately taken by new entrants to the labour market.

The life history method does add much valuable material to the analysis of employment patterns. However, there are some serious problems if this data is falsely assumed to contain sufficient information by itself to explain such employment patterns. The strengths are that it enables us to understand the implications of structural change at the actual individual level, and prevents false assumptions that the individual experience is represented by aggregate change. This was demonstrated most clearly in relation to the deindustrialisation thesis in the Lancaster economy, where it was shown that it was rare for individuals to have moved jobs from manufacturing to the service sector despite the change in the structure of the aggregate economy. Instead we were able to see women's attachments to particular occupations and industries, even across breaks in employment due to child bearing. The new service sector jobs were taken primarily by new young workers, not those displaced from the collapsing manufacturing sector. It would be false to think that the majority of individuals directly experienced deindustrialisation in their own employment histories.

Life history analysis is at its strongest when used together with a data set on structural change, such as in this example. It is weakest when it is used by itself, since there is a tendency to presume incorrectly that the data contains all the variables necessary to explain its patterns. In relation to women's employment problems arise when it is incorrectly assumed that interruptions to employment by domestic work are the main determinant of women's patterns of employment, neglecting structural factors in the labour market and political and legal factors. Women's employment patterns are determined by many factors, of which their location in the life cycle with its different domestic demands is merely one. In so far as there is a tendency within life history analysis to overemphasise the significance of this factor the methodology has serious shortcomings. In so far as it is used in conjunction with other data sources which capture other aspects of social and economic structure, it can lead to significantly improved analysis of women's employment.

This chapter has shown that it is necessary to examine the intersection of structural change in the economy with women's biographies if we are fully to understand the nature of their participation in employment. Further, a woman's early employment continues to have an impact on the nature of her employment in later life, showing commitment and continuity even over breaks from paid employment for child care.

7

GENDER POLITICS AND SOCIAL THEORY

INTRODUCTION

The significance of politics for the analysis of gender relations has often been underestimated. In particular, the balance that women choose between domestic and paid employment is crucially structured by the environment created by state policies. These include policies expressly oriented to the reconciliation of working and family life, such as publicly funded child care, as well as the regulation of gender relations in employment such as the Equal Pay and Sex Discrimination Acts. There are also important policies which have an indirect effect on the sexual division of labour through the regulation of the wider social environment within which men and women make gendered decisions. This includes policies regulating marriage, such as determining the conditions under which divorce can be obtained; those regulating aspects of sexual practice and fertility, such as the availability of legal abortion and contraception; the wider environment, such as policies towards women's safety and the policing of sexual harassment and other forms of male violence; and cultural institutions, such as the regulation of the circulation of pornographic imagery. These state policies are the outcome of political activity more broadly defined.

FOUR APPROACHES TO POLITICAL SOCIOLOGY

The treatment of gender in political sociology has undergone major changes in recent years. There are four types of approach. The first is to ignore gender as if it were not relevant or did not make any difference, or only refer to women in a brief aside or footnote. The second is the stage of critique when the flaws and fallacies which stem from ignoring gender are exposed. The third stage is to add on the study of women as a special case, as compensation for their previous neglect. The fourth is the full theoretical integration of the analysis of gender into the central questions of the discipline itself. These types of approach are, to a great extent, dependent upon the prior ones being carried out in turn. The flowering of empirical

137

work on women in politics cannot take place until the feminist critique is established. The last stage, of full theoretical integration, cannot take place until a body of empirical work which relates to both sexes, and not just one, has been built up. After discussing the early approaches, this chapter makes a case for the nature of the integration of gender politics into the main-stream political sociology.

The first approach – to regard women as irrelevant to politics – is illustrated by work such as Lipset's (1960) designation of societies as democratic even when the women in them did not have the vote. An example of the practice of mentioning women very briefly in a descriptive way is Dearlove and Saunders (1984) in their otherwise excellent study of British politics. They do not suggest that there is equality between men and women in contemporary Britain, noting that men dominate women and indeed describing this as patriarchy, however issues of gender politics are rarely mentioned. The area of voting studies is a little more varied (better examples include Britten and Heath, 1983; Heath, Jowell and Curtice, 1985). However, most studies merely state that women vote more conser-vatively than men (e.g. Butler and Stokes 1974: 160n), or that they vote on the basis of the class allegiances of their husbands (Sarlvik and Crewe, 1983: 91 do both), treating gender as tangential to the main issue.

The second phase, that of critique, has made much of the flaws in those voting studies which mention women only very briefly (Bourque and Grossholtz, 1974; Goot and Reid, 1975; Randall, 1982; Siltanen and Stan-worth, 1982). Bourque and Grossholtz (1974) find four types of distortion on the representation of women in political science: the fudging of foot-notes – in which inaccurate statements are made with substantiating foot-notes which are inaccurate; assuming male dominance without critical examination and for reasons which have no evidential basis; accepting masculinity as ideal political behaviour; and commitment to conventional feminine roles for women. Goot and Reid (1975) provide a comprehensive critique of the portrayal of women as, if not apolitical, then conservative. For instance, they argue that the notion that women vote more conserva-tively then men has an insubstantial empirical basis. This critique is further reinforced by Hills (1981) who suggests that in so far as women are more likely than men to vote for the Conservatives Party, this is primarily an age effect. Older people, especially those over 65, are more likely to vote conservatively than younger people.

The third phase in the development of scholarship on women and politics was to study women. This appeared as an obvious next stage; to study what had previously been neglected. In practice this has usually meant that women are studied whenever they engage in politics. This is generally held to be less often the case than for men. Hence one of the major issues generated by this body of work is the explanation of women's lesser participation in politics than men. This is usually conducted via a study of exceptions to this rule; women who do enter the political forum are studied in order to explain why most women do not. Writers in this school of thought explore the barriers to women's equal political participation and those unusual circumstances in which women are able to be politically effective. Barriers to women's political involvement have been variously analysed as stemming from their domestic responsibilities, the detailed arrangements of political institutions, and the socialisation of women.

This approach has been of immense importance in reorienting political sociology towards issues of gender politics, nevertheless it has its limitations. This school of thought both presents women's political activity as exceptional and restricts gender politics to women's activities. I shall show that women's political actions on their own behalf are much more historically widespread than these accounts suggest. Further, I shall argue that gender politics should be defined not in terms of the gender of the actors (the politics that women do), but rather in terms of the nature of the transformations in gender relations that these political practices seek to achieve. Feminist politics usually call forth resistance from those whose interests are challenged, and these patriarchal political practices are part of gender politics too. Examples of these will be explored in the next chapter on the notion of the backlash to feminist politics. I shall here support these claims with an account of the breadth and significance of first-wave feminist politics and the opposition to it. In the light of this analysis accounts of contemporary feminism as a 'new social movement' must fall, since feminism is not new; hence accounts of feminism as originating with recent developments in capitalism are also shown to be misplaced.

WOMEN'S POLITICAL BEHAVIOUR AS EXCEPTIONAL INDIVIDUALS

There is now a major set of writings which focus on the relative absence of women from the formal political elites (e.g. Currell, 1974; Diamond, 1977; Epstein and Coser, 1981; Hills and Lovenduski, 1981; Kirkpatrick, 1974; Norris and Lovenduski, 1995). The evidence presented substantiates the claim that women's lack of political achievement is often that of their relative absence from the formal political elites. Indeed the figures show that women are infrequently in these positions. Women in Britain after the 1987 general election formed only 6.6 per cent of Members of the House of Commons, and after that in 1992 were still less than 10 per cent, while in the US in 1981 women formed 4.4 per cent of the Members of the House of Representatives (Randall, 1982: 73). The underrepresentation of women in the legislatures of the world is not confined to Britain and the US, but is a common pattern. The highest representation is to be found in Sweden, but even there the figure is significantly less than half. The level of representation in local government is only slightly higher. Women formed 19 per cent of local elected councillors in Britain in 1985, and 7 per cent of US mayors in 1977 (EOC, 1986: 39; Randall, 1982: 74), and while it had risen a little by the 1990s, the proportion in the UK is still very low.

If the notion of the sphere of public politics is broadened to include the proportion of women representatives in trade unions and public bodies the picture in Britain looks little different. In January 1986 in NUPE, with nearly half a million female members who composed 67 per cent of the membership, women held only 31 per cent of the seats on the executive; in USDAW, with a female membership of nearly a quarter of a million – 61 per cent of the total – women held 19 per cent of the seats on the executive; in the NUT with over 150,000 female members, making 72 per cent of the total, women formed only 16 per cent of the executive (EOC, 1986: 44). In 1985 women comprised only 18.5 per cent of appointments to public bodies, rising to only 28 per cent in 1993, and in 1984 only 7 per cent of representatives on Industrial Tribunals (British Council, 1996: 15; EOC, 1986: 40, 41).

Currell (1974) states that women's 'rate of political participation is very low', that 'the norm for women still seems to be non-participation in political leadership', and that a women's political 'role is a departure', indeed a 'deviance', from the norm (Currell, 1974: 1, 3). She suggests that this is due to the problems women face as the child-bearing sex, and the different socialisation that girls receive which makes them more passive and submissive than boys. Currell states that the complex of factors around family and home was often cited by the women in her study as the reason why women were less successful in politics than men. She does note, however, that it is the articulation of this with the nature of political institutions which causes the difficulty, for instance in the need for at least partial residence in London for MPs, and also that some technical issues, such as the nature of the voting system in single- or multi-member constituencies, do make some difference.

Likewise Kirkpatrick (1974), analysing US politics, suggests that political behaviour by women is unusual, and similarly uses the lack of women's presence in the political elites as her evidence for this. Like Currell she concludes that the most important barrier to women's political behaviour is that of sex roles, especially that of being wife and mother for women in the contemporary US, but also that of the restriction of women to occupational categories which do not typically lead on to being a politician, unlike typical male jobs such as lawyer. Both Currell and Kirkpatrick base their arguments on studies of samples of women who have entered the political elites. They interviewed women politicians to find out what made them so unusual. Currell found that these women had succeeded where most other women had not, because they had specific circumstances which counteracted the usual difficulties. She found that women MPs were older and rarely entered Parliament until their child-bearing years were over. She suggested that the problem of lack of appropriate socialisation was negated when women were born into 'political families' in which girls as well as boys imbibed the activist political culture. The final route by which the 'exceptional' woman was able to enter politics was as a substitute for a close male relative, perhaps a husband who had died.

Stacey and Price (1981) take the argument about barriers to women's involvement in polities one stage further, suggesting that given the scale of the obstacles to women's involvement in polities it is surprising that women have come as far as they have, rather than that they have achieved so little. Stacey and Price suggest that the main problem for women is that they are still involved in a form of family which restricts their involvement in the public sphere as individuals, despite some improvements in the position of women in recent years. It is this sexual division of labour, and its related aspects, such as ideologies of appropriate feminine behaviour, which prevent women's equal involvement with men in public political life. Women's work in the home is seen as a major obstacle to success in public political life. Stacey and Price argue that women have historically only had political power when there has been no separation between the public and private spheres. They suggest that the barriers to contemporary political achievement by women are internalised as well as existing in the social structure.

Some more recent studies of the absence of women from the political elites, such as that by Norris and Lovenduski (1995) are more sophisticated in their data and analysis, but still follow this structure of argument. These writers all argue that women face difficulties in being as politically active as men, because of their position in the family, absence from relevant occupations, and gender socialisation. They vary in the extent to which they see the nature of the political institutions themselves creating difficulties for women to enter public life, such as needing a second home in London and the money to campaign to get selected by a party for a Parliamentary seat (Norris and Lovenduski, 1996).

WOMEN'S POLITICAL BEHAVIOUR AS COLLECTIVELY EXCEPTIONAL

Women's movements

The exceptional political behaviour by women so far examined has been that of individuals. Other writers have focused on exceptional political behaviour by women acting collectively. I shall examine three variants: Freeman's (1975) analysis of the rise of second-wave feminism; Castells' (1978, 1983) account of 'new social movements'; Eisenstein's (1981) account of the distinctively radical potential of second wave feminism.

Freeman (1975) suggests that the development of cooptable communications networks which can be precipitated into action around feminist goals is a necessary condition for the development of a feminist movement. She analyses the origin of second-wave feminism in such terms. The women's rights branch was formed out of a network of women set up as a by-product of President Kennedy's political manoeuvrings. The network was based on Kennedy's Commission on the Status of Women, which had been set up as an alternative to giving women the political office their campaign efforts on his behalf might otherwise be thought to have earned them. This group of women was precipitated into action by the refusal of the Equal Employment Opportunity Office to enforce the sex provision of Title VII of the Civil Rights Act soon after the publication of Betty Friedan's famous book *The Feminine Mystique*. The women's liberation branch of the movement was formed out of a network which originated in the wider Movement which was opposed to the war in Vietnam, and demanded civil rights for Blacks and democracy in the universities. It was precipitated by the sexual and personal insults hurled by apparently radical men at women in the Movement. Freeman gives an account of the unusual micro-structural configurations which led to the start of the two branches of the women's movement in the late 1960s in the US. Her explanation is premised upon political activity by women being unusual. She is explaining why second-wave feminism started, not why first-wave feminism stopped. It is this premise that I shall critically examine later.

'New social movements'

Castells also considers that women engage in political behaviour in exceptional circumstances. He analyses 'new social movements', which include struggles over issues which may be considered gendered, although he does not himself describe them as such. Rather he conceptualises them, especially in his early work, as struggles over collective consumption. In his later work (1983) he does have a somewhat broader viewpoint, but I shall start with his earlier work. In this he considers the means of collective consumption to be 'Housing, education, health, culture, commerce, transport, etc.' (Castells, 1978: 3). At a more theoretical level Castells suggests that this is the collective reproduction of labour power (Castells, 1978: 17,18,19). Castells argues that collective consumption, or the urban question, is an increasingly important political issue in advanced capitalist countries.

Castells argues that consumption is being transformed by long-run structural tendencies in capitalism: the concentration and centralisation of capital, the increasing strength of the worker movement, and the growing intervention of the state (pp. 16–17). He suggests that the changing form of capital requires smooth functioning of the supply of labour power. Yet certain of the needs of workers are not adequately met by the market. The intervention of the state to provide these facilities has a double causation:

capital's need for the provision of appropriate labour power, and popular demands (pp. 18,42).

He argues for an analysis of 'new urban social movements' (p. 177), since it is they who pose the questions of urban policy most forcefully. It is the sphere of consumption, within which they operate, rather than that of production, which is at the forefront of contemporary politics. Castells briefly cites feminism as one of these new urban social movements, since it challenges the logic of the urban structure (p. 177).

While Castells is correct to notice the relevance of feminism, its fleeting mention does not adequately deal with the gendered nature of so-called 'collective consumption'.

Castells' major error stems from conceptualising the production of labour power as consumption rather than production. The use of the concept 'consumption' implies a failure to recognise that the work that women do in the home as domestic labour is work. The term signals 'leisure', not 'work'. This is misleading, not only in that it is a misrecognition of the activities of women and a belittling of their contribution to the production of the world, but also in that it is problematic since it results in a failure to theorise the gender relations which shape the organisation of this work, and thus to recognise their significance.

Castells ignores the extent to which the issues which he names as collective consumption, as part of the circuit of capital, are part of a patriarchal system. What is for Castells a movement from individual to collective consumption within capitalism, is a movement which radically transforms certain aspects of gender relations: one from privatised labour within a patriarchal mode of production to socialised labour outside of the patriarchal mode of production. Castells' failure to appreciate the significance of the gender dynamic means that he gives an incorrect specification of the structural changes which generate the 'new urban social movements' in terms of capitalism, not patriarchy. Further, he does not analyse the gendered nature of the forces pushing for and against these transformations, and his account of the historical specificity of these changes is incorrect.

Feminist attempts to socialise women's domestic labour have existed since first-wave feminism. Castells is incorrect to suggest that movements for collectivisation of 'consumption' or, rather, domestic production, are new. First-wave feminists campaigned for public provision for education, for the public feeding of school children, for nurseries, for the public provision of health care among others (see accounts of these campaigns in Banks, 1981; Hayden, 1981; Middleton, 1978). I would argue that these efforts, by feminists, primarily at the local level, constituted an important political force behind the development of the welfare state.

Since Castells is wrong to imply that movements for the collectivisation of the production of labour power are new, he is thus incorrect to imply that feminism is a new urban social movement. He is right to notice that struggles over the collectivisation of the production of labour power are important, but wrong to analyse them only in terms of capitalist social relations.

Castells does modify his approach later on; by 1983 he recognises that there were struggles in 1915 in which women took part (the Glasgow Rent Strikes). He suggests that they mobilised on behalf of their families' needs as part of a class struggle. He still manages to ignore the more significant feminist politics of the time, in first-wave feminism, thus incorrectly stating that it was only recently that women had fought their domination by men. Castells also changes his analysis to include cultural identity and state politics as part of urban social movements. Yet again this is empirically incorrect, since while feminist movements have included identity as an issue, disputes over values form only a part of their agenda. So while the later Castells (1983) is more complex in his analysis than the earlier (1978), it significantly misrepresents the patterns and forms of women's politics and thus their explanation.

Radical women's movements as exceptional

Some writers on women and politics have taken the existence of first-wave feminism seriously, but consider only second-wave feminism to have been truly radical (Eisenstein, 1981; Klein, 1984). Eisenstein (1981) recognises that there was a major political movement of women at the turn of the century as well as a second wave some half-century later. She examines the varieties of feminist thought in both waves, especially in regard to the extent to which they represented liberal and radical political tendencies. She argues that women's political activity itself is not exceptional, but that *radical* political activity by feminists is.

Eisenstein argues that first-wave feminism was limited by a commitment to liberalism, although she does qualify this by noting that in so far as these liberal feminists recognised that women were barred from equal rights with men because they were women they were implicitly using a sex/class analysis, and hence incorporated some aspects of radical feminist thought. However, she suggests that they were primarily liberal in that they accepted a central feature of liberal thought, that of the separation of the public from the private and the restriction of women to the latter.

Eisenstein argues that second-wave feminism, while incorporating some aspects of liberal feminism, has the potential of going beyond this to radical transformative politics. She suggests that this is because of the different material conditions in which second-wave feminism is rooted. These new circumstances are those in which many women perform both unpaid house-work and paid work. These, suggests Eisenstein, generate contradictions in the position of women, which in turn generate a new form of conscious-ness. Further, she suggests that when these women start to become politically active they will move beyond mere liberal politics because their demands, however apparently mild and liberal, cannot be granted within the terms of the existing capitalist patriarchal society. Such contemporary liberal feminists do have a radical future because of the structural contradictions and possibilities inherent in contemporary society, unlike their predecessors of the earlier feminist wave.

These new circumstances are generated by the increasing participation of women in waged work, itself a result of the development of the capitalist economy. Thus Eisenstein is in fact arguing that second-wave feminism can be radical rather than liberal like the first wave, because of the changes in mid- to late twentieth century capitalism.

While providing an important and provocative account of feminist politics, which is exceptional in taking both first- and second-wave politics seriously, there are, however, some significant problems in this analysis. Eisenstein seriously underestimates the significance of radical currents in first-wave feminism. While not in error in her analysis of the first-wave feminist theorists that she discusses, she omits to consider other writers whom it would be much less possible to characterise as liberal. She does not discuss the feminist critique of sexuality and of marriage, nor the activities of women active in the labour movement. I would argue that second-wave feminism is not new in its radical nature, since first-wave feminism contained significant radical elements. (I shall present evidence for this argument later.) Hence her attempt to explain the newness of the radical thrust of contemporary feminism in terms of the development of the capitalist economy is misplaced, since this radicalism is not new. Developments in capitalism are not sufficient to explain the liberal or radical nature of feminism. Her argument that feminism can only be radical if the capitalist economy has pulled women into waged labour is incorrect.

LIMITATIONS OF THE THIRD APPROACH

The analyses of gender politics of the third approach have focused on the occasions when women have been politically active; they have treated these as exceptions to the general rule that women are less politically active than men, and have sought to explain them as deviations from this norm. The nature of the exceptions have been either individual, such as the entry of women into the formal political elites, or collective, as when women have combined to press for feminist demands. These analyses of gender politics, while significant advances on those accounts of politics which seriously neglect women's activities, have some problems themselves. First, they have an unduly restricted conception of gender politics; second, they are misconceived in their description of the extent and nature of gender politics.

Most accounts of gender and politics have focused on women rather than the nature of the goals demarcating the field. I think that it is better to define gender politics instead as those forms of political practice which seek to change gender relations for or against women's interests. These may be attempts to achieve feminist goals, or attempts to intensify patriarchal relations. That is, I am defining gender politics in terms of the gendered nature of the goals, not of the actors. Yet accounts of the goals of the politics under study are not a major focus for a significant number of the studies thus far considered.

The two types of study which together make up the majority of work on women and politics select their object of study in terms of the gender of the actor, rather than the aims of the politics. Both studies of women in political elites and women's patterns of voting do this. In the case of the elite studies there is little interest in the political consequences of this (Diamond, 1977 being an exception here); in the voting studies the only consequences considered are women's impact on class, not specifically gender, politics. Only in the third type of study, that of women's political movements, is the content of the politics the focus of much attention, and even here it is the gender of the actors that has determined the object of study rather than the political process and outcome.

This definition of gender politics has two implications. First, some significant aspects of gender politics are missed because of the overwhelming focus on the gender of the actors. There are significant gender politics which are not carried out by women as a whole, or separate groupings of women. Many policies have gender implications, and may represent the interests of the genders unevenly, without their being the explicit focus of women's political actions. Issues of taxation and economic policy are examples of this. The representation of men's interests over women's is clear here, although these issues are not always taken up by women as women.

Second, these studies omit men as actors in gender politics. Yet the patriarchal political practices are of vital significance to gender politics. It is as if the existing studies take men as gender neutral and only women as gendered subjects. This turns the study of women's politics into the study of a deviant minority. This is parallel to the way in which many studies of race conceptualise only people of colour as having ethnicity, and Whites are considered ethnically neutral. Yet men are active in gender politics, in much the same way that Whites are active in racial politics. The analysis of gender struggle must include patriarchal agents, usually, but not always men. The following two examples illustrate this point.

One, perhaps obvious, instance is that of the opposition to women gaining the vote in Britain. Women (and a very few men) did not struggle for the vote against a vague non-gendered object. Rather, men (and a very few women) struggled against these feminist demands. Those opposing the demand for the vote for women were not passive, but rather active participants in a battle which raged for decades. They banned women from attending meetings (for fear they would ask the male politicians whether

146

they would give votes to women), and forcibly ejected women from those meetings. (Male) police arrested protesters; (male) magistrates convicted protesters; (male) Members of Parliament passed Acts which regulated the imprisonment and temporary release of women suffragettes so that suffragettes would not have martyrs from the death of hunger strikers in the prisons; male by-standers beat up women attempting to present petitions to the Prime Minister (Banks, 1981; Harrison, 1978; Morrell, 1981; Pankhurst, 1977; Spender, 1983; Strachey, 1978). We cannot understand the suffrage struggle unless we understand the nature and extent of the opposition to feminist demands by patriarchal forces.

Another example is that of gender politics in the trade union movement. There have been attempts to understand the position of women in trade unions by looking at women unionists (e.g. Lewenhak, 1977; Soldon, 1978). These histories typically describe the slow unionisation of women, charting the successes that they have. These accounts provide invaluable basic data on women trade unionists and some of their activities. However, it is not possible to understand the position of women in trade unions, nor their politics, without examining the actions of existing trade unions towards women workers. The establishment of separate unions for women in the nineteenth and early twentieth centuries is inexplicable without an explanation of the refusal of many male trade unions to allow women to join them; for instance the Amalgamated Society of Engineers did not admit women until 1943. Further the difficulty women had in their battle for equal pay is inexplicable outside an analysis of the patriarchal practices of many male-dominated trade unions. Women's trade unions had, not untypically, two forces ranged against them, not only employers, but also organised competitive male workers. These are not simple forms of opposition to women; patriarchal strategies by male trade unions varied, for instance, as to whether they tried to exclude or merely segregate the women. The conditions which led to different types of patriarchal strategy need to be part of the analysis of women trade unionists. For instance, the main union of the skilled manual engineering workers was more successful in excluding women from 'their' work than were the organisations of the male clerks. The clerks, on being unsuccessful, despite protests which included strikes, turned early to a strategy of segregation of women clerks from the men, and the grading of men's work as higher than that of women. This strategy was not adopted by the main engineering union until 1943, when the war-time entry of the women and their recruitment by rival general unions led to a change of policy. After this date women were recruited into separate sections, not allowed to hold important union offices, and were represented by the men's officials. Simple accounts of the men as hostile to the women would fail to capture the significance of the different strategies open to the patriarchal forces, and their radically different outcomes for the women workers. Not only is it impossible to study women as a gender without

147

bringing men as a gender into the analysis, but we need to differentiate between patriarchal strategies (see Walby, 1986b for a fuller account of patriarchal strategies in the workplace).

Thus we see in both of these examples the importance of analysing patriarchal political practices as well as feminist ones in order to explain gender politics properly. The opposition of patriarchal forces to feminist demands must be analysed along with women's actions. By focusing too closely on women – by, for instance, taking all-woman samples, as in the analyses of women in political elites – these studies miss the extent of opposition among men to women's demands, and thus fail to appreciate the full range of political forces which affect how these female political actors behaved. It is not possible to explain why there are so few women in the political elites, in either Parliament or the trade union movement, without understanding the history of men's attempts to exclude women from participation in these political arenas. Gender politics involves two genders.

There is a further, and more major, problem with these accounts of women's politics; they very significantly underestimate the extent of women's political actions. This distorts the theoretical understanding of gender politics very seriously indeed. By underestimating the amount of women's agitation these theorists end up asking the wrong questions in their attempt to explain it. Most accounts of women's politics attempt to explain why there is so little of it. They ask why there are so few women in political elites and why the recent women's movement began. They take as a premise that women are much less politically active than men and try to explain this lesser activity. The premise is mistaken, hence the question is misplaced.

There are two main points here. First, women's lesser success than men in Parliament is not evidence of lack of political action. Just as one would not use the lower proportion of people of working-class origin or who are members of minority ethnic groups in national legislatures as evidence that these groups are politically inactive, the same should be understood for women. In all three cases – women, working class, and minority ethnic groups – one would not expect their proportionate representation in a body which represents the interests of the dominant gender, class and ethnic group. This underrepresentation is a result of their exclusion and oppression; it does not necessarily mean that they are politically quiescent.

Second, the amount of agitation by women on their behalf is seriously underrepresented in the social science literature. Mainstream political, sociological and historical texts are quite simply wrong in characterising movements for women's emancipation and liberation as small, narrow, of limited duration, and recent. I shall focus on three interpretations of first-wave feminism to substantiate this claim, with briefer reference to other waves of feminist activity.

148

First-wave feminism, as I shall call this movement, is more usually referred to as the suffrage movement. It is in fact frequently characterised as primarily a struggle for the vote in the mainstream texts; rarely are other issues mentioned, with the occasional exception of the reform enabling married women to own property. Thus the women's movement is described as campaigning on a very narrow range of issues. Further, it is often considered to represent the interests of only a narrow range of women: middle- and upper-class women. This latter view is supported in two ways: by reference to the married women's property acts, which are considered to be of interest only to women with inherited property, and by reference to the apparently middle- and upper-class composition of the movement.

I shall show that both these contentions are incorrect: the movement embraced a wide, not narrow, range of demands; it represented the interests of all women, not only those of the middle and upper classes. To do this it is necessary to describe the nature and range of first-wave feminism.

PUSHING BACK THE HORIZONS ON FEMINIST POLITICS

I have argued that one of the major problems in analyses of gender politics is that they ignore, or at best significantly underestimate, the radical nature of first-wave feminism. First-wave feminism was a large, multi-faceted, long-lived and highly effective political phenomenon. It can be dated as extending from around 1850 (when the Seneca Falls conference was held in the US and, in Britain, Employment Bureaux for women were set up by women concerned about the lack of access of middle-class ladies to appropriate employment) to 1930 (women between 21 and 30, and women without any property, only became enfranchised in 1928 in Britain). It was an international phenomenon (Evans, 1977; Lovenduski, 1986), and was represented in most Western nations. It contained a wide range of political positions and involved a large variety of campaigns. At minimum it may be considered to contain: evangelical feminism, socialist feminism, materialist feminism and radical feminism as well as liberal feminism (Banks, 1981; Hayden, 1981; Schreiner, 1978; Spender, 1983; Strachey, 1978). Campaigns included not only the famous one for suffrage but also for the containment of predatory male sexual behaviour (Christabel Pankhurst's slogan was 'Votes for women, chastity for man'); access to employment; to training and education; reform of the legal status of married women so they could own property; for divorce and rights to legal separation at the woman's behest as well as that of the husband; for the collective rather than private organisation of meal preparation among many others.

The campaigns around the containment of men's sexuality probably best illustrate my claim that the breadth and radical nature of first-wave feminism are neglected. In the last quarter of the nineteenth century feminists argued against the sexual double standard and men's sexual exploitation of women in explicit and controversial ways. The attempt to repeal the Contagious Diseases Act was merely one example. In this case the government, worried about the extent to which venereal disease was incapacitating the strength of its navy, sought to contain it by regulation of female prostitutes. The Acts made it possible for women deemed to be common prostitutes by the police to be seized, examined and incarcerated until deemed cured. Feminists such as Butler vigorously protested at the double standard by which women were to be controlled in order to protect men's health, when they saw men as responsible for the problem of venereal disease as well as women. The Acts were finally repealed after a highly controversial campaign in which Butler was threatened as she tried to address public meetings on the subject. Other feminist campaigns around sexual purity sought to raise the age of consent so as to protect young girls from being forced in prostitution. This was also successful, and the age of consent remains at 16 to the present day (Banks, 1981; Butler, 1986; Walkowitz, 1980).

While the dominant male discourse on sexuality entailed a clear dichotomy between the good woman and the bad, between virgin and wife on the one hand, and whore on the other, some feminist writers such as Hamilton (1981) argued that marriage was a trade and that there was little difference between a wife and a prostitute in the way that they traded their bodies for economic support, except that one was respectable and the other not.

These two issues were argued by feminists whose overall analysis was drawn from quite different perspectives. Butler can be characterised as an evangelical feminist in that she worked within a Christian framework and interpreted her own actions as following through the will of God. Hamilton, on the other hand, can be characterised as a materialist or radical feminist, and her work has clear parallels with that of Delphy (1984) today.

The actions of feminists in the labour movement are another such neglected area of agitation. Organisations such as the National Federation of Women Workers and the Women's Trade Union League set out to organise women workers so as to improve their rates of pay and conditions of employment. Most unions in the nineteenth century refused to admit women, so if they were to be unionised it had to be in newly created women's unions. These were encouraged by the National Federation of Women Workers and the Women's Trade Union League. These women activists in the trade union movement are often excluded from designation as part of first-wave feminism by definitional fiat. That is, trade unionist women are a priori categorised as part of the labour movement and not part of the feminist movement. Yet since they were clearly representing the interests of women as women this is inappropriate. These women had to deal with both male workers and employers in order to advance the interests of their members (Andrews, 1918; Drake, 1920; Lewenhak, 1977; Soldon, 1978; Strachey, 1978; Walby, 1986b).

The deprivatisation of women's domestic labour was another major area of political and theoretical activity among first-wave feminists (Gilman, 1966; Hayden, 1981; Schreiner, 1978). Leading first-wave feminists identified the exploitation of women's labour in the privatised context of the home as a major source of the problems facing women. This labour was theorised as work, and as subject to particular forms of exploitation. The barriers to women obtaining work outside the household of a type which would adequately support them, and their children if any, was considered to be a major reason for forcing women into marriage as a means of economic survival. The isolated and monotonous nature of the work were seen as further problems for women. Initiatives to remedy this varied from cooperatives in which housework was performed collectively, to the development of hot meals services for profit; that is they varied as to whether they took on all aspects of domestic labour or merely one, and as to whether this was to be organised cooperatively or for profit.

Access to higher education is one of the few campaigns of first-wave feminism which is sometimes noticed. In this women won the right to attend some universities. This was significant not merely in its own right, but also because it gave women access to those professions for which a university level training was a prerequisite, such as medicine.

The struggle for suffrage is the only campaign of first wave feminism which is universally acknowledged, yet even here there are problems in the conventional interpretation. It is customarily described as a battle fought largely by middle-class women around a liberal vocabulary of human rights; that is, the campaign is represented as that of middle-class liberal feminists. This is misleading. Working-class women were involved in this struggle, especially the organised women workers of the Lancashire cotton textile mills (see Liddington and Norris, 1978). While one section of the movement, that of the suffragists, did adhere to a liberal political philosophy, others such as the militant suffragettes did not. The latter groups had an analysis much more in keeping with that of contemporary radical feminists, seeing society as composed of two main social groupings: men and women. Parliament was described as a male club, with the differences between the two parties as of little significance to women. Militant tactics were not designed to win moderate male support, but both to gain greater female support by exposing what they saw as the charade of chivalry by provoking hostile male reactions, and to force the men into conceding the vote. Tactics such as the coordinated simultaneous smashing of all the windows in fashionable London shopping streets, burning 'votes for women' on golf courses by acid, setting fire to pillar boxes, defacing paintings, and hunger strikes when imprisoned do not correspond to most people's conception of liberal actions. This campaign for the vote was not restricted to small groups of women; one of the meetings in Hyde Park was of a quarter of a million people (Pankhurst, 1977; Spender, 1983; Strachey, 1978).

In short, first-wave feminism involved numbers of women much greater than conventional accounts suggest; these women were from a wider range of class backgrounds than usually suggested; the range of issues and campaigns were much more varied and wide-ranging than described. First-wave feminism was not a few middle-class liberal women who wanted the vote and a bit of education; it was a cross-class, multifaceted powerful political movement.

New questions

Yet questions remain. Why was there less visible militant feminism in the years after 1920? Was this merely appearance, or reality as well? Did the movement crumble internally because of bad tactics, such as the concentration on the vote (the most common view). Or did it fade because it became incorporated into various establishments? For instance, in the inter-war period many of the women's unions joined with the larger men's unions, which no longer refused them admittance. This might be considered as a victory for the women in gaining admittance, a sell-out by the leaders since the women lost their own independent voice or, most plausibly, a form of incorporation of these organised women workers into the trade union establishment with its own particular forms of compromise. The conventional debate on corporatism typically only considers the compromises between capital, labour and government. It is time to consider the incorporation of gendered political forces. A final hypothesis on the relative demise of first-wave feminism is that it collapsed because it was smashed by superior forces. Significant violence was used against the movement both by the organised state (for instance the Cat and Mouse Act in which women were arrested, imprisoned, force fed, released when nearly dead, and rearrested when recovered), and also by individual men who attacked and beat up feminist protesters (Morrell, 1981). A further interpretation is that it faded because it had been so successful; it had gained for women the basic rights of citizenship. Whichever of these four views on the facing of the first-wave of feminism is correct, the posing of such a question is a radical departure from the usual formulation of questions within the third phase. Rather than treating feminist activity as exceptional and those in need of explanation, it reverses the presumption and demands an explanation of periods of absence of feminist activity. This question is addressed in the next chapter.

Other feminisms

I have been arguing that mainstream political sociology has underestimated the significance of feminism by means of an examination of first-wave feminism. There are also other instances of feminism whose existence further supports the argument that the importance and extent of feminism is grossly neglected in conventional accounts.

These feminist movements both pre-date the first wave and exist in a wide range of countries. I have dated first-wave feminism as beginning in the middle of the nineteenth century. There is now widespread evidence of an earlier feminist wave in the middle of the seventeenth century in England (Rowbotham, 1972; Spender, 1983). Some of this protest may be considered to fall within the evangelical feminist tradition because of the important role of women preachers and prophets. More recently there is the development of scholarship about feminists in the Renaissance, about women who raised the 'Woman Question' in the fourteenth and fifteenth centuries (Kelly, 1984).

Feminist movements have not been confined to Britain and the US, despite my use of examples drawn primarily from these countries. During the Russian Revolution women played a leading role, not merely for workers' demands, but for feminist ones too. Likewise women have played important roles in the French and Chinese Revolutions and many wars of national liberation including those of Algeria and Nicaragua (Chafetz and Dworkin, 1986; Morgan, 1985; Rowbotham, 1972).

IMPLICATIONS

I hope to have shown that gender politics are much more extensive and significant than current theories of politics and of society presume. Women have agitated around their own interests over many more issues than is suggested by mainstream texts. Women's politics is not something exceptional to be explained as a deviation from the norm. Hence those theories which attempted to explain these exceptions are trying to do the impossible; to explain something which is not even the case. Their conception of the norm and the exception should be inverted.

There have been some attempts to move beyond the confines of the third approach. Spender (1983, 1984) has shown that feminist politics have a long, if neglected, history. She has argued convincingly that it is problematic to state that there was no feminism after the vote was won and that first-wave feminism included radicals as well as liberals. Harrison (1978), Morrell (1981) and Jeffreys (1985) have shown that first-wave feminism faced much opposition and that this affected its form and its extent. Miller et al. (1996) have used a broad definition of politics in their work on Northern Ireland, and demonstrated that women are as involved and active as men when this new definition is used, although they are less well represented in party politics.

In future the following points should be taken into account:

1 Politics includes gender politics. There are structured power relations between the interests of each gender which are contested in formal political arenas as well as in other social relations.

2 Gender politics have effects upon other forms of politics such as class politics and green politics.

3 Party politics and electoral politics are gendered as well as having a class dimension. Political issues usually have a gender dimension.

4 Gender politics include what men do as well as what women do. Men are often significant as anti-feminist political actors. Women may also adopt such a position.

5 Gender politics cannot be understood without an analysis of anti-feminist as well as feminist forces.

6 Gender political forces cannot be read off from biological categories of men and women. Women do not always support feminist positions; men do not always take anti-feminist positions. None the less there is a significant correlation between these positions and a person's sex.

7 There is more than one way of being a feminist. Significant differences between feminist tendencies have had historically significant effects.

8 Similarly there are significant differences between patriarchal political forces.

9 Gender politics are more complex than a simple division between varieties of feminist and anti-feminist political forces because there is a very important third position – that of the pro-women non-feminists who wish to defend and develop women's sphere of activity. The historical significance of this position has been very significantly underestimated and underanalysed.

10 Feminist politics are not unusual. We need to understand why they fade as well as why they rise.

What are the general implications of this? First, women are not as quiescent in their subordination as contemporary theories suggest. Women do resist, and theories of gender must take this into account rather than either presuming or trying to explain female passivity.

Second, it raises a new research agenda. While women have been politically active, they have not always met with success. This is more a consequence of male resistance than has previously been thought. The analysis of the political behaviour of men as patriarchal agents has been little studied. It needs to be. The patriarchal strategies are many and varied; the conditions which generate their forms and success and failure need analysis. We need analysis of the decline as well as rise of waves of feminism. Women's political resistance is not unusual. It is not necessary to study this as an aberration; rather the conditions which act as barriers to successful mobilisation, and the forces which push feminism into decline are the issue.

Third, it challenges mainstream accounts of what is meant by politics. Politics is more than class politics; it is gender politics too, and indeed ethnic politics as well. The tradition of stratification analysis in Britain has often been concerned with the relationship between changes in material position and political action. This is considered a key question for both those in the Marxist and in the Weberian traditions. The analysis here suggests that political action has been defined too narrowly, and should in future include gender politics as well as class politics. For instance we need to ask what difference material position makes to a person's gender politics. In the US a significant gender gap opened up under Reagan, with women less likely to support Reagan and his policies than men. Eisenstein (1984) has suggested that this is a consequence of women's awareness of gender issues in politics. Campbell (1987) suggested that there was a gender gap in British electoral politics but that this is now closing for reasons again connected to women's awareness of gendered political issues. Lovenduski (1995) has shown that in 1995 there is an age dimension which differentiates women, so that while older women are more conservative than men, younger women are more likely to vote Labour. Thus, even on the conventional terrain of the explanation of voting patterns, gender politics is now an issue in serious need of analysis. It is important in its own right and because it affects class relations and party politics as well.

A further implication is that the differences between the major political parties in Parliament do not make up the sum total of major political debate; elite studies and voting studies are not the total range for analysis of gender politics. The political structure of Parliament hinders the placing of gender politics at the centre of the Parliamentary political agenda. How this was achieved is an interesting issue for research. Gender politics have been kept out of the centre of Britain's leading political institution. That is no reason why it should continue to be kept out of the centre of Britain's leading social science debates. The analysis of gender *in* politics needs to go beyond the third phase of compensatory studies of women – of adding them on to a pre-defined field and treating gender politics as exceptional – and on to the fourth.

8

'BACKLASH' TO FEMINISM

INTRODUCTION

Gender politics, as was argued in the last chapter, are not only the activities of women asking for greater equality, but involve anti-feminist responses. 'Backlash' appears to be a recurring feature in the history of feminism. Feminist successes have often met, not only with resistance, but with renewed determination by patriarchal forces to maintain and increase the subordination of women. Gender politics includes not only the actions of women, but the reactions of men.

But is backlash simply inevitable and does it take an equal and opposite form to the initial political force? Is the form of backlash against feminist politics the same across different historical periods and different continents? Much recent feminist theory has emphasised the significance of diversity in women's experiences (Aaron and Walby, 1991; Barrett and Phillips, 1992; Begum, 1992; Brah, 1991; Spellman, 1988; Watt and Cook, 1991) and the difficulty of translation across historical periods (see Stanley, 1990). The postmodernist turn in feminist theory (Franklin, Lury and Stacey, 1991; Fraser and Nicholson, 1988) has urged hesitation over generalising beyond specific ethnic group or historical period, and argued for a focus on difference rather than commonality. However, this position sometimes underplays the significance of commonalities.

I shall address this question of diversity in response to feminist politics in the context of turn-of-the-century and contemporary feminism and compare the US and UK so as to illuminate contemporary concern with 'backlash'. I shall argue that feminism does have a continuing tradition, varied across nation, ethnic group, social class, and time, with enough commonalities to declare it a feminist tradition.

A second issue to be addressed is that of the conditions under which women are able to make effective political claims. It has sometimes been argued that women are relatively politically quiescent (see Chapter 7) and are responsible for their own oppression. This position tends to underestimate the significance of patriarchal backlash and the forms of men's oppositional and reactive patriarchal politics, especially in understanding the form and effectiveness of feminist movements (see Chafetz and Dworkin, 1987; Harrison, 1978; Kimmel, 1987; Walby, 1988). Chafetz and Dworkin (1987) note that feminism and other social movements have often been followed by a backlash; that the form, timing and extent of the backlash vary, according primarily to the strength and success of feminism; but that these will have a similar focus, namely the family. Kimmel (1987) however, suggests that there are different responses to the turn-of-the-century women's movement. So how do we understand backlash in historical context?

THE BACKLASH

Faludi has written a well-documented account of the contemporary form of backlash in the US (Faludi, 1991), which she has applied to the UK (Faludi, 1992). She argues that women in the UK and the US are seeing a reaction against the advances made by feminists in the last two decades. She suggests that backlash is not a new phenomenon, but that it occurs wherever feminists make advances.

One of the features of the contemporary backlash is that it works by reversal, by presenting the opposite as true. One of the ways that it works is as a journalistic examination of difficulties faced by women today which are then falsely represented as being a result of feminism. The feminist movement is blamed for the problems in women's lives, rather than being seen as a potential solution. Faludi argues that in reality the problems identified are due to aspects of gender inequality which have not yet been removed. She provides many examples of the way the debate as to the causes of women's problems has been reversed by the media, especially issues related to marriage and fertility. The following four examples are ones which Faludi herself headlines.

First, there was a story about a 'man shortage', in which a Harvard/Yale study was supposed to have shown that college-educated women were going to find it very difficult to find a husband if they delayed marriage, as increasing numbers of women were in fact doing. They suggested they had statistical evidence that a college-educated unwed woman at 30 had a 20 per cent likelihood of marriage, at 35 a 5 per cent chance and that at 40 this had reduced to 1.3 per cent (Faludi, 1992: 21). In fact, this was not true, as was shown later by more reliable studies and statistics. However, the press did not publicise these later, more accurate, findings.

Second, there was the issue of divorce, in particular of whether changes in divorce procedure hurt women. There had been a change in the law so that instead of would-be divorcees having to prove fault in the conduct of their spouse in order to obtain a divorce, there could be divorce based solely upon the breakdown of the marriage without the attribution of fault. Some research by Weitzman (1985), then at Stanford, suggested that women suffered a decline of 73 per cent in their living standard on divorce, while men received a 42 per cent rise, and suggested that the no-fault divorce laws had made the financial position of women on divorce worse than under the previous legal regime.

Faludi states that other studies show that these figures seriously exaggerated the decline in women's standard of living. Other larger sample surveys showed that if the investigation of living standards took place a few years after divorce rather than merely one year, then women were better actually better off after divorce. Indeed there were no actual data in Weitzman's book which directly compared the no-fault with fault-related divorce, rather she had made her case indirectly based on research which focused primarily on the new situation alone. Yet these criticisms of the thesis that no-fault divorce made the position of divorcing women worse received little publicity.

Third, there was the issue of fertility decline. There was a story that fertility rates among women in their thirties were so low that women who were deferring having children were risking never having them – it was claimed that among women aged between 31 and 35, 39 per cent were not to be able to conceive.

Again Faludi argues that the figures were unreliable, since the sample was very special and small. A larger study showed fertility was not a major problem with thirty-something women, but this finding was not seriously reported. In fact younger women in their twenties had been subject to a significant fall in fertility, largely due to diseases to which little attention had been given, but the problems of infertility among twenty-somethings was little reported.

Fourth, there were stories about burn-out. Women's mental health was alleged to be declining as a result of staying single and having stressful careers. In fact studies showed that single women had significantly better mental health than housewives who stayed home looking after children.

All these media stories suggested that women had better marry fast and early, stay married, have children early, rather than take high-powered jobs, if they wanted happy, fulfilled lives. They claimed to draw upon research. In fact, Faludi says, they were highly selective in the research findings reported and did not present the best state of scientific knowledge about the problems in women's lives. Faludi has hundreds of similar examples where the media picked up on academic studies to suggest that the position of women had changed for the worse as a result of feminist inspired changes, but other studies which showed these findings to be fallacious were poorly reported. She continues this theme of a conservative turn in the press with analysis of other media, including films, such as *Fatal Attraction*. Faludi argues that this media distortion of research on gender and women is a backlash against feminism and the changes which feminism has wrought in women's lives. She states that they are trying to turn the clock back on women's advances.

I want to engage in a two-way comparison in order to assess Faludi's account, first by comparing the present period with a backlash against an earlier feminist wave, and second by comparing Britain and the US. In her section on earlier backlashes in the US, and in the UK edition of her book, Faludi includes examples to parallel the US experience, thereby suggesting similarities. But are there also important differences?

Chafetz and Dworkin (1987) suggest that, although there are differences in the form of the backlash, depending largely on the strength of feminist movement, there are no significant differences in content: 'The passage of nearly 100 years has apparently done little to change the ideological focus of the opponents of women's movements' (1987: 52). Kimmel (1987), however, suggests that men's responses to turn-of-the-century feminism are diverse, including two quite different antagonistic stances. He suggests that there was an anti-feminist backlash, as evidenced in anti-suffrage organisations, such as the Man Suffrage Association and the Illinois Association Opposed to Women's Suffrage; as well as a masculinist reaction which did not see women as the enemy, but nevertheless opposed creeping cultural feminisa-tion, shown in organisations such as the Boy Scouts in America. He also identifies a third response among men, a pro-feminist response, which was less influential, instanced by the leaders of the newly opened women's colleges such as Matthew Vassar, the Socialist Party, and the sex radicals of Greenwich Village. So there are disagreements here over whether the contemporary backlash is simply a repeat of previous examples of backlash. To explore this further I shall examine the causes of the end of first-wave feminism, and, in particular, the place of backlash in this.

Why did first-wave feminism end?

A variety of reasons have been put forward as to why first-wave, or turn-of-the-century, feminism ended, and indeed arguments that it did not end. I shall present three main approaches, with several sub-variants, followed by two versions of the argument that it did not in fact end.

Successful conclusion

First-wave feminism ended because it achieved its objects. This view repre-sents the movement as one in which the main goal was the winning of suffrage, with a secondary interest in equal rights, such as access to uni-versities and to property rights. The majority of women in Britain won the vote in 1918, that is women over 30 with a little property, and the remainder gained suffrage in 1928. At the end of the nineteenth century women had gained the right of entry to some universities and married women had won the right to possess property. Many other legal barriers were removed in the 1919 Sex Disqualification Removal Act (e.g., women were to be allowed to sit on juries). These were major victories in the acquisition of civil and political rights by women. Hence it could be argued that turn-of-the-century feminism ceased because it had achieved it main aims.

This is probably the dominant historical interpretation of turn-of-the-century feminism. The problem with this account is that the demands of first-wave feminism were not in fact so narrow, and that while these and indeed many other demands had been won by 1918, many had not. For instance, women had not obtained equal access to employment, equal pay, or freedom from men's violence and sexual abuse (Butler, 1986; Strachey, 1978).

Organisational failure

A second interpretation is that the movement ceased as a result of internal organisational failure. It is suggested that while initially turn-of-the-century feminism was a broad movement with varied aims, by the early twentieth century it had narrowed its goals, prioritising suffrage. So when the vote was won, they had serious organisational difficulties reorienting to the new circumstances, which led to their failure. An example is that of the attempt to transform the suffrage organisations into associations oriented to issues beyond the vote. The main suffrage organisation in Britain, the National Union of Women's Suffrage Societies, became the National Union of Societies for Equal Citizenship in 1919, and then the Townswomen's Guilds. In the US a similar transformation occurred. In each case the new organisation chose to focus on education rather than campaigning. They lost political focus and momentum, and ceased to be recognisably feminist organisations, fading away. This view sees the end of the movement as a result of poor political organisation and strategy.

A further variant on organisation failure is that this wave of feminism came to an end because of internal divisions. Women were badly split over different opinions on war and peace. The women's movement divided bitterly over the Great War of 1914–18. One grouping, including some of the suffragettes with Christabel and Emmeline Pankhurst, supported the war as an essential patriotic campaign, and argued for the cessation of suffrage activities for its duration. Another group, including the socialist-oriented Sylvia Pankhurst, opposed the war and argued for pacifism. A large and effective women's peace movement was established (Wiltshire, 1985). This issue split the feminist voice, and it was difficult to reconstitute the groupings and momentum after the war. Clearly the divisions over the war were a problem. However, these should not be overstated.

The third variant of the argument that first-wave feminism ceased as a result of organisational failure relates to the possible cooption of early leaders. Some women did acquire leadership positions in the early twentieth century, for instance as Members of Parliament and trade union leaders. For instance, Margaret Bondfield became a Labour Minister, but cut married women's rights to benefits in the Great Depression. Were these women simply coopted by the dominant male structures which they joined? For example, there were a series of amalgamations of women's trade unions with men's trade unions in the 1920s and 1930s. Prior to this, in the nineteenth century many men's unions had refused to allow women to join (Drake, 1920). But by the early twentieth century this patriarchal exclusionary strategy was being modified. These amalgamations might be regarded as strengthening the representation of women's interests, since they gave women trade unionists access to the financial reserves of the larger and more wealthy male unions. However, they also involved the loss of autonomy of the women's unions and the loss of the independent voice of women trade union leaders on the national stage.

Rather than interpreting the process as primarily one of cooption of the women's leaders, it is more appropriate to examine the changing gender strategies of the period as a whole. The 1920s and 1930s were periods in which the exclusionary strategy of organised male labour towards women workers was being replaced by one in which women were included, but segregated. The worst of the exclusionary practices were overcome by these amalgamations, but at a price. This constituted a major shift in patriarchal strategy, so that it was no longer in direct confrontation with the feminist strategies, or independent women's unions. Rather, this was a process of development of new forms of incorporation of women, but usually in subordinate positions. For instance, these newly merged unions were led by men not women. It is inappropriate to interpret these changes in too voluntarist a manner, as the selling out of the women's leaders, rather we have a major change in gendered strategies by many groups of men and women.

These last three explanations share a common position of seeing the failure of first-wave feminism to survive as a major force after the granting of suffrage as a result of the organisational failure of the women activists. The next approach is different in focusing on the opposition to these women – that is, backlash.

Backlash

There are two main versions of the backlash argument in relation to first-wave feminism. The first is that the turn-of-the-century women's movement was smashed by the repressive powers of the state. The militant phase of the suffrage movement, which entailed actions such as the simultaneous smashing of all the windows in Regent Street, the burning of pillar boxes and the burning of 'votes for women' in golf courses, as well as more self-sacrificial gestures such as chaining themselves to the gates of Buckingham Palace, met with strong repression. Demonstrations were broken up with police violence; mob violence against suffrage demonstrators was not prevented; suffrage activists were imprisoned and, when they went on hunger strike, forcibly fed (Morrell, 1981). When close to death they were let out only until they were well enough to be reincarcerated under the notorious Cat and Mouse Act. This view maintains that the repressive power of the state was successful in deterring a reintroduction of the guerrilla tactics of the militant suffragists after the war. These tactics had been essential in raising the profile of the movement, even though the majority of women in the movement did not engage in them.

The second version of the backlash argument focuses on the shift in sexual discourse which led to the portrayal of the husband-free women of the suffrage movement as unnatural because they did not engage in sex with men. 'Experts' on sexuality, such as Freud, introduced new ideas and norms about appropriate sexual conduct. The Freudianisation of the understanding of sexuality made heterosexual sex appear to be necessary for a healthy life style. Thus as women won demands on a political level, they were faced with increasing pressures to marry and engage with men at a sexual level, and this undercut the independence which women had been developing (Faderman, 1981; Jeffreys, 1985; Millett, 1977).

However, while this argument accurately describes a change in sexual discourse it tends to underestimate the opportunities as well as problems opened up for women. This new discourse also included some new freedoms and spaces for women to make demands within heterosexual relations.

Continuation

There are many approaches to explaining the end of first-wave feminism as a vibrant political force: feminists were successful; they made strategic and organisational mistakes; they met backlash. These explanations all engage with something significant, though the significance of backlash is often underestimated. Turn-of-the-century feminism met an enormous backlash, both very directly in the repressive power of the state, and, slightly less directly, in the cultural attack on the life style and sexual identities of women not attached to men. There were attempts to incorporate women, especially at the level of the labour movement, and internal divisions led to organisational splintering, for example as a result of their differences over the First World War. But feminists did have enormous successes.

A very different interpretation is that first-wave feminism did not end in 1918, or even 1928, but has been a continuing force. This focuses on continuing campaigns to improve women's position. Women have argued for health care, especially for that of mothers and children. Women have fought for access to contraception and abortion. Women continued to fight for school meals for children, for free school milk. Women campaigned for the right to divorce men on the same grounds as men could divorce women, and for easier divorce. The political actions of women were crucial in building foundations of what we used to call the welfare state. The welfare state was not an achievement of an ungendered labour movement – represented as a male labour movement – but an alliance between feminism and the labour movement (see Banks, 1981; Middleton, 1978; Spender, 1984).

Women in the labour movement in particular continued to campaign for women's issues, though these were often represented as matters of class rather than gender. Women fought for equal pay, gaining a Royal Commission in 1946, and equal pay for women civil servants in the 1950s (Walby, 1986b).

While it is now clear that some political activity by women did continue throughout the period between 1920 and 1968, many of these women did not call themselves feminist. For instance, most of the women trade unionists who fought for equal pay did not do so. If self-identification takes priority, then should they be excluded from the feminist heritage? Or should the social science evaluation of their struggles as being on behalf of women be sufficient to have them included? Certainly they have been important in pursuing policies for women.

CHANGES IN THE FORM

The question of the definition of 'feminist' is as important in considering the range of political practices today as in the inter-war period. There are still women who say 'I am not a feminist but...' and then say and do things usually identified as feminist (Pilcher, 1995). So feminism is not dead, even if the word is not used in some quarters. Many policy demands that were once considered radical and feminist are no longer described as feminist. Who would now call someone who believes in equal pay feminist? Yet before 1975 this was not law and was controversial. Is this a feminist success? Definitions of feminism are important for the assessment of the impact of any backlash, since if issues such as these are excluded from a feminist project then the impact of that project will appear more limited.

But is the backlash the same in both periods and in both the US and UK? Are Faludi, Chafetz and Dworkin right to suggest that there was a common focus on pushing women back into marriage? While this theme is clearly present, I think this argument oversimplifies the situation. In particular, it underestimates the significance of attempts to allow women into the public sphere, while subordinating them there, especially in relation to employment.

I will now compare the form of the opposition to feminism in the contemporary US and UK. There are some features which can be misunderstood because the notion of forward and backward for women is insufficiently theorised. And there is the question of whether Faludi has sufficiently grasped the specificity of the European configuration of gender relations in general and the New Right in particular.

Faludi suggests that the push backwards is on women to go back to the home, to be fertile, and to raise babies, to look after husbands, to marry and stay married. While this is clearly anti-feminist, it is not the only way in which patriarchal oppression can be intensified. There has been a regrouping of the patriarchal forces which oppose feminist successes in reducing gender inequality. The metaphor of 'backlash', and Faludi's analysis, tend to suggest simply back and forth, which is insufficient to catch the changes that are actually going on. Partly, it is a question of UK/US differences; partly, her account is just too simple. For example, the resurgence of the Right in the UK is different from that in the US.

During the 1980s, Britain, like the US, had a conservative government. There were some similar concerns relating to sexuality and fertility, such as attempts to restrict abortion and attempts to restrict homosexual expression via Clause 28 (see Franklin, Lury and Stacey, 1991). There have also been fundamentalist developments in some religious groupings (Sahgal and Yuval-Davis, 1992). But these developments were much weaker and less successful than in the US. Pushing women back into the home has not been a major feature of governments in the UK. During this period women's participation in paid work has dramatically increased; the rates of divorce and unmarried motherhood have soared, dramatically changing household structure, so that women live without men much more frequently. This is not a case of women simply being pushed back into the home. But nor is it simply progress, since a significant wages gap remains, female-headed households are typically very poor, and older women in part-time work have particularly poor conditions of employment. Certain dimensions of women's autonomy have increased, removing certain forms of control, even as some women face acute poverty. The position of women is increasingly polarised as to whether or not they have access to good employment. This is compounded by the reduction in welfare provisions which are disproportionately used by women with little or no income from paid work.

Thatcherism, and then Majorism, are best seen not as representing a 'turn-the-clock-back' type of backlash, but rather as pursuing a project of public patriarchy, rather than private patriarchy. Women are not pushed back into the domestic sphere, though the conditions of lone mothers are poorer. However, the entry to the public is on poor conditions for those women without qualifications and labour market experience (see Walby, 1990). Gender inequality can be intensified without a return to private patriarchy. It is necessary to distinguish between the different forms of patriarchal systems, rather than conflate them all into a monolithic model.

There are increasing divisions between women in these forms of patriarchal pressure, with an exacerbation of class and 'race' inequalities. For instance, a polarisation in women's wages between those few, younger, highly educated women who are gaining entry to the professions and well-paid occupations on the one hand, and older women, with fewer skills recognised by the labour market, who take the very badly paid, insecure, part-time jobs, as they re-enter the labour market after a period of full-time child and husband care. Class relations between women in the form of the differential access to well-paid, service-class occupations on the one hand, and badly paid, part-time jobs on the other, have shifted. But crucial to understanding this is the change in the form of patriarchal relations: from private to public patriarchy. This was also true of turn-of-the-century feminism.

CONCLUSIONS

What are the implications? The previous historical instances of 'backlash' need to be understood, not underestimated. Turn-of-the-century feminism was ferociously attacked. This is one of the most significant reasons why it lost momentum and went underground in the period between 1920 and 1968. But it was not defeated. Some accounts of the demise of turn-of-the-century feminism blame feminists for making mistakes which led to its demise – that they were responsible for bad organisation, internal divisions, selling out and inappropriate goals. Such an approach underestimates the historical significance of the backlash phenomenon, then and now.

However, in order to understand this opposition it is necessary to take account of the nuances of the different forms of the backlash. Anti-feminism can take many forms other than 'turning the clock back' and pushing women back into the home. It is possible to intensify the exploitation of women in the public sphere. The history of change in gender relations is not one of women leaving or being pushed back into the home; nor of simple progress or regress; but one of a complex interrelationship between a variety of feminist and patriarchal forces and forms of gender regime.

9

IS CITIZENSHIP GENDERED?

INTRODUCTION

Is citizenship gendered or is it beyond such particularism? Is it a concept which can be successfully universalist, or is it always affected by deeply rooted social divisions of gender, class and ethnicity? These issues relate to both a political project for which the concept of citizen serves as a unifying symbol, and an intellectual understanding of social integration. In contemporary Britain the term 'citizenship' has been used to indicate a populist notion of fairness and justice for all Britons, as in the development of 'Citizens' Charters'. The intellectual focus of British social science debate on the topic has often been concerned with the extent to which class restricts effective access to citizenship, as in the debates around T. H. Marshall's work (Mann, 1987; Marshall, 1950; Turner, 1990), although there is also an interest in the relationship of citizenship to social cohesion (Marquand, 1988; Pahl, 1991; Taylor, 1991; Turner, 1991a, 1991b).

Gender is absent from many discussions of citizenship. Despite the fact that women do not have the same access to citizenship as men, the significance of, and reasons for this are rarely explored (with some key exceptions e.g. Lister, 1990). The inclusion of gender, even if merely to note that women have a different relationship to citizenship than men, is a necessary initial corrective. However, there is a question as to whether 'citizenship' is so imbued with gender-specific assumptions related to the public sphere and the nexus of the market and state that it is necessarily only a partial rather than a universalistic project. A further question concerns the significance of citizenship in the development of contemporary forms of gender relations, and hence of social relations more broadly. This is the issue of whether the achievement of citizenship by women has a significant impact on the form and degree of gender inequality.

MARSHALL'S HERITAGE

Much of the recent social science debate on citizenship is concerned with the relationship of class to social integration, and omits gender. T. H.

Marshall developed a theory of citizenship which he saw as both socially progressive and politically moderate, believing in the possibility of justice and rights in a mixed capitalist economy (Marshall, 1950, 1975, 1981). Most of Marshall's analysis was related to the changing structure of social classes in relation to citizenship and capitalism. While I shall adopt Marshall's definition of citizenship, I take issue with his theory of its development.

According to Marshall, citizenship has

> three parts, or elements, civil, political and social. The civil element is composed of the rights necessary for individual freedom – liberty of the person, freedom of speech and thought and faith, the right to own property and to conclude valid contracts, and the right to justice... the institutions most directly associated with civil rights are the courts of justice. By the political element I mean the right to participate in the exercise of political power, as a member of a body invested with political authority or as an elector of the members of such a body. The corresponding institutions are parliament and councils of local government. By the social element I mean the whole range from the right to a modicum of economic welfare and security to the right to share to the full in the social heritage and to live the life of a civilised being according to the standards prevailing in the society. The institutions most closely connected with it are the educational system and the social services.
>
> (Marshall 1950: 10–11)

These rights were considered to have been steadily built up, first civil rights, then political, lastly social:

> it is possible, without doing too much violence to historical accuracy, to assign the formative period in the life of each to a different century – civil rights to the eighteenth, political to the nineteenth, and social to the twentieth.
>
> (Marshall 1950: 14)

Civil rights include *habeas corpus* and, in the economic field, the right to work in an occupation of one's choosing (p. 15).

Yet women in Britain before 1928 and in the US until 1920 did not have many of the features of either civil or political citizenship. They lacked 'liberty of the person' in that they did not have the right to control their own bodies in situations where they wished for abortion or contraception. Married women lacked the right to live anywhere other than where their husbands insisted. Married women, until late in the nineteenth century, did not have 'the right to own property and to conclude valid contracts', losing this right on marriage. Married women did not have 'the right to justice' in that they did not have the right to be free from the physical coercion of their husbands nor to refuse him sexual intercourse. Women certainly did not have 'political citizenship' either, since the vote was only granted to women in stages between 1918 and 1928. Women did not have the 'civil' right to work at the occupation of their choice, since there were so many restrictions on the forms of employment open to women, ranging from the marriage bar in many white-collar employments, to lack of access to skilled manual labour since they were denied access to apprenticeships (Banks, 1981; Drake, 1920; Holcombe, 1983; Walby, 1990).

Marshall's concept of citizenship opens the way to discuss degrees of citizenship obtained by different social groups at different times. That Marshall does not take advantage of this is no reason why we should not do so today.

Mann (1987) criticises Marshall's conception of three stages of the attainment of citizenship for its evolutionism and Anglocentrism, choosing instead to emphasise the importance of military and geo-political formations. Mann is correct to make this point, but I think he does not follow it through sufficiently in that he underestimates the significance of ethnicity and 'race', and ignores other social divisions, such as that of gender. There are occasions where a descriptive qualification is made, but it is of little analytic significance. For instance, discussing the case of the US, Mann proposes:

> In the US labour was eventually absorbed into the liberal regime. A broad coalition, from landowners and merchants down to small farmers and artisans, had made the Revolution. White, adult males could not be easily excluded from civil and political citizenship. By the early 1840s all of them, in all states, possessed the vote – 50 years earlier than anywhere else, 50 years before the emergence of a powerful labour movement. Thus the political demands of labour could be gradually expressed as an interest group *within* an existing federal political constitution and competitive party system....As the (white) working class was civilly and politically *inside* the regime, it had little need for the great ideologies of the proletariat excluded from citizenship – socialism and anarchism.
>
> (1987: 342, emphasis in original)

In this paragraph there is an illegitimate sliding between what are quite distinct categories, especially between on the one hand 'labour' and on the other 'white, adult males'. The paragraph opens with a reference to 'labour' in the first sentence. The second sentence refers to 'a broad coalition, from landowners and merchants down to small farmers and artisans'. The third sentence refers to 'white, adult males'. In the fourth, 'them' refers to the 'white, adult males' of the third sentence. The fifth returns to the opening concept of 'labour'. In the next paragraph the subject shifts yet again, this time to 'the (white) working class'.

Yet 'labour' and 'white, adult males' are quite different groups since the former includes women and Blacks and the latter does not. Some women are engaged in waged and unwaged labour, so are part of 'labour' and, presumably the 'working class'. This slide is problematic, since White adult males were a minority of the population and a minority of labour. Yet Mann seeks to generalise from this minority category to the larger concept of 'labour'. While 'white, adult males' were 'inside the regime', 'labour' was not. The social base that Mann identifies as the basis for his analysis of political forces is seriously mis-described and mis-conceptualised.

It is thus inappropriate to describe the US in the 1840s as a 'liberal' society – when civil and political citizenship were granted to a minority of the adult population on the basis of ascriptive criteria of sex and 'race'. The US did not become a full 'democracy' with civil and political citizenship rights for all adults until the late 1960s, after both the struggle which won White women's suffrage and the civil rights movement of the 1960s which gained effective suffrage for Blacks. This has major implications for a theory of democracy, citizenship and political structure. While Mann explains the present US state as a result of early inclusion of 'labour', I would argue the opposite – the US state is a result of a slow inclusion of different categories of person, including 'labour', into citizenship.

Mann makes some interesting points about the significance of the military in relations of power. Yet he makes no reference to the fact that the military is a highly gendered institution (see Enloe, 1983). If his thesis about the importance of the military is accepted, then so also must the significance of gender.

Turner (1990) also draws on Marshall's concept of citizenship as a valuable analytic tool, and similarly criticises it for its ethnocentrism, indeed criticising Mann for not going far enough in his criticisms of Marshall. Turner is interested in the application of Marshall's three-fold notion of citizenship to the current period. In particular he is interested in the last part of the schema – that of social rights, which he considers have been guaranteed, until recently, by the 'welfare state'. Using a variety of historical examples ranging from the Greek city-state to revolutionary France, Turner suggests that a typology of forms of citizenship is more appropriate than a single entity. He uses this to discuss the specific historical social forces under which different forms of citizenship arise. Turner argues for the significance of two dimensions: first, whether the pressure for citizenship is from above or below; and second, its orientation to public/private space. He suggests that a combination of pressures from below and a positive orientation to public space gives rise to revolutionary forms of citizenship, such as that found in the French tradition. Pressure from below combined with a less positive orientation to the public gives rise to liberal pluralism, as in the American instance. When the move for citizenship comes from above and is combined with a positive evaluation of the public there is passive democracy, as in the British case. When the move above is combined with a negative evaluation of the public this is considered to give rise to fascism, as in the German case.

The second issue on which Turner is critical of Mann is his neglect of 'private/public' structuring, which Turner considers to be very important. 'If we regard the historical emergence of the public as in fact the emergence of the political, then the structural relationship between the private and the public, and their cultural meanings, is an essential component in any under-standing of the relationship between totalitarianism and democracy' (1990: 211). This issue is discussed with reference to concepts of 'the rights of the individual' (p. 200) and 'private life' (p. 201), which are opposed to those of 'state' (p. 201) and 'totalitarianism' (p. 200). The dichotomy is set between the 'individual' and the 'state' as in 'private life emerges as a sanctuary from state regulation' (p. 201). Turner closely links 'private' with 'family', as in 'the private space of the family' (p. 209).

There is a problem in Turner's concepts here in his elision of the distinc-tion between 'individual' and 'family' via the concept of 'private'. In so doing he erases women. He treats the 'family' as if it has a unitary being and set of interests. This is incorrect because of the distinct interests of wives and husbands (see Acker, 1973; Delphy, 1984; Pateman, 1988). 'Private' appears to have two meanings – on the one hand, the autonomy of the 'individual'; on the other hand, freedom from state interference. I would suggest that Turner conflates these meanings. Turner's attempt to extend this sense of 'private' to the 'family' is illegitimate. The 'family' is not an 'individual' – it is composed of several people, who are not 'private' from each other. Women are not free from interaction with and dominance by men. The 'family' is not 'private' for women. The 'family' may or may not be free from 'state' interference, but that is a separate issue. That is, while the dichotomies of state/individual and of state/family are legitimate, it is not appropriate to conflate the individual with the family. The phrase 'the private space of the family' is nonsensical, since it denies the social relations within the family, illegitimately conflating the woman with her husband. This conflation is further evidenced by Turner's adoption of the male view-point on the activities within the household when he asserts that 'in modern societies...the private is seen as the space of personal leisure and enhance-ment' (p. 222), thereby denying the salience of the household as a site of domestic labour by women.

The neglect of the analysis of gender and the exclusion of women from citizenship in societies which granted full citizenship to adult men is sur-prising in Turner's case, given his interest in the public/private structuring of social relations, since the role of this structuring in the exclusion of women from citizenship has been subject to extensive debate. Indeed some political theorists have argued that it is precisely this public/private divide that has made women's participation in formal politics so difficult (see Eisenstein, 1981; Okin, 1989; Pateman, 1988). Yet Turner does not describe, let alone explain, the exclusion of women from citizenship at some times and their inclusion at others.

The Marshall/Mann/Turner writings on citizenship are interesting in grasping an important concept in political practice and debate. However, they do so at the expense of reducing it to a narrow form of class analysis. Citizenship is a broader concept than class rights. It should be retained with its modern connotations of all adults participating in a full democracy, otherwise the analysis is only relevant to the Greek city-state type of citizenship and unfitted to a gendered, ethnically diverse Europe and world of the 1990s.

I would like to suggest an alternative approach to the analysis of citizenship. In this approach the differential access of inhabitants of a given territory to civil, political and social citizenship would be a key feature. Rather than this differential participation being considered 'a complication', it should become a central issue. It is not something to be left to 'further development of the theory of citizenship' (Turner 1990: 212), but must be an integral part of its initial, central, conceptual make up.

There is usually no one key period of nation-formation, despite the assumptions behind the work of Mann (1987) and Turner (1990) that there is a critical period of nation-formation (or state formation or nation state formation). This incorrect assumption is key to Mann's discussion of the societal variations in the development of the political institutions which constitute democracy. It is also a key assumption in Turner's discussion of the moments of formation of different forms of citizenship. Yet in many countries citizenship did not arrive at one moment for all people; rather, different groups gained different aspects of this in different periods. Countries vary as to whether White men, White women, men and women of minority ethnic groups, gained citizenship at the same time or not.

In most first world countries there is a period of several decades between the granting of political citizenship to men and to women. This is quite different from the circumstances of many third world countries where women won the franchise at the same time as men, at the moment of national independence from colonial power. The winning of civil citizenship, while completed for most first world men before political citizenship, is barely completed for women in these countries, since only recently have women won control over their own bodies, the ability to disengage from marriage and the right to engage in all forms of employment. That is, for first world women political citizenship is typically achieved before civil citizenship, the reverse of the order for men. This exists in direct contradiction of Marshall's thesis. Rather than the notion of one critical period of 'nation-formation', it is more appropriate to talk of 'rounds of restructuring' of the nation state (cf. Massey, 1984). It is useful in carrying the notion of change built upon foundations which remain, and that layer upon layer of change can take place, each of which leaves its sediment which significantly affects future practices.

In most Western nation states White women won political citizenship after some considerable struggle. In the case of the UK the struggle for the vote and political citizenship was part of a wider struggle over issues which fit Marshall's category of civil citizenship. These included: the right of access to education; to own property; to terminate a marriage; to bodily integrity, such as the right not to be beaten by a husband; to professional employment; to sit on juries; to join the police (see Banks, 1981; Strachey, 1978; Walby, 1988). Some of these rights were won before suffrage, some in the decades following. For British women, political and civil citizenship were won as part of the same wave of political action, with at least as many aspects of civil citizenship being won after political citizenship as before. This contradicts Marshall's (1950) thesis that civil citizenship is won before political. In the case of British women, political citizenship was at least as often the power base from which women were able to win civil citizenship, as vice versa.

The structuring of the private and public spheres is of critical concern to the position and citizenship status of women (see Eisenstein, 1981; Okin, 1989; Pateman, 1988). Citizenship, especially its political aspect, has historically been bound up with participation in the public sphere. European women have historically been structured out of the public by the restrictions on their paid employment, restrictions on speaking in public, threats of violence if unaccompanied in public spaces, and their confinement to domestic duties (Cockburn, 1983; Hanmer and Saunders, 1984; Smart, 1984; Spender, 1983). It has only been by leaving the private sphere of the home that women have been able to gain some aspects of citizenship.

Some turn-of-the-century feminists believed that these changes would lead to the elimination of gender inequality. A more appropriate interpretation is that they shifted the form and degree of patriarchy without eliminating it. Contemporary Britain has moved towards a public, rather than private form of patriarchy (see Walby, 1990). Women's previous confinement to the domestic has been reduced, but structured gender inequality still exists. Social citizenship has been slower to follow. The development of the welfare state has been a significant element in this. Women played a more significant role in the struggle for this than is sometimes suggested (see Banks, 1981; Middleton, 1978).

WOMEN AND CITIZENSHIP

But is the relationship of women to citizenship simply one in which they have been slower than men to become 'citizens'? This implies that the citizenship project is as open to women as it is to men, if certain overt forms of discrimination are removed. It implies, further, that there is a single model of citizenship to which women can aspire alongside men, that is, a certain modernist universalism about the citizenship project.

This notion of a single model of citizenship has been brought into doubt by some recent feminist work (Bubeck, 1991; Lister, 1990, 1992; Nelson, 1984; Pateman, 1991; Ungerson, 1990, 1991; Wilson, 1991). The different experiences and structural position of women are seen to militate against their full access to the rights of citizenship. This work, which draws either implicitly or explicitly on the notions of the different levels of citizenship articulated by Marshall, focuses particularly on the rights contained within the notion of social citizenship. One of the problems identified here is that social citizenship usually depends upon being a worker for full access to such rights. Significant aspects of income maintenance payments by the state, pensions, and related welfare provision are provided as a result of waged employment. Those who do not make provision via employment can fall back on only very meagre levels of support.

Pensions, for instance, are provided typically as part of a scheme with an employer. Occupational pension schemes involve payments by both employer and employee which are protected from tax. Women, with a primary orientation to the care of children, husband, and elderly relatives, do not have direct access to pensions of the same level. They may derive pension benefits via their husbands, so long as they stay married, or they may have to fall back on poverty-level state benefits. Even women who do have paid employment may find that their pension is small, since part-time workers are rarely members of occupational pension schemes, and interruption of employment for a period of child care can play havoc with such pension entitlement.

There is a question as to whether access to a decent pension is compatible with the role of carer which many women take up. Is being a carer compatible with being a full citizen? If not, then what should change? Should women only be entitled to citizenship if they behave like men and have lifetime commitment to paid employment? And if so, what are the implications for those who need caring? Or should the rules of the welfare system be changed so that paid employment is not the only or main route of access to decent support in old age? (Bubeck, 1991; Lister, 1990, 1992; Nelson, 1984; Pateman, 1991; Ungerson, 1990, 1991; Wilson, 1991).

The value placed upon caring becomes a key question here. The role of carer is disproportionately taken by women (Abel and Nelson, 1990; Finch and Groves, 1983; Glendinning, 1990; Mayall, 1990; Morris, 1990). Yet this role as carer places women at a disadvantage in access to income (Glendinning, 1990); and more broadly in relation to political and social citizenship (Lister, 1990; Nelson, 1984).

Lister (1990) argues that financial dependency is an obstacle to women's citizenship. She shows how the government, in its discussions of the 'problem of dependency', considers only the public form of dependency on the state, and neglects the salience of women's private dependency in the family on the arbitrary will of another. Lister discusses Hurd's notion of the 'active citizen' promulgated when Home Secretary in 1988, which, while suggesting the centrality of the ideal of neighbourliness, still manages to neglect women carers, who logically ought to be exemplary representatives of this constituency. Poverty and lack of time and money curtail women's access to the political rights of citizenship. Lister suggests that excessive calls on women's time for unpaid work limit women's effective participation in the political rights of citizenship.

Turning to social citizenship – by which Lister effectively means the welfare state, and in particular welfare payments – she suggests that the structure of payment of these benefits is detrimental to women because it is predicated on married women's dependence. The changes which are needed here to secure social citizenship for women are three-fold. First, a change to individual rather than household entitlement. Second, a change so that the right to benefit is not dependent upon contributions, since that would be affected by labour market position where women are disadvantaged. (The one example of a non-contributing benefit is the rather small and currently vulnerable child benefit.) Third, Lister suggests that a coherent child care policy is needed to facilitate women's participation in the labour market.

Lister's article exemplifies the dilemmas in much current feminist analysis of social citizenship. On the one hand she argues that the solution is for women to stop being exploited at home and enter the labour market, on the other that women's position as carer should be supported. Lister argues that on the one hand:

> Women's position as the economic dependent of a male partner; as double-shift worker juggling the responsibilities of paid employment and caring work; or as welfare benefit recipient struggling to raise children in poverty or to manage on an inadequate pension, is incompatible with the full exercise of the social and political rights of citizenship. If women are to be fully integrated into full democratic citizenship, radical changes in personal and domestic life are required.
>
> (1990: 464)

Yet that on the other, the institutions of the 'public sphere' must do more to accommodate the sexual division of labour so long as it shapes and constrains the lives of women and limits their access to the 'public' sphere (p. 464). And she calls for changes 'to reflect the value to society as a whole of caring work, whether it be done in private or public sphere' (p. 464).

Lister demands both the entry of women into the public, as the only way that their second-class status can be ended, and that women's presence in the private realm of caring be accommodated. Perhaps she is deliberately asking for both, but these are quite different strategic responses. Indeed

174

they underlie many of the issues in the feminist debate on gender and citizenship. Should women seek support for their existing roles in the family as carers, or should they be seeking to leave such roles behind and enter paid employment? Women's greater commitment to caring is at the same time positively valued and a source of disadvantage to women. The suggestion that women should become more like men in order to obtain economic and social rights is contentious within the debate on gender and citizenship.

This issue of whether women are intrinsically different from men and should value this difference, or are basically the same and should claim the same rights on the basis of this similarity, is a key philosophical, theoretical and political division in feminist analysis and practice (Eisenstein, 1984; Meehan and Sevenhuijsen, 1991). It underlies the debates on the issue of citizenship and caring and has fuelled discussions on the analysis of the effectiveness of divergent feminist strategies since the turn of the century (Banks, 1981; Hewlett, 1986; Littleton, 1987; Segal, 1987; Sklar, 1973; Weitzman, 1985). On the one hand, there is the desire to claim the same rights and privileges as men – for instance, equal pay and pensions, the vote and political representation. On the other, there is the wish to protect things women hold – for instance, protective legislation at work, abstention from military conscription.

HOW IMPORTANT IS CITIZENSHIP FOR GENDER?

The question of the relationship of citizenship to gender can be asked in the reverse direction. What is the place of citizenship in the analysis of gender relations? How important is it for patterns of gender relations? This can be considered, following Marshall, in three arenas: civil, political and social.

Civil citizenship

Marshall described civil citizenship as being related to individual freedom – including liberty of the person, freedom of speech, the right to own property, and the right to justice (Marshall, 1950: 10). Yet these are rights which most women did not obtain until after political citizenship, and some, such as the right to justice from male violence, are still not fully obtained (see Adler, 1987; Edwards, 1989). Many of the first-wave feminists who struggled for the rights Marshall would consider the marks of civil citizenship came to argue that they could not win them without political citizenship. That is, they reversed the order that Marshall suggested was general, but is in fact merely typical for White men, in which civil rights preceded political rights. Most aspects of civil citizenship were won after suffrage was obtained. They are important, but in the case of women, are largely

175

contingent upon success in obtaining political citizenship, the struggle for which is therefore even more significant.

Political citizenship

Interpretation of the significance of political citizenship depends upon the theory of the state and politics within a theory of gender relations. Much feminist theory in the 1970s argued that the realm of the political was much wider than was usually considered, and that the state did not play as large a role as conventional theories suggested (Millett, 1977). However, there is currently some reassessment of this position within feminist theory, partly as a result of the success of some feminist movements to win changes they desire (Sawer, 1990; Watson, 1990).

Political citizenship is more important than has often been considered in analyses of changes in gender relations (Walby, 1988, 1990). The successes of turn-of-the-century feminism are rarely noted in accounts of changes in gender relations, despite the impact of the movement on women's formal political rights, access to education and employment, civil rights, such as the right to sit on juries, and to leave unwanted marriages (compare Strachey (1978) with Bergmann (1986)). Political citizenship was the basis of the transformation from private to public patriarchy (Walby, 1990). Without these political victories neither civil nor social citizenship would have occurred.

Social citizenship

There is a tension between social citizenship for women and their location as carers in the family, as discussed above. The concept of citizenship depends upon the public sphere; the term has no significant meaning in the private. So what can be the relationship between that private realm of the family and citizenship? Is the family intrinsically an obstacle to the inclusion of all people as citizens? Or can it be accommodated, or even embraced? The answer to this depends upon the theorisation of the family, in particular the relationship between gender inequality and the family. This depends on the theorisation of women's interests. Some of the dilemmas these issues raise in feminist theory have already been explored above.

For most social theorists, social citizenship is bound up with the provision of welfare, with the provision of an infrastructure which enables people to be guaranteed a minimum of provision of necessities. Hewlett (1986) compares the welfare position of women in the US and Europe and suggests that European women have higher levels of provision than those in the US. European women have been more successful in issues such as publicly funded child care and legal entitlements to hold on to a job through pregnancy. This is not due to any greater strength of European feminism, but due to the different strategy that they have followed on behalf of women. Hewlett argues that European feminists have adopted a 'difference' position to a greater extent than feminists in the US, who adopted more of a 'sameness' strategy, and have done better by women because of that.

However, there are problems in the analysis of the history of European feminism. For instance, European feminists are currently eagerly participating in the 'sameness' strategy through the utilisation of sex discrimination legislation emanating from the EC (CREW Reports, *passim*). European feminists were less enthusiastic, or perhaps simply less strongly divided, than their US counterparts about protective legislation. Hewlett misconstrues European feminism by viewing it through the lens of the US sameness/difference debate. Rather, the explanation of the different achievements of US and European feminism lies more in the nature of the alliances which feminists have made in Europe. UK feminists have long engaged with the labour movement and won, in alliance, those welfare demands that Hewlett sees as a consequence of the 'difference' strategy. This is part of a collective strategy of the working class, from which women not only benefited, but in which they took a leading role. In alliance with some middle-class feminist organisations, they demanded social provision such as health care, child and maternity welfare schemes, free school milk. These demands were steadily implemented from the turn of the century onwards (see e.g., Mark-Lawson, Savage and Warde, 1985; Middleton, 1978). This alliance was absent from the US because there was no lasting labour movement of any size. The US and UK histories of social citizenship are thus based on different political contexts, with distinctive dilemmas.

Economic citizenship?

Much of the writing on women and social citizenship has taken a focus which concentrates on women's welfare needs, rather than women's social and economic contributions. However, the concept of social citizenship has also been used to illuminate the notion of social integration, of the ability to take part in the full range of societal activities. This has been developed by Marquand (1988) in his account of the need for full social and political citizenship in order to secure economic participation and economic efficiency and success. Marquand has interestingly inverted the old dilemma of efficiency or equity into an argument that greater participation is needed for economic efficiency. His argument could have been made more strongly if he had included a gender dimension. The cessation of exclusion of women from effective participation in paid work, or their full economic citizenship, is a contributor to a country's economic success. A focus on social integration and social cohesion as concerns of citizenship might then include women's economic participation.

177

CONCLUSIONS

We should not only ask how gendered is citizenship, but also the symmetrical question: how important is citizenship for gender? I would answer this question unequivocally – political citizenship has been central in the transformation of the forms of gender relations over the last century.

Today, citizenship means universalistic democratic rights of social and political participation. In popular political discourse it entails the full integration of all adults regardless of 'race', ethnicity, sex, or creed. In this way it is a modernist, universalistic concept. However, it is also a national project, a location which places limitations on its universalism. Nevertheless, the new meaning of the term citizen, with its attempt at a democratic and universalistic project, rather than the limited notion utilised in ancient Greek city-states from which women and slaves and aliens were excluded, is useful for social science. Access to citizenship is a highly gendered and ethnically structured process. Yet the concept is potentially suited to the conceptualisation, investigation and theorisation of the varying degrees of social integration and participation in contemporary society.

The development of social citizenship for women is linked to, but different from, that for men. Similarly, the social citizenship of men has been affected by women's demands for welfare. Access to welfare benefits is so significantly structured by employment that women and men typically have a very different relationship to them. Women's caring work in the family is a major barrier to women's full social citizenship.

The question of citizenship belongs not only to the classic debates about the balancing of liberal freedom with the demands of a capitalist economy, of the relationship between the labour market and the state, of efficiency and equity, that is, of class and capitalism; it is also about the major structuring principles of gender. When half the population might be denied effective citizenship because of gender, then gender matters to citizenship. The question of the relationship of the public and private is not incidental.

The male-dominated family-household is incompatible with full citizenship. Social citizenship for women is incompatible with, and unobtainable under, women's confinement to the family and the vagaries of a dependency relationship upon a private patriarch. Political citizenship for women has had a destabilising effect on private forms of patriarchy and thus traditional forms of the family. Citizenship is about gender and the transformation of the form of patriarchy as much as it is about class, nation/ethnicity and capitalism.

The introduction of the different levels of citizenship is not only about the development of capitalism, but about the transformation of patriarchy. The civil and political rights and the development of the possibility of social citizenship through the welfare state are essential foundations of the transformation from private to public patriarchy. The welfare state acts as a mechanism of welfare payments from which women disproportionately benefit, in that they receive more in benefits than they pay out in taxes (LeGrand *et al.*, 1992), and, despite all the many problems of poverty levels of income support, it does constitute an alternative to the private patriarch, albeit a public one (Borchorst and Siim, 1987; Hernes, 1987). This financial alternative to dependence on an arbitrary individual patriarch is important in the transformation of the form of gender relations, even if it does not lift women out of poverty. The welfare state has socialised some forms of previously privatised domestic labour, through schools, nurseries, hospitals and other forms of publicly provided care, albeit at levels which do not satisfy women's demands. It is the socialised provision as much as the welfare transfers, which is crucial in socialising women's domestic role. Given the significance of these transformations for gender relations it is not surprising that women played an active role in struggling for these changes.

Thus the development of social citizenship is constituted at least as much by changing gender relations as it is by changing class relations. Citizenship is about a transition from private to public patriarchy, not only the civilising of capitalism.

10

WOMAN AND NATION

INTRODUCTION

Gender relations are differentiated in many ways, including ethnicity, 'race', nation, religion and linguistic community. These are actively constructed social and political categories and projects. The focus in this chapter will be on 'nation' in the context of these other forms of group identities.

The literature on nations and nationalism rarely addresses the question of gender, despite a general interest in the differential participation of various social groups in nationalist projects. A key issue in the analysis of nation has been the conditions under which an ethnic group can claim and possibly achieve the status of nation and then of nation state (see Smith, 1971, 1986). Nationalist movements necessarily draw upon their relevant constituency in uneven ways, and there has been much analysis of the differing class compositions of such movements, their levels of education, and a variety of socio-economic and cultural variables. However, this body of literature has engaged but little with the differential integration of women and men into the national project. Most texts on nationalism do not take gender as a significant issue (see Gellner, 1983; Kedourie, 1966; Smith, 1971, 1986). Rare and thus important exceptions to this absence are Enloe (1989), Jayawardena (1986) and Yuval-Davis and Anthias (1989).

There has been a revival of interest in the related concept of citizenship, which historically has formed a link between 'nation' and 'state'. 'Citizenship' has been introduced in the context of macro-societal comparisons in order to facilitate discussions of the social conditions under which different forms of democracy have been attained (see Mann, 1987; Turner, 1986, 1990). It is of interest here because of its link with 'nation' and the possibility that the concept offers assistance in dealing with degrees of integration into the national project. However, the existing literature, despite this potential, rarely deals with gender.

There are five main positions on the issue of the intersection of gender with citizenship, ethnicity, nation and 'race'. First, there is the argument that gender, while existing, does not affect the nature of citizenship/ethnic/national/'race' relations (e.g. Mann, 1986b). This is sometimes expressed via a suggestion that there either is patriarchy or there is not, with little attempt to use or build the necessary concepts for a more sophisticated position (compare Mann, 1986a and 1986b; Turner 1986). Second, there is a symmetrical argument that citizenship/ethnic/national/'race' do not significantly affect the nature of gender relations (e.g. Daly, 1978). This is the argument that gender inequality has common features in all societies and all historical periods, and that women share a common oppression despite their documented differences of ethnicity/nationality/'race'. This position is not to be confused with the notion that ethnicity is irrelevant to the analysis of social relations. Third is the argument that these systems of social relations should be added together, so as for instance to talk of the double burden that Black women suffer from both racism and sexism. This also suggests that racism is an extra layer of oppression some women have to bear and produces differences and inequalities between women. Fourth, there is the argument that ethnic/national/'race' differences mean that the institutions which are central for White women's oppression are not central to those of women of other ethnicities (e.g. hooks, 1984). For instance, the family can be considered to have different significance for gender relations in different ethnic groups. This means that there is not a common form of gender differentiation and inequality across different ethnic groups. Fifth, there is the argument that gender and ethnic/national/'race' relations affect each other, leading to dynamic analyses of the shifting forms of gender and of ethnic/national/'race' relations (e.g. Anthias and Yuval-Davis, 1989; Enloe, 1989; Jayawardena, 1986). This entails an analysis of the causal interconnections between gender and ethnic/national/'race' differentiation and inequality. Overlying all of these five positions is a further variable of the different significance of class and capitalist relations within each of these analyses. This varies independently of the five perspectives.

GENDER, NATION AND NATIONALISM

While many texts on the nation have ignored gender, several very important contributions have addressed this issue: Yuval-Davis and Anthias (1989), Jayawardena (1986) and Enloe (1989). In the introduction to their volume, Anthias and Yuval-Davis (1989: 7) suggest that there are five major ways in which women are involved in ethnic and national processes:

1 as biological reproducers of members of ethnic collectivities;
2 as reproducers of the boundaries of ethnic/national groups;
3 as participating centrally in the ideological reproduction of the collectivity and as transmitters of its culture;

4 as signifiers of ethnic/national differences – as a focus and symbol in ideological discourses used in the construction, reproduction and trans- formation of ethnic/national categories;
5 as participants in national, economic, political and military struggles.

The papers in the collection illustrate these themes excellently. They provide evidence that women and gender relations are indeed used in the ways that the editors suggest. They show that gender is important for ethnic/national practices and that ethnic/national practices are important for gender relations.

The volume shows the significance of demographic factors such as birth rate for some ethnic/national projects, and hence the pressure in historically specific moments, placed, on women to breed or not to breed 'for the good of the nation/"race"'. Klug convincingly illustrates both pressures in her case study of Britain (1989), and de Lepervanche in hers of Australia (1989), where White women have been encouraged to produce more children and Black women not to, and Yuval-Davis shows similar issues in the pro- grammes of both Israeli and Palestinian nationalists. The flexibility of the discourse of motherhood rather than its biological fixity is the theme of Gaitskell and Unterhalter's (1989) comparison of the changes in the idea of motherhood for Afrikaner nationalism and the African National Congress over the course of the twentieth century.

Anthias suggests that women were used as symbols of national identity in the case of Greek-Cypriot nationalism. This theme is continued by Kan- dyoti (1989) writing on the case of Turkey, although she also raises the question of whether women will always be passive symbols rather than actively engaging themselves in 'the woman question'. Here she raises the question of the extent to which one idea of gender is used by nationalism, and the extent to which the woman question has a dynamic which shapes history itself. In Obbo's paper on Uganda (1989), women appear to have their interests as women under attack, not only as a pawn in a nationalist project. This again suggests that it is insufficient to think of nationalism affecting gender in a one-way relationship. Finally, in Afshar's paper (1989), women unequivocally leave the world of symbols and appear fighting for their gendered interests in the context of Islamic revival in Iran.

Thus Anthias and Yuval-Davis' five major roles of women in ethnic/ national processes have empirical support from papers in their book. How- ever, there is a question as to whether these five encompass all the major ways that gender and ethnic/national relations intersect. While they are important, some additions should be made.

First, this categorisation privileges the ideological or cultural level in three out of the five practices; of the other two, one is biological, the other is 'national economic, political and military struggle'. The division of labour is curiously absent from this list, unless it is considered to be subsumed under biology or culture. Is the specificity of the gender division of labour in different ethnic/national groups considered to be relevant to ethnic/national divisions only at the symbolic level? Or is the category 'biological reproducers' meant to carry an analysis of women's labour? This latter is surely difficult, since birthing is only one part of women's labour, albeit a significant one.

A second and related point which is underemphasised in this summary is that conflict, and the maintenance of boundaries, between ethnic/national groups is also a conflict between different forms of social hierarchies, not only different cultures. Even the most cohesive ethnic/national group almost always entails a system of social inequality, and one where the dominant group(s) typically exercise(s) hegemonic control over the 'culture' and political project of the 'collectivity'. It is a sociological orthodoxy that societies typically have a system of social inequality and that the dominant group tries to exercise hegemonic control over the ideas current in that society. Ethnic/national conflicts, then, may be expected to benefit the interests of the members of that grouping differentially. Different genders (and classes) may therefore be differentially enthusiastic about 'the' ostensible ethnic/national project, depending upon the extent to which they agree with the priorities of 'their' political 'leaders'. It may be that there is unanimity on 'the' ethnic/national project by members of both genders and all social classes, but this is unlikely, and it is at least a question to be investigated.

Indeed, Yuval-Davis and Anthias' volume itself contains evidence of the varying commitment of women, and indeed of different groups of women differentiated by class, education, urban/rural residence and so forth, to the ethnic/national project of 'their' community leaders. Some of the strongest papers are about this tension between (highly differentiated) gender groupings and the ethnic/national project, as in the case of Afshar on Iran. Sometimes the gender discourse would shift, as nationalist movements shifted ground (as in the case of Gaitskell and Unterhalter's analysis of the changes in Afrikaner Nationalism and the African National Congress).

While Anthias and Yuval-Davis emphasise the participation of women in the ethnic/national project, albeit in different ways, I have suggested emphasising the question of women's differential involvement. The national project may affect women and men differently (and sub-groups of these) and hence engender different degrees of enthusiasm.

The significance of feminist demands in the shaping of nationalist demands is discussed by Jayawardena (1986). She argues that feminists were active in pushing for the emancipation of women in Third World nationalist movements at the end of the nineteenth and beginning of the twentieth centuries. She shows that there have been important feminist components of nationalist movements in Third World countries in the late nineteenth and early twentieth centuries. She discusses evidence of the interconnections between feminism and nationalism from Egypt, Iran, Afghanistan, India, Sri Lanka, Indonesia, the Philippines, China, Vietnam, Korea and Japan. All these countries had been subject to imperialism, and the feminism that she finds is bound up with anti-imperialist nationalist movements.

Jayawardena discusses the suggestions from Third World writers that feminism is merely Western, decadent, foreign, suitable only for the bourgeoisie, and a diversion from the struggle for national liberation and socialism. She also discusses the parallel view from the West that feminism is a product of Europe and North America, and that if it is to be found elsewhere then it is merely an imitation. Contrary to both these positions Jayawardena argues that feminism has endogenous roots in Third World countries, and that it is not imposed from the West. However, she does not want to deny that the impact of the West was important in creating social changes which indirectly led to feminism:

> Feminism was not imposed on the Third World by the West, but rather... historical circumstances produced important material and ideological changes which affected women, even though the impact of imperialism and Western thought was admittedly among the significant elements in these historical circumstances. Debates on women's rights and education were held in 18th-century China and there were movements for women's social emancipation in early 19th-century India; the other country studies show that feminist struggles originated between 60 and 80 years ago in many countries of Asia.
>
> (1986: 2–3)

Jayawardena wants to argue that feminism should not be reduced to Westernisation, but that this does not mean that Westernisation was not relevant. She goes on to argue that women's emancipation movements were conducted in the context of nationalist struggles:

> [They were] acted out against a backdrop of nationalist struggles aimed at achieving political independence, asserting a national identity, and modernising society.
>
> (1986: 3)

> ...struggles for women's emancipation were an essential and integral part of national resistance movements.
>
> (1986: 8)

> The organisation of women around their own demands was closely inter-related with the nationalist movements. They rarely organised autonomously, but more usually as wings or subsidiaries of male-dominated nationalist groups.
>
> (1986: 259)

In a similar manner Jayawardena argues that the expansion of capitalism was an important factor in the creation of the material circumstances which led to both the movement of women into the public sphere and to feminism, but that it did not simply cause feminism. Rather it created the conditions under which feminist demands were possible.

> The basic reforms that involved the freeing of women from pre-capitalist social constraints of various kinds, giving them freedom of mobility, bringing them out of seclusion and facilitating their work outside the home, were in keeping with strategies of capitalist forms of economic production and capitalist ideology. In many countries, the periods of reform coincided with attempts to develop capitalism and to harness the supply of cheap female labour into factory production and the service sector of the economy.
>
> (1986: 256)

Jayawardena is clear that there are significant class variations in the way that these economic and social changes affected women. It was the women of the bourgeoisie and petty bourgeoisie who benefited most from the development of education and the opening of the professions to women. Hence Jayawardena is arguing not only that feminist and nationalist movements were closely interconnected, but that they cannot be understood outside of an understanding of imperialism and both local and international capitalism.

Although Jayawardena does not make this point, it is interesting to note that many Third World countries granted formal suffrage to women at the same time as men, at the point of national independence. The histories of Third World democratic practices are thus very different from those in the First World, where men's and women's suffrage were typically separated by several decades. Citizenship and nationalism and gender are closely interconnected.

While Jayawardena and Yuval-Davis and Anthias focus on the relationship of woman to nation, Enloe (1989) focuses on the significance of gender for the relations between nations. She examines both the international order and transnational entities, and demonstrates how they cannot be fully understood outside of an analysis of gender relations. Enloe makes her argument by examining the gendered nature of the institutions which make up the international order. Enloe looks at sex and the international tourist trade, arguing that the forms of the development of tourism cannot be understood outside of the various constructions of gender and sexuality which affect practices ranging from package tours for 'the respectable woman', to sex tourism for men (cf. Mitter, 1986; Urry, 1990).

Enloe examines the way the hierarchical relations between nations and the construction of gendered cultural forms mutually affect each other. For instance, images of women in colonised countries were often constructed and purveyed in a manner which simultaneously eroticised and exoticised them while justifying imperial domination in the name of 'civilisation'. 'Oriental' women 'needed' male European 'protection':

> European 'Orientalism' nurtured an appreciative fascination with these cultures while justifying European rule in the name of 'civilization'. The image of the tantalizingly veiled Muslim woman was a cornerstone of this Orientalist ideology and of the imperial structure it supported.
>
> (1989: 44)

Enloe is arguing that support for a particular kind of gender relations was used as a justification for colonial domination. The notion of 'civilisation' was saturated with ideas about correct gender relations and forms of sexual relations:

> Ladylike behaviour was a mainstay of imperialist civilization. Like sanitation and Christianity, feminine respectability was meant to convince both the colonizing and the colonized peoples that foreign conquest was right and necessary.
>
> (1989: 48)

Not only was femininity an imperial issue, so also was masculinity. Enloe suggests that British leaders were concerned to ensure appropriate forms of masculinity to sustain the Empire. In particular she suggests that the Crimean and Boer Wars led to initiatives to 'improve' the forms of masculinity. The founding of the Boy Scouts in 1908 by Robert Baden-Powell was to counter the spread of venereal disease, intermarriage of the races and falling birth rates which were allegedly leading to the decline of the British Empire: 'Baden-Powell and other British imperialists saw sportsmanship combined with respect for the respectable woman as the bedrock of British imperial success' (Enloe, 1989: 50).

Enloe shows that nationalist movements have often grown out of men's rather than women's experiences: 'nationalism has typically sprung from masculinized memory, masculinized humiliation and masculinized hope' (p. 44) She suggests that nationalisms would be different if women's experiences were foregrounded in the building of this culture and project. She goes on to suggest that if this were to happen, then the nature of the relations between states, and the international order itself, might be different:

> If more nation states grew out of feminist nationalists' ideas and experiences, community identities within the international political system might be tempered by cross-national identities.
>
> (1989: 64)

Enloe discusses the international division of labour in which women's labour in the Third World is constructed as cheap. She examines the various

patriarchal practices which make women's labour 'cheap', such as maintenance of 'family' relations and the suppression of women's unions. The
international significance is demonstrated by an examination of the uses
to which this labour is put by transnational corporations. National boundaries are becoming less significant for multi-national capital and hence for
women as workers.

Enloe's argument about the significance of gender to issues of nation and
the international is often conducted through an analysis of sexuality. This is
the case when she discusses the international tourist industry, Hollywood
cinema, the role of women on military bases who work as prostitutes, and
the women who are wives of diplomats. This is not always the case,
however, as in Enloe's discussion of women who work in the world fac-
tories of Asia and as domestic servants. Her conclusion is that the personal
is not only political, but also international. The personal and gender is
everywhere, even in the international order.

Enloe's argument that gender is pertinent to nations and to the international order is convincing at both a theoretical and empirical level. She
is able to show how the building blocks of the international order are
gendered, and how this affects international relations. Implicit in her
analysis are theories of both the international order and of gender. In
her account Enloe appears to privilege the sexual and cultural levels,
with the sexual division of labour taking a lower level significance. In so
far as Enloe includes all paid work, housework, sexuality, culture, violence
and the state in her analysis of women and the international order, I am
in agreement with her. I hesitate at the apparent privileging of the sexual
and cultural levels rather than the economic. A fuller account might also
have discussed the gender structuring of the international institutions themselves. These were curiously absent, apart from occasional reference to
the IMF.

TO WHAT EXTENT DO WOMEN SHARE THE SAME NATIONAL PROJECT AS MEN?

In the second half of this chapter I shall discuss the extent to which women
share in the same group identity as men, and in particular the same national
project. By national project I mean a range of collective strategies oriented
towards the perceived needs of a nation which include nationalism, but
may include others. I shall argue that there are often differences between
men and women on these issues and I shall suggest some reasons for this. I
shall discuss the reasons why women and men have different identifications
with national projects and may have different commitments to different
types of macro-level groupings. This will be approached in three stages.
First, via a discussion of the extent to which and conditions under
which national projects are simultaneously gender projects. Second, via a

discussion of the interconnections and distinctions between nationalism, militarism and gender. Third, via a discussion of whether gender relations share the same spatial ordering as class and ethnic relations, and whether women and men have commitments to social phenomena which have different spatial scales. This last will be discussed with the assistance of two examples: gender, the nation and the EU; feminism, nationalism and Westernisation.

Nationalism and women

Are women as committed to nationalist/ethnic/'racial' projects as men? Is their project the same one as men's? Do women's nationalist/ethnic/'racial' and other large-scale social projects have the same, or more global, or more local boundaries than those of men?

Anthias and Yuval-Davis (1989) are concerned with the way in which women are part of the national project, especially the way women are differently but equally engaged in this project: sometimes voluntarily, – perhaps eagerly involved in the struggle (role number 5 – see discussion of Anthias and Yuval-Davis, pp. 181–3 above); sometimes coerced, as sometimes happens when they are considered to be the breeders of the 'race' (role number 1); most often in a day-to-day way, as reproducers of the culture via socialisation of children (numbers 2/3); sometimes passively, as symbols (number 4). It appears that Anthias and Yuval-Davis argue that women are just as committed to the national/ethnic project as men, but they sometimes express their commitment in different ways.

I have queried this. Sometimes women may support a *different* national project from that of men. There is a struggle to define what constitutes *the* national project, and women are, typically, heard less in this than men. Thus gender relations are important in determining what is constituted as *the* national project. Where the national project includes women's interests then women are more likely to support it. Jayawardena's work on feminism and nationalism in Third World in the early twentieth century shows how integrated these projects can be, though only as a result of women's struggles.

Is there reciprocal impact between gender and ethnicity/nation/'race'? While Yuval-Davis and Anthias have clearly shown the impact of nation on gender, I think there is a mutual influence (see the discussion below of militarism and nationalism, pp. 190–2). Further, women's differential commitment to the ethnic/national project affects the project itself, and its relationships with other ethnic/national groups.

The question of *whose* national project has already been discussed in relation to the work of Enloe (1989). In the example which follows I am arguing for a recasting of the theorisation of 'nation-formation' in order to take this point into account.

Critical period of state formation or rounds of restructuring?

One of the assumptions behind the work of Mann (1987) and of Turner (1990) is that there is a critical period of nation-formation (or state formation or nation state formation). This is key to Mann's discussion of the societal variations in the development of what he considers to be the key political institutions which constitute democracy. It is also a key assumption in Turner's discussion of the moments of formation of different forms of citizenship.

I am arguing that there is often no one key period of nation-formation. In many countries citizenship did not arrive at one moment for all people, but different groups gained different aspects of this in different periods; that countries vary as to whether White men, White women, men and women of minority ethnic groups, gained citizenship at the same time or not. Mann and Turner falsely universalise from White men's citizenship experiences. As Smith (1986) has shown, there is a very long period of formation of the ethnic groups which go to make up a nation.

Turner seems to suggest that in the US citizenship and democracy were won in the 1840s, when White men won suffrage. Yet Black men did not get the vote technically until the 1880s, and in practice, given the Jim Crow laws, not until after the Civil Rights movement at the end of the 1960s. White women did not get the vote until 1920 and Black women, while technically getting the vote in 1920, in practice had to wait until further rounds of struggle brought them the franchise at the end of the 1960s together with Black men. The history of the citizenship rights of the native American Indians, of course, is one of loss of citizenship after conquest. Thus there are five significant dates: the conquest period, the 1840s, the 1880s, 1920 and the late 1960s, each with an associated period of social struggle. Do we have several stages in nation building? It remains true of course that the formal institutional structure that constitutes the apparatus of democracy in the US was set up in the second wave of struggle, but these empty institutions do not a democracy make.

In most First World countries there is a period of several decades between the granting of political citizenship to men and to women. This is quite different from the circumstances in many Third World countries where women won the franchise at the same time as men at the moment of national independence from colonial power. The winning of civil citizenship, while completed for most First World men before political citizenship, is barely completed for women in these countries, since only recently have women won control over their own bodies, the ability to disengage from marriage and the right to engage in all forms of employment. That is, for First World women political citizenship is typically achieved before civil citizenship – the reverse of the order for men. This in direct contradiction of Marshall's thesis (see pp. 166–8 above).

Rather than this notion of one critical period of 'nation-formation', it is more appropriate to talk of 'rounds of restructuring' of the nation state. I borrow the term from Massey's (1984) work on economic restructuring. It is useful in carrying the notion of change built upon foundations which remain, and that layer upon layer of change can take place, each of which leaves its sediment which significantly affects future practices.

It matters whether the 'citizenisation' of society involves all adults at once or only a fragment of them at a time. In the US the gap ranges over well over a hundred years from 1840 to the late 1960s. In Britain the gap was shorter – a few decades separated adult men's suffrage from that of all women in 1928. In many newly independent African and Asian societies suffrage for both sexes was granted simultaneously at the time of independence in the 1950s and 1960s. It is perhaps salutary to remember that in the early 1960s some African and Asian states had full universal suffrage while that in the US was only partial. Indeed the granting of full citizenship to all was one of the ways in which previously dominated colonies could make a claim to nationhood.

The restructuring of states in terms of degrees of democracy has some interesting global patterns. Most European and North American states granted citizenship by degree to different layers of the population between the eighteenth and mid-twentieth centuries. Most post-colonial states granted full citizenship at once in the mid-twentieth century. Some countries have lost democracy. This usually occurs all in one go, as when there is a military coup in which all people simultaneously lose the right to vote. However, since 1979 there has been a serious exception to this situation, with the loss of civil and political rights to women alone, with the rise of Islamic fundamentalism where the Islamic priesthood has taken power (e.g. in Iran).

Women, militarism and nationalism

The relations between gender and nationalism may be mediated through the differential relations of women and men to militarism. The most famous linking of these themes is by Virginia Woolf in *The Three Guineas*, where a female pacifist says:

> As a woman I have no country. As a woman I want no country. As a woman my country is the whole world.
>
> (Woolf, 1938: 109)

Women are frequently, though by no means universally, thought to be more pacifist and less militaristic than men (see Cudworth, 1988; Oldfield, 1989). Some writers have argued that women's greater pacifism is a result of a specific aspect of gender ideology (see Ruddick, 1989). Whether or not this is the explanation, empirically the fact remains that there is a difference in the extent to which men and women take up arms for nationalist projects, support peace movements and support politicians who favour military build up (Campbell, 1987; Cudworth, 1988; Eisenstein, 1984; Enloe, 1983). The issue here is whether there is a connection between this lesser militarism and support for nationalism. Does women's greater non-violence have an effect upon their view of the 'national' project, in that they are less prepared to pursue nationalist goals by force than men? Does this then make them appear less nationalistic, in that they are less prepared to use a particular means of pursuing that goal, and does this mean that they are actually less nationalistic? That is, is women's lesser militarism a cause of lesser nationalism? Or does it mean that women support a different nationalism? Or that women are greater supporters of transnational projects?

A leading example which suggests a link between women's non-violence and greater internationalism is that of the women's peace camp at Greenham Common in the 1980s, which was part of a loose international grouping of women's peace camps opposed to nuclear weapons, war and the social systems which breed militarism. Women's peace initiatives here may be seen to affect the nature of the national project. Another contemporary example of a group which links anti-militarism with internationalism is that of the Green movement. This is a political grouping, finding expression in both parliamentary and other political arenas, which is committed to ecologically sound policies and which includes a feminist programme as an integral part of their politics. They are seriously internationalist in outlook, finding voice in both the Third World (see Shiva, 1989) and the first – the Green Party fought EU elections as a European party to a greater extent than any other political grouping. Here, ecological politics, feminism and internationalism converge into a unitary political programme. Further evidence of the link between women and pacifism is to be found in opinion polls which regularly show, at least in Britain and the US, that women are less likely to support militaristic defences of the nation (see Eisenstein, 1984).

Another possibility is that the link between nationalism and militarism works the other way around. Here women's greater commitment to peace and opposition to militarism might be thought to be linked to their lesser commitment to 'their' nation. Do women more often think that war for nationalist reasons is not worth the candle because they have less real interest in a 'victorious' outcome, since it would make less difference to their place in society than to men? While some men will move from being the rulers to being subordinate, this is likely to be true of almost no women. Conversely, is the gap between women and men's militarism less marked in societies where women have a greater stake as a result of less gender inequality?

There are a number of ways in which gender and nationalism are mediated by women's typically lesser support for militarism. We see here women's greater commitment to international peace and co-operation than to militaristic nationalism. The Green slogan of 'think globally, act locally' is very close to typical feminist and women's practice.

Boundaries for gender relations

Women's political activity can thus be on a different spatial scale to that of men. I am suggesting that women's political activities are typically more local than those of men, and less nationalist. In order to discuss this issue further I shall explore the differential significance of a number of large-scale political entities for women and men.

Women are less often than men to be found in formal electoral politics. Women are more likely to be found in the elected assemblies of local rather than national government. In Britain women constituted 6.6 per cent of Members of the House of Commons after the 1987 election, and still less than 10 per cent after that in 1992, while they formed 19 per cent of local councillors after the 1985 elections. Indeed it is popularly believed that women do not engage in large-scale national organisations. However, there are such women's organisations. There are mass, national, women's organisations, for example Women's Institutes, Town's Women's Guilds, Mothers' Union. So the argument about the different spatial scales of men's and women's political organisations should not be exaggerated. It is, nevertheless, often thought that women are more active on a smaller territorial scale than men.

I have been using a variety of concepts and categories to differentiate between different social patterns and groups – the notions of ethnic group, 'race' and nation. There are also a number of others – religion, empire, common language. These have been largely used to differentiate between groups of men. The question in relation to gender is then logically – are the concepts which denote difference between men the same as the concepts which usefully denote difference between women? Are men and women divided up in identical or different ways? Are women as attached and defensive of 'their' ethnic, or other, group as men?

There are a number of possible answers to this. First, if it is held that men and women have identical interests, then there would be little possibility of separation. However, this is a largely discredited idea. Men and women do occupy different social positions and thus do have different interests. But do these differences make for differences at the level of ethnicity/nation/ 'race'? Second, if women suffer from ethnic domination or benefit from ethnic dominance to the same extent as men, then they may have similar ethnicity/nation/'race' interests. Third, different ethnicity/nation/'race's have different patterns of gender relations, some of which may be seen as preferable to others. This is likely to give rise to different gender opinions as to the merits of a given ethnicity/nation/'race' project. This is still dependent upon the same ethnicity/nation/'race' boundaries as those experienced by men, but may entail differential evaluation of the ethnicity/nation/'race' projects by men and women (or, more likely, some men and some women). Fourth, given that ethnicity, nation, 'race', religion, language and other signifiers of boundaries between social groups often overlap, but are not usually coterminous, then there is the possibility that some of these boundaries may have more salience for women and some for men. One example of this is that a religious signifier might be more important to women than a 'national' signifier, but not for men, so that if those two systems were in conflict, men and women may diverge. Issues of militarism and nationalism may be affected here. Fifth, different gendered discourses may hold a greater or lesser commitment to large or small groups. (Gilligan (1982) has suggested that women have different criteria of moral evaluation.)

Women, nation and Europe

The shifting relations between a state, the UK, and a supra-national body, the European Union (EU), illustrates the issue of different bounded units having varying gender relations. It also demonstrates the importance of not considering a state to have only one critical period of formation, as was argued above. Gender, ethnicity and class have different relationships to the 'nation', the state and to supra-national state-like institutions. This is because the determinants of gender, class and ethnicity are different. Hence the nation state has a different place in their construction.

An example of this can be seen in the development of the EU. The central EU institutions have long supported the practice of 'equal opportunities' (see Gregory, 1987; Hoskins, 1985). This was formally built into the EU in the Treaty of Rome, which operates effectively as a constitution for the supra-national EU. These formal rules have been brought into effective operation partly by the actions of some of the officials of the EU. It is also obviously the case that it is not in the interests of those countries which have institutionalised equal opportunities practices to allow others to continue to use subordinated female labour which could undercut their industries. Recalcitrant nation states have been brought into line by the use of rulings from the European Court and Directives from the EU Commission, with consequent changes to national legislation.

The UK state has not passively accepted these changes but has a long and complicated history of resistance interleaved with compliance. For instance, the UK Government's representatives on the EU bodies have typically resisted the expansion of equal opportunities policies. They have used their right of veto to prevent the EU extending equal opportunities policies to parental leave, and part-time workers. Hence the UK Government's preferred policies on gender have affected the workings of the EU.

Nevertheless, many policies have been imposed on a reluctant UK government. One of the most important was the 'equal value' amendment to the equal pay legislation. This significantly widened the ways in which a woman could claim equal pay. No longer did she have to find a man doing the 'same or similar' work, which was very difficult given the extent of occupational segregation. Now she could claim equal pay with a man whose work was of the same value as hers (usually to be determined by some method of job evaluation). In the US in those places where such policies have been introduced it has often led to 20 per cent increases in women's pay. Tens of thousands of these cases are currently wending their way through the British industrial courts.

Here we see a supra-national body challenging and changing the gender relations of a nation state. There are two key elements in the explanation of this. First, the differential representation of women's interests at the level of the supra-national body, the EU, as compared to the national, such as the British state. Second, the relations between the EU and the British state.

Gender relations in Britain today cannot be fully understood outside of an analysis of the relations between the British state and the EU, that is, issues of 'nation' and 'state' are significant determinants of the changes in contemporary British gender relations. The greater the loss of the independence of the British state *vis-à-vis* the EU, the greater has been, and is likely to be, the strengthening of equal opportunities legislation and practices. Women have an interest in the loss of British sovereignty on this issue.

Feminism, nationalism and Westernisation

Another example of a transnational category which is of relevance to gender relations is that of 'Westernisation'. The issue of whether there is a link between feminism and Westernisation is important for issues of political mobilisation around nationalist projects, and around both feminist and anti-feminist ones (see Jayawardena, 1986). Is feminism transnational or is it nationally or ethnically specific?

Third World critics of feminism have often suggested first, that it is Western in origin, and second, that this renders it less relevant than if it were nationally endogenous. There are really two further questions here. Is feminism a transnational political movement? Is it Western in origin? It is the case that the kinds of demands which are called for by feminists are not nationally specific. It is also the case that feminists have typically read the work of feminists in other countries. But it is also the case that much feminist writing originated in the West: this is not to say that feminism is not generated by local conditions however. Indeed Jayawardena (1986) argues strongly that feminist movements in the Third World have been generated by Third World women in their own interests, as was discussed above. Evans (1977) shows that the first-wave of feminism was not only

194

found in many European countries including Russia, and also in Australasia and North America, but that there were international feminist organisations as well.

The question is, of course, whether women share similar forms of subordination in different countries. If they do, then it is likely that women in many countries will articulate similar demands. It is then logical that literature written and tactics generated in one country will be pertinent in another. That is, there are internationally valid forms of feminism. The evidence from writers such as Jayawardena and Evans is that feminists across the world have believed that there are such commonalities. That is, feminism and patterns of gender relations have significant transnational aspects.

However, the significance of the 'accusation' that feminism and the movement of women into the public sphere are Western phenomena should not be underestimated. In this case whether it is true or not does not necessarily diminish the significance of this assertion in the context of national struggles. Whether or not male elites have the ability to characterise women's public presence as Western is often a matter of local struggle. Further, the meaning of 'Western' is variable. Sometimes the epithet 'Western' has been conflated with that of 'modern' (as in the case of Turkey under Ataturk, and Iran under the Shah), in which case it has assisted the implementation of policies likely to increase the public presence of women. On other occasions the epithet 'Western' is conflated with that of 'hated alien and imperialist oppressor', in which case it has assisted policies likely to hinder the presence of women in public (e.g. Iran under Khomeini). Thus the conflation of feminism or the public presence of women with 'Westernisation' may assist or hinder such a change, depending on other circumstances. An analysis of which circumstances lead in which direction needs not only an analysis of gender, but also of ethnicity/nation/'race' and the international order.

CONCLUSIONS

Gender relations in the UK are subject to more than one polity, both the UK state and the European Union; are subject to global as well as national pressures; and involve several ethnic and religious communities and identities. There is not a simple unit of analysis, rather complexity deriving from multiple power sources some of which are in competition with each other.

Gender cannot be analysed outside of ethnic, national and 'race' relations; but neither can these latter phenomena be analysed without gender. It is not a case of simply adding these two sets of analyses together, but rather that they mutually affect each other in a dynamic relationship.

Patterns of gender relations sometimes take the same spatial units as those of class and ethnicity, nation and 'race', but often they do not. It appears, from the available evidence, as if women's political activities have tended to be both more global and more local than men's (as a proportion of their total political activity). However, this conclusion must remain tentative in the light of the limited evidence. Women have less often than men engaged at the level of the nation. Commonalities in the nature of gender relations sometimes transcend national frontiers and ethnic and 'racial' specificity. At the same time, the 'personal' is as political as ever.

The relationship between feminism and nationalism is crucially mediated by militarism, since men and women often, but not always, have a different relationship to war. This may mean that women are simultaneously both less militaristic and less nationalistic because militarism is often seen as an integral facet of a national project.

A national or ethnic project will have been struggled over by social forces differentiated in many ways, especially by class and gender. Thus relations between nations are partly the outcome of many locally specific gendered struggles.

The struggle for citizenship is today a democratic project. In popular political discourse it entails the full participation of all adults regardless of 'race', ethnicity, sex, or creed. It is also a national project and indeed a project by which the 'nation' seeks to obtain legitimacy as a project in the eyes of both that country's inhabitants and the 'international community'. Social scientists should pay regard to the new meaning of the term citizen, rather than the limited notion utilised in ancient Greek city-states from which women, slaves and 'aliens' were excluded.

These struggles for democratisation in which women are engaging, if unevenly, are important for the understanding of changes in gender relations. Political citizenship, as was argued in previous chapters, has been important in securing changes in the nature of the gender regime. The polities within which these struggles take place are more than just the nation state, involving a supra-state as well as organised ethnic and religious communities.

11

GENDER AND EUROPEAN UNION INTEGRATION: TOWARDS A POLITICAL ECONOMY OF GENDER

INTRODUCTION

Contemporary gender relations in the UK cannot be understood without recognising the impact of the European Union, a gendered supra-state. The increasing integration of the European Union is changing the nature of gender relations in the UK, especially in employment. Much current labour market regulation, especially that concerning gender relations, is dependent upon the Treaties and Directives of the European Union. Some of these legal changes have already had significant impacts on gender relations in employment already, as was shown in Chapter 2. The further planned integration of the European Union will have increasing effects on gender relations in Member States, primarily as a result of its regulation of labour markets and other economic matters.

The gender project of the European Commission is significantly different from that of several of its Member States. While there are divisions within the European Union institutions and politicians over the nature of is gender project – for instance the European Parliament sought a stronger Social Charter than the Council of Ministers – nonetheless, there is a general tendency within the institutions of the European Union, led by DGV in the European Commission, to promote a more public rather than domestic gender regime, in particular by encouraging the equal participation of women with men in employment and related arenas. Member States of the European Union vary significantly in their gender regimes, with a wide spectrum between more public and more domestic forms. These involve different types of household structures, levels of integration of women in employment, patterns of political representation of women, religious institutions, and other aspects of social relations. The integration of the European Union especially through the development of the Single European Market and its policies for social cohesion have varying effects upon the different social constituencies in Europe. In particular, the policies represented in the Maastricht Treaty have different implications for women in countries with different levels of social protection and labour market regulation, for example, tending to raise the level of protection and regulation in the UK (despite the UK opt out from the Social Chapter) and that of many Southern European countries, though not sufficiently so as to converge with those in Scandinavian countries, such as Denmark and Sweden.

Traditionally, it has been supposed that women's interests have been more successfully articulated at a local rather than national political level, as a consequence of the limitations on the types of political process in which women are able to engage because of women's position within the domestic domain, as discussed in Chapter 7. Yet it appears that an equal rights type of representation of women's interests is being articulated more successfully at the level of the emerging supra-state of the EU than at the level of some constituent Member States, in particular that of the UK. That is, there are overlapping and divergent spatially specific political bodies which embody and articulate gendered interests.

This concluding chapter will examine the actual and potential impact of the changing structure of the national and the EU supra-state on gendered employment practices, as well as the refocusing of social theory which is necessary to understand contemporary gender relations in such a European context. It will examine the extent to which increasing EU integration might affect participation rates of women in paid employment, the size of the wages gap between women and men, the security of women's labour contracts and the conditions of employment. It will consider whether the political pressures for equal opportunities represented in the Social Chapter of the Maastricht Treaty and Article 119 of the Treaty of Rome are likely to be fully realised. It will argue for the importance of the polity if we are to understand contemporary economic and gender relations.

There are two major economic and social policy dimensions to increasing EU integration: first, the policy promoting competitiveness and deregulation which is represented in the creation of the Single European Market (Cecchini *et al.*, 1988) and the White Paper on 'Growth, Competitiveness and Employment' (European Commission, 1993); and second, the social policy oriented to promoting social cohesion and social integration represented in the Social Charter, the Social Chapter of the Maastricht Treaty, Article 119 of the Treaty of Rome, and the 1994 White Paper on Social Policy (The Community Charter of the Fundamental Social Rights of Workers, 1990; European Commission, 1994a). There is a tension between these two policy dimensions even though they were originally conceived as each necessary for the sustainability of the other. The social policies have been especially important in providing a platform for equity and justice for women workers. However, there is a question as to whether such positive social and equal opportunities policy changes for women are being undermined by the policy for increasing competitiveness by deregulation.

EUROPEAN UNION INTEGRATION

The development of a Single European Market from 1992 was considered by some industrialists, academics and politicians as essential if Western European economies were to meet the increased global competition from the US and Japan which had larger internal markets from which to develop firms to sell into an increasingly global market. But the more historic impetus behind the creation of the Common Market was at least as much political as economic – that of preventing further wars within Europe, especially between Germany and France. The social policies were considered essential to providing equity alongside efficiency by the socialist contributors to this project, notably Jacques Delors (Ziltener and Bornschier, 1995). The policy to increase the competitiveness of the West European economy in a global context was recognised to have negative implications for some workers, especially those in declining industries and regions who could suffer social exclusion as a consequence of their subsequent unemployment. The social policies were designed to counter the growth of social exclusion, especially that around unemployment, and to promote the social cohesion seen as essential for a stable, civilised and productive society.

The relative significance of these two dimensions in the current institutional development of the European Union is subject to debate. Streeck and Schmitter (1992) argue that the current round of increased European integration is bound up with a project of deregulation, and with the interests of international finance capital. The Single European Market is seen as a policy designed to remove barriers to the free movement of goods, services and people. For instance, the recently decided practice of mutual recognition of qualifications effectively amounts to deregulation of professional qualifications. Streeck and Schmitter argue that employers have resisted the building of European level organisations capable of engaging in binding agreements, and that they seek European integration in order to remove or by-pass the controls on employers set up in a number of European states at national level. They suggest that the attempts to build a European level corporatism had their hey-day in the 1970s and are now defeated. For instance the attempt to impose German patterns of codetermination in the 1970s failed. The attempt by the European Trade Union Committee (ETUC) to obtain binding agreements failed, winning instead only consultation. For Streeck and Schmitter integration is deregulation. Ziltener and Bornschier (1995) however, argue that the social dimension has always been a central part of the project of the European Union, even though the establishment of this social policy has been less full than intended. They argue that the social dimension is a cornerstone of the project of the European Union, not merely a flanking exercise. They suggest that Jagues Delors played a central role, and sought to implement the ideals he brought from his French socialist background. Their argument rests particularly on the importance of the political entrepreneurship of Delors and other post-war socialists at least as much as on structural and economic arguments.

The nature of the economic and social policies of the European Union are crucial for the regulation of gender relations in Member States, though this is given little attention by the aforementioned writers. These economic strategies are highly gendered, even though they are usually articulated in gender-free language. There are several ways in which these policies and their implications are gendered, including: the differential impact on sex-segregated industries; the differential impact on highly qualified as compared with vulnerable workers (in practice a gendered divide); and their impact on welfare regimes which typically disproportionately support women.

DEREGULATION, COMPETITIVENESS AND THE SINGLE EUROPEAN MARKET

The Single European Market leads to disparate increases and decreases in employment levels in different industrial sectors. Since women's employment is highly segregated (see Chapter 5; Crompton and Sanderson, 1990; Hakim, 1979; *Social Europe* 1993; Walby, 1988), this differential impact on industrial sectors has divergent effects on men's and women's employment. This disparate impact across the European Union has been shown in the case of banking (Jortray, Meulders and Plasman, 1991) as compared with textiles (Meulders and Plasman, 1990; Rubery, Humphries and Howell, 1992). If women are concentrated in sectors which are likely to face significant rationalisation – that is overall reductions in employment in order to secure efficiency gains – then women bear disproportionate employment losses, while if they are in expanding sectors female employment is likely to grow disproportionately. There is a further question as to whether the gender composition of different sectors itself is affected by these changes.

The development of Single Market policies focused around deregulation on a European level has disadvantageous consequences for workers who are more marginal or more vulnerable, if the rate and mode of economic growth does not compensate. Women are much more likely than men to be in atypical forms of employment such as working part-time rather than full-time hours, working as family aides, or on temporary contracts (Dahrendorf, Kohler and Piotet, 1986; Drew, 1992; Emerek, 1994; *Labour Force Survey*, 1994).

The impact of European integration on gender rates of employment depends upon which macro-economic policy is dominant. Lindley (1992) distinguishes between an efficiency scenario as a result of vigorous product market competition and the promotion of labour market flexibility; a cost-cutting scenario, resulting from fierce price competition; and a quality scenario, in which a high-value-added/high-skill European economy is the result of the increasing integration (Lindley, 1992: 12). Lindley, amongst others, sugests there will be different outcomes in different sectors of the economy, including cost-cutting in textiles and clothing (Rubery, Humphries and Howell, 1992), and a potential quality scenario in tourism and leisure (Parsons, 1992).

While it is important to distinguish between the different macro-economic regimes, there is a question as to whether Lindley has sufficiently differentiated the impact of the Single European Market and its associated policies for deregulation from those policies for social cohesion. While Lindley usually states that he is assessing the impact of the Single European Market only, he is ambiguous as to the extent to which he takes into account the impact of the social policies as represented in the Social Chapter. Sometimes these are noted and are integrated as contributing to the 'quality' rather than the 'cost-cutting' or 'efficiency' scenarios. Sometimes they are considered to be exogenous to the process at hand. Sometimes they are dismissed as unlikely to have much impact on equity between the sexes. Yet the degree to which the Social Charter and Article 119 are implemented could make an important difference to the relations between the sexes both outside and inside of employment. In short, Lindley has produced excellent accounts of the likely impact of the Single European Market alone, but not of the Single European Market and the Social Charter combined.

SOCIAL COHESION AND EUROPEAN UNION SOCIAL POLICY

EU social policy is a further major source of change. Such policies include not only those related to the equal treatment of women and men as laid down in Article 119 of the Treaty of Rome, but also a more broadly defined social policy, as developed in the Social Charter, the Social Chapter of the Maastricht Treaty, and described in the White Paper on European Social Policy (The Community Charter of the Fundamental Social Rights of Workers, 1990; European Commission 1994a, b and c). These two policy areas, of equal opportunities and social policy are closely interconnected. For instance, many of the forms of labour market regulation are particularly beneficial to women workers, since they are typically in more vulnerable positions than male workers and have less collective bargaining power to acquire good conditions of employment.

The equal opportunities policy obtains its authority from the Treaty of Rome, the founding Treaty of the EU, and in some ways the EU's *de facto* constitution, where Article 119 lays down that there shall be equal treatment of men and women in employment-related matters. This has underpinned a comprehensive advocacy of equal opportunities policies within the EU institutions (European Commission, 1990, 1994b, 1994d; European Parliament, 1994a, 1994b). This has included the European Court of Justice decision in the early 1980s that the legislation of the UK and some other EU countries needed to be strengthened so as to provide for equal pay for work of equal value, not merely like work, which led to the Conservative Government in the UK passing the Equal Value Amendment in 1984, and also Directives and Recommendations from the EU Commission and Council of Ministers (see Gregory, 1987). Even though the UK Government rejected the Social Chapter at Maastricht it remains bound by Article 119.

The treatment of part-time workers provides an example of the impact of Article 119. The UK Government resisted attempts to give part-time workers full-time rights, but in 1995, as a result of a ruling in the House of Lords, it was obliged to bow to the superior law of the European Union, and reverse its policies and laws. This was because it was determined that part-time workers should be given the same rights as full-time workers, on the grounds that to treat part-time workers, who are almost entirely female, differently from full-time workers constituted unlawful indirect sex discrimination under Article 119. As was seen in Chapter 2 on employment and Chapter 3 on flexibility this division between part-time and full-time work for women in the UK has been a very important division in the UK labour market, entailing a combination of low wages and fewer fringe benefits for women in this effectively female segment of the labour market. That such poor conditions are not the inevitable lot of part-time workers is shown by research in the Nordic countries (Natti, 1993) which demonstrates that part-time work can sometimes be a bridge rather than a trap for women, if part-timers are employed under the same rather than worse conditions than full-timers. Indeed Natti argues that in Sweden and Norway part-time work has become normalised and gaps in the rate of unionisation and in continuity of jobs have narrowed. In 1994 the UK Government lost a case in the House of Lords in which European law was used to declare illegal some of the distinctions in conditions of employment which led to fewer benefits to part-time workers (as described in more detail in Chapter 2). Part-time workers must in future receive most of the same rights as full-time workers, since to do otherwise is to treat a largely female group worse than a more male group.

A related dimension of concern in EU social policy is that of the 'reconciliation of working and family life' (Drew, Emerek and Mahon, 1995). This extends the remit of the EU, which was initially considered to extend only to matters more narrowly related to the economy, to the highly gendered issue of the relationship of the domestic and employment. An example of such policy development is the creation of EU policy on parental leave, which provided a floor under the provision of maternity leave throughout the EU, although the attempt by the European Commission to do likewise for paternal leave was limited by the UK 'opt-out'.

It is in this area of gendered social policy that the suggestion has been raised, initially by Nordic analysts, but by many French in autumn 1995, that EU convergence may not mean harmonisation at the highest level of provision, but rather at the lowest common one, as a result of the EU monetary and fiscal regime. It has been argued that the intended common EU fiscal regime, with its restrictions on taxation such as VAT, will prevent the collection of sufficient revenue to finance such welfare expenditures (Borchorst, 1992; Dahlerup, 1992; Melby, 1992). In France, fear that the drive for a Single European Currency was leading to such a conservative fiscal regime that expenditures on welfare were being cut, led to widespread social and political unrest, especially among some trade unions in the autumn of 1995. However, whether monetarist and conservative financial policies are caused by the European Union, or are the agenda of specific national politicians is unclear, though it is the case that the conditions laid down for monetary union have been used by national politicians as a rationale to curtail welfare expenditures. Since women are disproportionate recipients of such expenditures this matter is a gender issue.

The full and effective implementation in the UK of the Social Charter and the policy thrust that it represents would probably lead to significant changes in gender relations in the labour market. However, there is both political and procedural resistance to full harmonisation of European social policy both from countries who think that the Social Charter went too far and those who think it did not go far enough. The UK Conservative Government did not accept the Social Chapter of the Maastricht Treaty on the grounds that it was too interventionist. The first Danish referendum on Maastricht in 1992 further slowed this down this momentum for change, since some Danes, especially women, were concerned that closer EU integration might undermine their higher level of social provision (Borchorst, 1992; Dahlerup, 1992). This was followed by further uncertainty caused by turbulence in the financial markets resulting from speculation against the devaluation of currencies during the autumn of 1992. Further, in France in autumn 1995 there was resistance to cuts in provision which were introduced ostensibly in order to achieve EU policy goals.

Procedural, rather than directly political, resistance is found within the complex and slowly changing legal structures within the EU. There is a significant distance between the passing of a clause of a Treaty and its having direct impact on the resolution of conflicts at individual level. Fitzpatrick (1992) describes the hierarchy of Community law as one in which the top layer is the Treaty of Rome (where Article 119 ensures the basis for claims for equal treatment of men and women in employment, recently added to by the Treaty of Maastricht), followed by the legally binding Directives, and then by Recommendations. The mechanisms by which the ostensibly binding Treaty articles and the Directives are given effect are four-fold. First, there is the direct enforcement of the Treaty against recalcitrant Members States by the EU Commission. Second, there is the legal principle of direct effect whereby there is direct enforcement of the Treaty Articles in national courts, but to achieve this the provision must be clear and unambiguous. Third, there is the legal principle of indirect effect, whereby national courts are expected to interpret national legislation in a manner that it is consistent with the EU Treaty. Fourth, there is state liability, whereby a state may be sued if it has failed to pass the necessary legislation and procedures through which legal remedy could be sought on matters pertaining to the EU Treaty (Fitzpatrick, 1992). There are many contested cases currently in the courts relating to these provisions. The success of the mechanisms remains an open question. On the one hand several Member States were sued by the EU Commission over their narrow definition of equal pay, and forced to introduce domestic legislation which widened this to equal pay for work of equal value, not only like work. On the other, there appear to be significant discrepancies between countries in the extent to which equal opportunities laws are enforced (European Commission, 1994b).

There is a question as to why such equal opportunities policies have such a strong legal foundation within the EU and why the 1950s produced such a potent equal opportunities article in an international treaty. The 1950s, when the Treaty of Rome was being drawn up was not renowned as a high-point of feminism. Yet Article 119 is of enormous importance for policies on gender and employment. This should be seen as the working through of the implications of women winning political citizenship in much of Western Europe during the early decades of the twentieth century, and the continuing pressure of women in the labour movement. It is part of the overall shift from a domestic to a public gender regime, one aspect of which was for women to be welcomed into paid work, but at lower rates of pay and segregated from men.

The development of the social policy dimension of the European Union is of enormous potential significance to gender relations in employment and hence in the wider society. Potentially, the political level may provide women with more rights and opportunities than they are able to achieve simply as a result of their labour market position.

THEORETICAL DEVELOPMENT

Four major changes in the theorisation of gender relations in employment need to occur in order to understand current changes resulting from the impact on the UK of increasing European integration. First, there needs to be a recognition of the crucial significance of the gendered polity for the gendered labour market. Second, an understanding of the diversities of women's lives – originating in different gender regimes as well as in different ethnicities, classes and other social divisions – is necessary before divergent strategies for equal treatment and special treatment can be analysed effectively. Third, the gendered nature of the shift from Fordist to post-Fordist methods of production in some sectors of the economy needs to be more fully understood before its implications for both employment and organisational strategies can be evaluated. Fourth, the analysis of the relationship between social citizenship, economic efficiency and macro-economic policy necessary for the construction of notions of a stakeholder society needs to take into account the gendering of these processes. In short, we need a properly gendered political economy.

Politics and economics

This book has argued that there are potentially significant changes to gender relations in employment resulting from changes in the state. The economic policies of the EU, and their implementation, are major issues for gender relations. We need to address the questions of the gendered relationship between politics and economics; the extent of the impact of politics on gender relations in the economy; the ways in which this impact occurs, and how the relationship is mediated.

This shifts the focus away from some of the more traditional debates on gender relations in employment. The relationship between women's domestic activities and their paid employment is mediated not only by their human capital but by social policies which structure the environment as well. However, the significance of the gender segregation of the workforce remains (Treiman and Hartmann, 1981; Reskin and Roos, 1990; *Social Europe*, 1993; Walby, 1988), especially that of industrial segregation (see Chapter 5), because of the differential impact of the Single European Market on industrial sectors. A focus on EU processes shifts the emphasis in the debates on gender and the labour market towards understanding new forms of regulation of the labour market and thus of the gendered polity. We need to understand the impact of different modes of regulation of labour markets on gender relations within them, how far the political and legal framework affects gender relations in the labour market and the nature of the intersection of gendered politics and gendered economics.

These changes in the gendered polity and society have generated a number of further initiatives around issues of equal opportunities. There has been a major growth in workplace-based policies to ensure equal treatment of men and women in the workplace, involving policy statements and equal opportunities officers within companies, indeed we have even seen the growth of specialist management consultancies in equal opportunities. Some policies are little more than attempts to keep within the law, while others are more developed attempts to utilise fully the skills of their female workers. These may be seen as a response to political pressure, the EOC's admonishment, the pressure of women workers, or as simply the need of employers to recruit and keep labour, which just happens to be female and thus requires different attention. However they are explained, it is the case that we have seen a remarkable explosion of equal opportunities policies in UK companies over the last few years. There is a question as to the difference they can make and under what circumstances they make an impact (Cockburn, 1991; Marcus, 1996; Rutherford, 1996). Again we see that the impact of a politically/legally based intervention on the economy is a crucial issue in understanding gender relations in employment.

Diversity and equal treatment

The policies of the European Union which seek to deliver equal treatment for women and men interact unevenly with the diversity and inequality among and between women. This book has argued that there is currently a change taking place in the form of gender regime from a more domestic to a more public form. As a consequence there co-exist older women who have planned their lives around the opportunity structures of a more domestic gender regime which no longer exists, and younger women who plan their lives around the opportunities and constraints of a more public form of gender regime. This creates differences and inequalities between women in many dimensions of their lives, most obviously in their labour market capacities, but also in their engagement with domestic activities and their political and cultural orientations. These differences and inequalities are further entwined with the more widely recognised inequalities and diversities involved in ethnicity, class, region and other social divisions.

There is more than one way of doing gender politics for the benefit of women, as was seen in Chapter 7 on gender politics and social theory and Chapter 9 on citizenship and gender. There is a division into at least two major strategies: one which seeks to give women the same privileges as men, via equal opportunities; a second which seeks to offer justice to women by focusing on special treatment of their special needs. The former, that of equal opportunities, is embedded in the founding Treaty of the European Union, and, further, is focused upon delivering this within the arena of employment and related areas. This is a strategy which has delivered equal opportunities policies in employment, underpinned by the law, and given results including the narrowing of the wages gap between full-time women and men workers. Its extension to part-time workers is currently underway. The strategy of special treatment is undermined by the equal treatment provisions of the Treaty of Rome. For instance, provisions which allowed women to retire and receive pensions earlier than men – at 60 rather than 65 – have been found to be illegal under EU law. Further, preferential treatment of women in recruitment, even when done to rectify a gender imbalance, has recently been found to be against European law.

The question as to whether the strategy of either equal treatment or special treatment is more effective in delivering justice to women has divided feminists since the turn of the century. The arguments range from the philosophical and theoretical to the political and legal. As was seen in

Chapter 9, the equal rights discourse draws on a universalist conception of human rights to underpin its view of citizenship, while some feminists have sought to emphasise the difference of women from men and the special needs that women have as a consequence. Examples of historical debates include protective legislation for women workers and maternity rights (Banks, 1981; Eisenstein, 1984; Meehan and Sevenhuijsen, 1992).

The impact of the EU equal treatment strategy on gender inequality depends both upon the centrality of employment to women, and the assumption that women and men are essentially similar. These assumptions might be considered either insufficient or indeed problematic in the context of the diversity of women's lives, especially those women who, for reasons including perhaps generation or ethnicity, are more oriented to domestic activities and to the maintenance of a different life style from men. However, equal treatment policies are part of the shift in the form of gender regime from domestic to public – partly a cause of and partly a strategy for justice within the latter. Given that the Treaties of the European Union have become a *de facto* constitution, in the sense of a superior set of law, then equal treatment is here to stay in the Member States of the EU. Special treatment is unlikely to continue to be a viable political strategy in this politico-legal context. A further question becomes that of the breadth of the remit of the European Union and how widely economic issues become defined. Women will experience this as either an opportunity or a constraint according to their position.

Post-Fordism

There is a question as to whether recent changes in employment, and indeed society as a whole, may be characterised as a movement from Fordism to post-Fordism (see Bagguley et al. 1990; Pollert, 1991; Wood, 1989; Walby and Greenwell et al., 1994). Post-Fordism is a debate which has been largely, but not entirely, ungendered (see Jenson, 1989; and Chapter 3 in this volume). The questions here are first, whether changes in gender relations are affected by the shift to post-Fordism and, second, what difference this makes to the debates on EU regulation and equal opportunities policies.

The post-Fordist thesis has several forms. An element key to them all is to stress the way new technology has opened up an era of flexible rather than mass production, of production oriented to specialist niche markets rather than mass consumption, where workers become more flexibly multi-skilled, rather than trained in a narrow rigid specialism; where there are a variety of labour contracts, rather than a full-time permanent contract directly with the main employer. A further characteristic is a tendency to decentralise certain aspects of decision making, although financial control remains centralised. This has been variously interpreted as producing the possibility of a freer, richer form of work (Piore and Sabel, 1984) or as merely the super-exploitation of workers on insecure contracts (Pollert, 1991). In between we have Atkinson (NEDO, 1986) and others describing the forms of both functional and numerical flexibility which divide the workforce into a core of multi-skilled flexible workers and a periphery of less skilled workers on insecure or even sub-contracted contracts. The explanation of these changes is also varied ranging from crises in production under Fordism by Marxists such as Aglietta (1979), to the powers of new technology, as in the case of Piore and Sabel, to the exigencies of economic circumstances, as in the case of Atkinson.

These debates raise two key issues for us here. First, whether the distinctive forms of labour contract under which many women work, such as part-time working, are attributable to post-Fordism. Second, the impact of increasingly decentralised decision making on the effectiveness of equal opportunities policies which were designed around centralised Fordist structures.

The first issue of the relationship between post-Fordist changes and the gendered nature of employment was addressed in Chapter 3 on flexibility. The key here is the interpretation of the growth of part-time work, which can be seen as a form of numerical flexibility in that it enables employers to employ labour at precisely those moments when it is needed and not otherwise. In this way the drive for flexibility by employers is a gendered process. Rather than seeing the increase in part-time work as a gendered outcome emerging from ungendered causes, as Atkinson *et al.* argued, it was shown that these changes were linked to wider changes in gender relations and the development of gender-specific forms of politico-legal governance of the labour market. For instance, the UK has a distinctive pattern of part-time work, higher than much of the rest of Western Europe as a result of its historically differential regulation of part-time as compared with full-time work which left part-time workers more vulnerable. (In the Nordic countries part-time work has a very different structure.) Many of the changes conventionally assumed to be caused by non-gendered processes, are actually part of structural changes in the form of gender relations. The movement from Fordism to post-Fordism cannot be understood outside of an understanding of these changes in the forms of gender relations from a more domestic to a more public gender regime.

Most equal opportunities strategies in the UK presume a Fordist structure of employment, and operate through a mode of regulation which is adapted to a Fordist regime. Most company-based equal opportunities policies utilise centralised monitoring and a bureaucratic structure of equal opportunities officers in order to introduce policies. They depend upon notions of uniformity of process and criteria and the reduction of *ad hoc* personnel decision making. In effect they raise the level of decision making on personnel issues upwards through the company hierarchy. These policies are underpinned by a legal process which is heavily bureaucratic and oriented upwards.

Equal opportunities policies oriented to Fordist modes of regulation are developing just at the time that the governance of the economy is shifting in a post-Fordist direction. This raises the question as to whether they will have less impact as a consequence. For instance, most equal opportunities policies operate only within a specific employment establishment. If work is sub-contracted out, either to another plant, or to another employer operating within the same plant, then that work is not included in the unit within which equal opportunities comparisons may be made. Lower wages may be paid to those on the sub-contracted work than on the work in the main plant, as is regularly the case under compulsory competitive tendering, thus avoiding union-negotiated rates in the old main plant. While unions operate on the basis of greater collective strength and the avoidance of undercutting, employers seek variability, sub-contracting work outside the parameters of the negotiated agreement.

This issue is particularly pertinent for the question of the unit within which equal pay comparisons can be made under UK legislation. Sub-contracting, which is a central strategy of flexibility, thus avoids worker organisations which are organised at the main plant. Attempts to extend the conditions of employment in house to all out of house tenders in National Health Service hospitals subject to compulsory competitive tendering have met fierce opposition. However, this process is tempered by EU attempts to insist that the conditions of the original employer are transferred to that of the new employer (the transfer of undertakings). Nevertheless, the attempt to break up the national wage agreements which have been common in the public sector further threatens to undermine the basis of equal value and other equal treatment claims.

Barth and Mastekaasa (1992) show that differences in men and women's pay between establishments are important in the private, but not the public, sector in Norway. National agreements are strong enough to eliminate this dimension of the wages gap in the nationally organised public sector. It is likely, though they do not suggest it, that this pattern would be found in many Western and Northern European countries. If there is a continuing decline in the public sector, then this might exacerbate the wages gap between men and women.

What if any is the relationship between increasing EU integration and post-Fordism? In some ways the deregulation project of the Single European Market and that of the Social Charter pull in different directions. Many of the policies embodied in the Social Charter are Fordist: there is a rhetoric of creating a level playing-field, and evening-up conditions of employment; there are pressures for uniformity of treatment; for reducing differentiation; and of the development of legal/bureaucratic structures to implement these policies. On the other side, deregulation and post-Fordism are characterised by variation; localism; niche-specialised markets; and decentralisation. The outcome of the intersection of these two trajectories is unclear.

Social policy as employment policy

The increased representation of women's political interests at the level of the state and the supra-state of the EU has been of immense significance in recent developments. Chapter 7 on gender politics and social theory, Chapter 9 on gender and citizenship and Chapter 10 on woman and nation showed the importance of women's struggles in the development of the modern state and its policies. However, the debate on the development of different forms of welfare state regimes has often focused on class relations (Esping-Andersen, 1990; Jessop *et al.*, 1991) and underestimated the significance of the gender dimension in both the creation and the impact of welfare provision, though there exceptions to this view (see Sainsbury, 1994; Skocpol, 1992).

EU social policies impact on the gendered labour market, especially those often thought of as 'welfare', and particularly those which provide infrastructure that is helpful for women in employment, such as parental leave and child care. The understanding of the gendered nature of state welfare regimes is crucial to understanding the potential impact of increasing European integration.

The macro-economic strategies of deregulation and of stakeholding are gendered in quite different ways. While neither appears to have any inevitable outcome as to the proportion of women in paid employment, they do tend to lead to different forms and levels of participation. The former is consistent with a greater polarisation between those women working full-time at more skilled jobs and those who work part-time under poor conditions. The conditions under which women are best able to use their skills fully in employment are those where there are effective ways of reconciling working and family life (see Drew, Emerek and Mahon, 1995). This reconciliation requires certain infrastructural supports for women's employment (McLoone and O'Leary, 1989), such as systems of parental leave, care for children and the frail elderly, life-long opportunities for learning and training, as well as equal opportunities policies, and that these are extended to part-time as well as full-time workers. These forms of social protection and labour market regulation are more consistent with the stakeholding approach than the deregulation approach.

Such policies are sometimes assumed to be subsumed within an overall welfare package which is then seen as simply welfare for the needy or regarded as a drag on competitiveness and economic growth, or welfare policies may be seen as extras won by the working class, or as luxuries to be afforded when the economy is doing well. Rather they should be seen as crucial infrastructure, enabling women to participate successfully in paid employment, and as important in the 'reconciliation of working and family life' (Drew, Emerek and Mahon, 1995; McLoone and O'Leary, 1989). They are infrastructural developments which facilitate the full utilisation of the skills and abilities of those people who choose to combine paid employment with the essential work of caring for the young, sick and old, that is, disproportionately, but not entirely, women.

There is a question as to whether increasing political integration within the EU will lead to harmonisation upwards (as is claimed within the European Commission), or downwards (as is feared by many Nordic women and French people) on issues of welfare provision (Borchorst, 1992; Dahlerup, 1992). The mechanisms through which such gendered interests might be represented within the EU are complex. Women are typically less well represented in corporatist bodies and at international levels than at the local, yet women's voices on behalf of equal opportunities policies appear to be more clearly heard in Brussels than in London. The position of women and the representation of gendered interests within the political structures of international or supra-national bodies as compared to the national is crucial to future developments in the EU.

CONCLUSIONS

Changes in the forms of gender relations in the labour market are significantly affected by the increasing integration of the EU, but the form and degree of the changes depend not only upon development of the Single European Market and its impact on differently gendered industrial sectors, but upon the extent to which the programme represented in the Social Charter and the Social Chapter of the Maastricht Treaty is implemented at national level.

These changes in gender relations in employment in the EU highlight the significance of political and policy issues in the determination of gender relations in employment. This contradicts the assumption in many early debates that patterns of gender relations in the labour market were primarily determined by the interaction of the household and the workplace. The significance of the polity can be seen more clearly because of the rapidity with which decisions taken at the political level affect employment. This is not a new phenomenon, merely something that is becoming more obvious in the context of rapid changes.

The full implementation of Article 119 and the Social Chapter are likely to affect significantly gender relations in employment in the UK and the rest of the EU, however, there is a question as to the extent to which this implementation will happen. There are many political, legal and procedural points at which this issue is subject to high levels of contestation.

A further doubt as to the impact of the EU on gender relations is over whether equal opportunities policies are undermined by a shift to a post-Fordist economic structure, since they are often built on an expectation of a Fordist regime. There is a question as to whether equal opportunities strategies, at either legal or company level, designed with centralised Fordist structures in mind, have been left behind with the demise of institutional mechanisms of implementation. This issue is a result of the shift in the locus of power in a decentralised direction, just as those supporting women's interests are beginning to run a centralised equal opportunities strategy through employment structures. However, while the locus of personnel policies has shifted in a decentralised direction, thus removing some of them from the initial strategies of equal opportunities activists, the development of new EU legal mechanisms is proceeding apace to address the new forms of organisation of the economy.

The political citizenship which women formally won seventy or so years ago is having a destabilising effect on patriarchal relations via a universalist discourse of equal rights – and the entrenchment of this in the Treaties which act as a *de facto* constitution for the EU. The conventional view – that women's interests are best represented at the local level and are progressively less present the further up the national and international scale we go – is contradicted by the EU, where women's interests have been institutionalised in the central institutions at the level of the emerging supra-state to a greater extent than that of most, but not all, Member States. Many women in the UK, though not Scandinavia, are seeing a reduction in gender inequality as a result of increasing EU integration. The formation of the EU supra-state in a period after women have won effective political citizenship is leading to a more effective institutionalisation of women's interests than occurred in those national states formed before women achieved political citizenship.

However, the transformation of gender relations is affecting women very unevenly. Younger women who are highly educated and gain good jobs are reducing the gender gap, but those who leave school without qualifications, who fail to get good jobs, and who engage in motherhood without male support, and older women who never had such educational and employment opportunities fare badly in the new form of public gender regime, where successful activity in the labour market is the key to other social resources.

APPENDIX
Labour markets with female majorities in employees in employment, 1991

001	Haddington
004	Hawick
005	Peebles
016	Cumnock and Sanquhar
025	Fraserburgh
031	Buckie
033	Forres
034	Badenoch
035	Wick
038	Lochaber
040	Skye and Wester Ross
041	Edinburgh
043	Dunoon and Bute
044	Campbeltown
045	Crieff
046	Dumbarton
048	Irvine
050	Greenok
051	Kilmarnock
052	Girvan
055	Blairgowrie and Pitlochry
058	Islay/MidArgyll
059	Sutherland
068	Liverpool
069	Wirral and Chester
076	S.Tyneside
083	Keighley
086	Wakefield
091	Weston-Super-Mare
099	Guildford and Aldershot

Source: Department of Employment 1991 Census of Employment

BIBLIOGRAPHY

Aaron, Jane and Walby, Sylvia (eds) (1991) *Out of the Margins: Women's Studies in the Nineties*, London, Falmer Press.

Abbott, Pamela and Wallace, Claire (1990) *An Introduction to Sociology: Feminist Perspectives*, London, Routledge.

Abel, Emily and Nelson, Margaret (eds) (1990) *Circles of Care: Work and Identity in Women's Lives*, New York, State University of New York Press.

Abercrombie, Nicholas and Urry, John (1983) *Capital and the Middle Classes*, London, Allen & Unwin.

Acker, Joan (1973) 'Women and stratification: a case of intellectual sexism' in Joan Huber (ed.) *Changing Women in a Changing Society*, Chicago, University of Chicago Press, pp. 174–83.

Adam, Barbara (1990) *Time and Social Theory*, Cambridge, Polity Press.

——(1995) *Timewatch: the Social Analysis of Time*, Cambridge, Polity Press.

Adams, Parveen (1979) 'A note on sexual divisions and sexual differences', *m/f* 3, 51–9.

Adams, Parveen and Minson, Jeff (1978) 'The "subject" of feminism', *m/f* 2, 43–61.

Adams, Parveen, Coward, Rosalind and Cowie, Elizabeth (1978) 'm/f', *m/f*, 1, 3–5.

Adkins, Lisa (1995) *Gendered Work: Sexuality, Family and the Labour Market*, Buckingham, Open University Press.

Adler, Zsuzsanna (1987) *Rape on Trial*, London, Routledge.

Afshar, Haleh (1981) 'The position of women in an Iranian village', *Feminist Review* 9, 76–86.

——(1989) 'Women and reproduction in Iran' in Nira Yuval-Davis Nira and Floya Anthias (eds) *Woman–Nation–State*, London, Macmillan.

Afshar, Haleh and Magnard, Mary (eds) (1994) *The Dynamics of 'Race' and Gender: Some Feminist Interventions*, London, Taylor & Francis.

Aglietta, M. (1979) *A Theory of Capitalist Regulation*, London, New Left Books.

Alcoff, Linda (1988) 'Cultural feminism versus post-structuralism: the identity crisis in feminist theory', *Signs* 13 (3), 405–36.

Amsden, Alice H. (ed.) (1980) *The Economics of Women and Work*, Harmondsworth, Penguin.

Amos, Valerie and Parmar, Pratibha (1984) 'Challenging imperial feminism', *Feminist Review* 17, 3–20.

Anderson, Michael, Bechhofer, Frank and Gershuny, Jonathan (eds) (1994) *The Social and Political Economy of the Household*, Oxford, Oxford University Press.

Andrews, Irene Osgood (1918) *Economic Effects of the War Upon Women and Children in Great Britain*, New York, Oxford University Press.

216

Anthias, Floya (1989) 'Women and nationalism in Cyprus' in Nira Yuval-Davis and Floya Anthias (eds) *Woman–Nation–State*, London, Macmillan.

Anthias, Floya and Yuval-Davis, Nira (1983) 'Contextualizing feminism – gender, ethnic and class divisions', *Feminist Review* 15, 62–75.

——(1989) 'Introduction' in Nira Yuval-Davis and Floya Anthias (eds) *Woman–Nation–State*, London, Macmillan.

Anthias, Floya and Yuval-Davis, Nira, in association with Harriet Cain (1992) *Racialized Boundaries: Race, Nation, Gender, Colour and Class and the Anti-racist Struggle*, London, Routledge.

Anthony, Sylvia (1932) *Women's Place in Industry and Home*, London, George Routledge & Son.

Arber, Sara and Ginn, Jay (1991) *Gender and Later Life: a Sociological Analysis of Resources and Constraints*, London, Sage.

——(1995) 'The mirage of gender equality: occupational success in the labour market and within marriage', *British Journal of Sociology* 46 (1), 21–43.

Bagguley, Paul (1991) 'The patriarchal restructuring of gender segregation: a case study of the hotel and catering industry', *Sociology* 25 (4), 607–25.

——(1995) 'Protest, poverty and power', *Sociological Review* 43 (4), 693–719.

Bagguley, Paul, Mark-Lawson, Jane, Shapiro, Dan, Urry, John, Walby, Sylvia and Warde, Alan (1990) *Restructuring: Place, Class and Gender*, London, Sage.

Bagguley, Paul and Walby, Sylvia (1988) *Women and Local Labour Markets: a Comparative Analysis of Five Localities*, Lancaster Regionalism Group Working Paper.

Banks, Olive (1981) *Faces of Feminism: a Study of Feminism as a Social Movement*, Oxford, Martin Robertson.

Barrett, Michele (1980) *Women's Oppression Today: Problems in Marxist Feminist Analysis*, London, Verso.

——(1987) 'The concept of difference', *Feminist Review* 26, 29–41.

Barrett, Michele and Coward, Rosalind (1982) 'Letter', *m/f* 7, 87–9.

Barrett, Michele and McIntosh, Mary (1979) 'Towards a materialist feminism?', *Feminist Review*, 1, 95–106.

Barrett, Michele and Phillips, Anne (eds) (1992) *Destabilizing Theory: Contemporary Feminist Debates*, Cambridge, Polity Press.

Barth, E. and Mastekaasa, T. (1992), 'Public and private sectors in the Nordic countries', paper presented to the First European Sociology Conference, Vienna.

Becker, Gary S. (1965) *Human Capital*, Chicago, Chicago University Press.

——(1981) *A Treatise on the Family*, Cambridge, Mass., Harvard University Press.

Beechey, Veronica (1977) 'Some notes on female wage labour in capitalist production', *Capital and Class* 3, 45–66.

——(1978) 'Women and production: a critical analysis of some sociological theories of women's work' in Annette Kuhn and Ann Marie Wolpe (eds) *Feminism and Materialism: Women and Modes of Production*, London, Routledge, pp. 155–97.

——(1982) 'The sexual division of labour and the labour process: a critical assessment of Braverman' in S. Wood (ed.) *The Degradation of Work?*, London, Hutchinson, pp. 54–73.

Begum, Nasa (1992) 'Disabled women and the feminist agenda' in Hilary Hinds, Ann Phoenix and Jackie Stacey (eds) *Working Out: New Directions for Women's Studies*, Basingstoke, Falmer Press.

Berelson, B. (1975) *The Great Debate on Population Policy*, New York, The Population Council.

Bergmann, Barbara (1986) *The Economic Emergence of Women*, New York, Basic Books.

Bhaskar, Roy (1979) *The Possibility of Naturalism*, Brighton, Harvester.

Bhavnani, Kum-Kum (1993) 'Towards a multi-cultural Europe? "Race", nation and identity in 1992 and beyond', *Feminist Review* 45, 30–45.

Bhopal, Kalwant (1996) 'Women in South Asian Households in Britain', unpublished PhD thesis, Department of Sociology, University of Bristol.

Bird, Derek and Corcoran, Louise (1994) 'Trade union membership and density 1992–3', *Employment Gazette*, June 1994, 189–92.

Blackaby, F. (ed.) (1978) *De-Industrialisation*, London, Heinemann.

Bongaarts, John (1993) 'The supply–demand framework for the determinants of fertility: an alternative implementation', *Population Studies* 47, 437–56.

Borchorst, Anette (1992) Personal communication.

Borchorst, Annette and Siim, Birte (1987) 'Women and the advanced welfare state – a new kind of patriarchal power' in Anne Showstack Sassoon (ed.) *Women and the State: the Shifting Boundaries of Public and Private*, London, Hutchinson pp. 128–57.

Bornschier, Volker and Fielder, Nicola (1995) 'The genesis of the Single European Act: forces and protagonists behind the relaunch of the European Community in the 1980s: the Single Market', paper presented at the Second European Sociology Conference, Budapest.

Bose, Catherine (1979) 'Technology and changes in the division of labour in the American home', *Women's Studies International Quarterly* 2, 295–304.

Boserup, Ester (1970) *Woman's Role in Economic Development*, London, Allen & Unwin.

Bourke, Joanna (1993) *Husbandry to Housewifery: Women, Economic Change and Housework in Ireland, 1890–1914*, Oxford, Clarendon Press.

Bourque, S. and Grossholtz, J. (1974) 'Politics as unnatural practice: political science looks at female participation', *Politics and Society* 4 (4)

Bowers, J. (1970) *The Anatomy of Regional Activity Rates*, National Institute of Economic and Social Research Regional Papers, Cambridge, Cambridge University Press.

Brah, Avtar (1991) 'Questions of difference and international feminism' in Jane Aaron and Sylvia Walby (eds) *Out of the Margins: Women's Studies in the Nineties*, London, Falmer Press, pp. 168–76.

——(1993) 'Re-framing Europe: en-gendered racisms, ethnicities and nationalisms in contemporary Western Europe', *Feminist Review* 45, 9–29.

Brah, Avtar and Shaw, Sobia (1992) *Working Choices: South Asian Young Muslim Women and the Labour Market*, Research Paper No. 91, London, Employment Department Group.

Brannen, Julia and Wilson, Gail (eds) (1987) *Give and Take in Families: Studies in Resource Distribution*, London, Allen & Unwin.

Brannen, Julia, Meszaros, George, Moss, Peter and Poland, Gill (1994) *Employment and Family Life: a Review of Research in the UK (1980–1994)*, Research Paper No. 41, London, Employment Department.

Braverman, Harry (1974) *Labor and Monopoly Capital: the Degradation of Work in the Twentieth Century*, New York, Monthly Review Press.

British Council (1996) *Network Newsletter*, March.

Bruegel, Irene (1979) 'Women as a reserve army of labour: a note on recent British experience', *Feminist Review* 3, 12–23.

Brittan, Arthur and Maynard, Mary (1984) *Sexism, Racism and Oppression*, Oxford, Blackwell.

Britten, Nicky and Heath, Anthony (1983) 'Women, men and social class' in Eva Gamarnikow, David Morgan, June Purvis and Daphne Taylorson (eds) *Gender, Class and Work*, London, Heinemann, pp. 46–60.

Brown, Colin (1984) *Black and White Britain: the Third PSI Survey*, London, Heinemann.

Bubeck, Diemut (1991) 'Do women care too much? Care, gender and justice', paper presented to LSE Gender Group seminar, London.

Butler, David and Stokes, Donald (1974) *Political Change in Britain: the Evolution of Electoral Choice*, London, Macmillan.

Butler, Josephine (1986) *Personal Reminiscences of a Great Crusade*, London, Horace Marshall & Son.

Campbell, Beatrix (1987) *Iron Ladies: Why Do Women Vote Tory?*, London, Virago.

Carby, Hazel (1982) 'White woman listen! Black feminism and the boundaries of sisterhood' in Centre for Contemporary Cultural Studies, University of Birmingham, *The Empire Strikes Back: Racism in '70s Britain*, London, Hutchinson.

Castells, Manuel (1978) *City, Class and Power*, London, Macmillan.

——(1983) *The City and the Grass Roots: a Cross Cultural Theory of Urban Social Movements*, London, Edward Arnold.

Cecchini, Paolo, Catinat, Michael and Jacquemin, Alexis (1988) *The European Challenge 1992: the Benefits of a Single Market*, Aldershot, Gower.

Chafetz, Janet Saltzman and Dworkin, Anthony Gary (1986) *Female Revolt: Women's Movements in World and Historical Perspective*, Totowa, NJ, Rowman & Allanheld.

——(1987) 'In the face of threat: organised antifeminism in comparative perspective', *Gender and Society* 1 (1) 33–60.

Charles, Nickie (1995) 'Feminist politics, domestic violence and the state', *The Sociological Review* 43 (4) 617–40.

Cockburn, Cynthia (1983) *Brothers: Male Dominance and Technological Change*, London, Pluto Press.

——(1991) *In the Way of Women: Men's Resistance to Sex Equality in Organizations*, Basingstoke, Macmillan.

The Community Charter of the Fundamental Social Rights of Workers (1990) in *Social Europe* 1/90, 45–50.

Cooke, Phillip (1982) 'Dependency, supply factors and uneven development in Wales and other problem regions', *Regional Studies* 16 (3), 211–27.

——(1983a) *Theories of Planning and Spatial Development*, London, Hutchinson.

——(1983b) 'Labour market discontinuity and spatial development', *Progress in Human Geography* 7, 543–65

——(ed.) (1989) *Localities: the Changing Face of Urban Britain*, London, Unwin & Hyman.

Cowan, R.S. (1983) *More Work for Mother: the Ironies of Household Technology from the Open Hearth to the Microwave*, New York, Basic Books.

Coward, Rosalind (1978) 'Sexual liberation and the family', *m/f* 1, 7–24.

——(1982) 'Sexual violence and sexuality', *Feminist Review* 11, 9–22.

——(1984) *Female Desire*, London, Granada.

Cowie, Elizabeth (1978) '"Woman as Sign"', *m/f* 1, 49–64.

CREW Reports, published since 1980 by Centre for Research on European Women, Brussels.

Crompton, R. and Jones, G. (1984) *White-collar Proletariat: Deskilling and Gender in the Clerical Labour Process*, London, Macmillan.

Crompton, Rosemary and Mann, Michael (eds) (1986) *Gender and Stratification*, Cambridge, Polity Press.

Crompton, Rosemary and Sanderson, Kay (1986) 'Credentials and careers: some implications of the increase in professional qualifications among women', *Sociology* 20 (1), 25–42.

——(1990) *Gendered Jobs and Social Change*, London, Unwin & Hyman.

Cross, M. (1985) *Towards the Flexible Craftsman*, London, Technical Change Centre.

Cudworth, Erika (1988) 'Feminism and Non-Violence: a Relation in Theory, in Herstory and Praxis', unpublished MSc dissertation, Department of Government, LSE.

——(1996) 'Feminism and Environmentalism', unpublished paper, School of Sociology and Social Policy, University of Leeds.

Currell, Melville E. (1974) *Political Woman*, London, Croom Helm.

Curson, C. (ed.) (1986) *Flexible Patterns of Work*, London, Institute of Personnel Management.

Dahlerup, Drude (1992) Personal communication.

Dahrendorf, Ralf, Kohler, Eberhard and Piotet, Francoise (eds) (1986) *New Forms of Work and Activity*, Luxembourg, European Foundation for the Improvement of Living and Working Conditions.

Daly, Mary (1978) *Gyn/Ecology: the Metaethics of Radical Feminism*, London, Women's Press.

Danielli, Ardha (1994), 'Gender and Industrial Relations', unpublished PhD thesis, University of Bristol.

Davies, Hugh and Joshi, Heather (1994) 'Sex, sharing and the distribution of income', *British Journal of Social Policy*, 23 (3), 301–40.

Davies, K. (1990) *Women and Time: the Weaving of the Strands of Everyday Life*, Aldershot, Avebury.

Davies, Richard, Elias, Peter and Penn, Roger (1994) 'The relationship between a husband's unemployment and his wife's participation in the labour force' in Duncan Gallie, Catherine Marsh and Carolyn Vogler (eds) *Social Change and the Experience of Unemployment*, Oxford, Oxford University Press, pp. 154–87.

Davis, Angela (1981) *Women, Race and Class*, London, The Women's Press.

Dearlove, John and Saunders, Peter (1984) *Introduction to British Politics: Analysing a Capitalist Democracy*, Cambridge, Polity Press.

de Lepervanche, Marie (1989) 'Women, nation and state in Australia' in Nira Yuval-Davis and Floya Anthias (eds) *Woman–Nation–State*, London, Macmillan.

Delphy, Christine (1984) *Close to Home: a Materialist Analysis of Women's Oppression*, London, Hutchinson.

Delphy, Christine and Leonard, Diana (1992) *Familiar Exploitation: a New Analysis of Marriage in Contemporary Western Societies*, Cambridge, Polity Press.

Department for Education (1995) *Education Statistics for the United Kingdom 1994*, London, HMSO.

Department for Education and Employment (1996) *Education Statistics for the United Kingdom 1995*, London, DFEE.

Derrida, Jacques (1976) *Of Grammatology*, Baltimore, John Hopkins University Press.

Dex, Shirley (1983) 'The second generation: West Indian female school leavers' in Annie Phizacklea (ed.) *One Way Ticket: Migration and Female Labour*, London, Routledge, pp. 53–71.

——(1985) *The Sexual Division of Labour: Conceptual Revolutions in the Social Sciences*, Brighton, Wheatsheaf.

——(1987) *Women's Occupational Mobility: a Lifetime Perspective*, London, Macmillan.

——(1989) Personal communication.

——(1991) 'Life and work history analyses' in Shirley Dex (ed.) *Life and Work History Analyses: Qualitative and Quantative Developments*, London, Routledge.

Dex, Shirley and Shaw, L. (1986) *British and American Women at Work: Do Equal Opportunities Policies Matter?* London, Macmillan.

Diamond, Irene (1977) *Sex Roles and the State House*, New Haven, Yale University Press.

Dobash, R. Emerson and Dobash, Russell P. (1992) *Women, Violence and Social Change*, London, Routledge.

Drake, Barbara (1920) *Women in Trade Unions*, London, Labour Research Department and Allen & Unwin (reprinted by Virago, 1984).

Drew, Eileen (1992) 'The part-time option? Women and part-time work in the European Community', *Women's Studies International Forum*, 15 (5/6), 1–8.

Drew, Eileen, Emerek, Ruth and Mahon, Evelyn (1995), 'Report for the European Foundation for the Improvement of Living and Working Conditions on European Research Workshop on Families, Labour Markets and Gender Roles', mimeo, Trinity College Dublin.

Drucker, Peter F. (1993) *Post-Capitalist Society*, Oxford, Butterworth Heinemann.

Duncan, O.D. and Duncan, B. (1955) 'A methodological analysis of segregation indices', *American Sociological Review* 20, 200–17.

Duncan, Simon (1991a) 'The geography of gender divisions of labour in Britain', *Transactions of the Institute of British Geography* 16, 420–39.

——(1991b) 'Gender divisions of labour' in D. Green and K. Moggart (eds) *A New Metropolitan Geography*, Sevenoaks, Kent, Edward Arnold, pp. 95–122.

Dworkin, Andrea (1981) *Pornography: Men Possessing Women*, London, The Women's Press.

Edwards, R. (1979) *Contested Terrain: the Transformation of the Workplace in the Twentieth Century*, New York and London, Basic Books and Heinemann.

Edwards, Richard C., Gordon, David M. and Reich, Michael (1975) *Labour Market Segmentation*, Lexington, Mass., Lexington Books.

Edwards, Susan S. M. (1989) *Policing 'Domestic' Violence: Women, the Law and the State*, London, Sage.

Eisenstein, Hester (1984) *Contemporary Feminist Thought*, London, Allen & Unwin.

Eisenstein, Zillah R. (1981) *The Radical Future of Liberal Feminism*, New York, Longman.

——(1984) *Feminism and Sexual Equality: Crisis in Liberal America*, New York, Monthly Review Press.

Elger, T. (1982) 'Braverman, capital accumulation and deskilling' in Stephen Wood (ed.) *The Degradation of Work?*, London, Hutchinson, pp. 23–53.

Ellis, Valerie (1991) *The Role of Trade Unions in the Promotion of Equal Opportunities*, London, Equal Opportunities Commission/Social Science Research Council.

Elson, Diane and Pearson, Ruth (1981) '"Nimble fingers make cheap workers": an analysis of women's employment in Third World export manufacturing', *Feminist Review* 7, 87–107.

Emerek, Ruth (1994) 'A/typical working time: examples from Denmark', paper presented to European Research Workshop on Families, Labour Markets and Gender Roles, European Foundation for the Improvement of Living and Working Conditions, Dublin.

Employment Department (1995) *Local Areas in G. B. 1991 Census of Employment*, Employment Department Statistical Services Division D4.

Employment Gazette, London, Employment Department/Department for Education and Employment.

England, Paula (1982) 'The failure of human capital theory to explain occupational sex segregation', *Journal of Human Resources* 17, 358–70.

Enloe, Cynthia (1983) *Does Khaki Become You? The Militarisation of Women's Lives*, London, Pluto Press.

——(1989) *Bananas, Beaches and Bases: Making Feminist Sense of International Relations*, London, Pandora.

Epstein, Cynthia Fuchs (1970) *Woman's Place: Options and Limits in Professional Careers*, Berkeley, University of California Press.

Epstein, Cynthia Fuchs and Coser, Rose Laub (eds) (1981) *Access to Power: Cross-national Studies of Women and Elites*, London, Allen & Unwin.

Equal Opportunities Commission (EOC) (1983) *Women and Trade Unions: a Survey*, Manchester, EOC.

——(1985a) *Women and Men in Britain: a Statistical Profile*, Manchester, EOC.

——(1985b) *Research Bulletin*.

——(1986) *Women and Men in Britain: a Statistical Profile*, Manchester, EOC.

——(1987) *Women and Men in Britain: a Statistical Profile*, Manchester, EOC.

Ermisch, John F. (1981) 'Economic opportunities, marriage squeezes and the propensity to marry: an economic analysis of period marriage rates in England and Wales', *Population Studies* 35, 347–56.

——(1983) *The Political Economy of Demographic Change: Causes and Implications of Population Trends in Great Britain*, London, Heinemann.

Ermisch, John F. and Ogawo, Naohiro (eds) (1994) *The Family, the Market and the State in Ageing Societies*, Oxford, Clarendon Press.

Esping-Andersen, Gosta (1990) *The Three Worlds of Welfare Capitalism*, Cambridge, Polity Press.

European Commission (1990) *The Impact of the Completion of the Internal Market on Women in the European Community* by Pauline Conroy Jackson, Brussels, EC.

——(1993) *Growth, Competitiveness, Employment: the Challenges and Ways Forward into the 21st Century*, White Paper, Brussels, EU.

——(1994a) *European Social Policy: a Way Forward for the Union*, White Paper, Brussels, EU.

——(1994b) *Sex Equality Legislation in the Member States of the European Community* by Barry Fitzpatrick, Jeanne Gregory and Erika Szysczak. DGV, EC.

——(1994c) *Equal Treatment After Maastricht: Special Report of the Network of Experts on the Implementation of the Equality Directives* by Sacha Prechal and Linda Senden, DGV, EC.

European Parliament, Directorate General for Research (1994a) *Measures to Combat Sexual Harassment at the Workplace: Action taken in the Member States of the Eruopean Community*, Working Paper in the Women's Rights Series, EP.

—— (1994b) *Women's Rights and the Maastricht Treaty on European Union*, paper in the Women's Rights Series, EP.

EUROSTAT (1993) *Labour Force Survey: Results 1991*, Luxembourg, EUROSTAT.

——(1995) *Demographic Statistics 1995*, Luxembourg, EUROSTAT.

——(1996) *Labour Force Survey: Results 1994*, Luxembourg, EUROSTAT.

Evandrou, Maria and Winter, D. (1994) *Informal Carers and the Labour Market in Britain*, London, Suntory Discussion Paper WSP/89.

Evans, Richard J. (1977) *The Feminists: Women's Emancipation Movements in Europe, America and Australasia 1840–1920*, London, Croom Helm.

Faderman, Lillian (1981) *Surpassing the Love of Men: Romantic Friendship and Love Between Women from the Renaissance to the Present*, London, Junction Books.

Faludi, Susan (1991) *Backlash: the Undeclared War Against American Women*, New York, Crown.

——(1992) *Backlash: the Undeclared War Against Women*, London, Chatto & Windus.

Feldberg, Roslyn and Glenn, Evelyn Nakano (1979) 'Male and female: job versus gender models in the sociology of work', *Social Problems* 26 (5) 524–38.

Fielding, A. and Savage, M. (1987) *Social Mobility and the Changing Class Composition of South-East England*, Working Paper in Urban and Regional Studies No. 60, University of Sussex.

Finch, Janet and Dulcie Groves (eds) (1983) *A Labour of Love: Women, Work and Caring*, London, Routledge.

Fitzpatrick, Barry (1992) 'Enforcing Community sex equality law in the UK courts', paper presented to National Pay Equity Campaign Seminar, LSE.

Flax, Jane (1987) 'Postmodernism and gender relations in feminist theory', *Signs* 12 (4) 621–43.

Folbre, Nancy (1994) *Who Pays for the Kids? Gender the Structures of Consent*, London, Routledge.

Forbes, Ian (1991) 'Equal opportunity: radical, liberal and conservative critiques' in Elizabeth Meehan and Selma Sevenhuijsen (eds) *Equality Politics and Gender*, London, Sage, pp. 17–35.

Foucault, Michel (1981) *The History of Sexuality, Volume One: An Introduction*, Harmondsworth, Pelican.

—— (1987) *The History of Sexuality, Volume Two: The Use of Pleasure*, Harmondsworth, Penguin.

Frank, A. Gunder (1967) *Capitalism and Underdevelopment in Latin America*, New York, Monthly Review Press.

Franklin, Sarah, Lury, Celia and Stacey, Jackie (eds) (1991) *Off-Centre: Feminism and Cultural Studies*, London, Harper Collins.

Fraser, Nancy and Nicholson, Linda (1988) 'Social criticism without philosophy: an encounter between feminism and postmodernism', *Theory, Culture and Society* 5, 373–94.

Freeman, Jo (1975) *The Politics of Women's Liberation: a Case Study of an Emerging Social Movement and its Relation to the Policy Process*, New York, Longman.

Froebel, Folker, Heinreichs, Jurgen and Kreye, Otto (1980) *The New International Division of Labour: Structural Unemployment in Industrialised Countries and Industrialisation in Developing Countries*, Cambridge, Cambridge University Press.

Gage, Matilda (1980) *Woman, Church and State: the Original Exposé of Male Collaboration Against the Female Sex*, Watertown, Mass., Persephone Press (originally published in 1893).

Gaitskell, Deborah and Unterhalter, Elain (1989) 'Mothers of the nation: a comparative analysis of nation, race and motherhood in Afrikaner Nationalism and the African National Congress' in Nira Yuval-Davis and Floya Anthias (eds) *Woman–Nation–State*, London, Macmillan.

Gallie, Duncan, Marsh, Catherine and Vogler, Carolyn (eds) (1994) *Social Change and the Experience of Unemployment*, Oxford, Oxford University Press.

Gallie, Duncan and White, Michael (1993) *Employee Commitment and the Skills Revolution: First Findings for the Employment in Britain Survey*, London, PSI Publications.

Gellner, Ernest (1983) *Nations and Nationalism*, Oxford, Blackwell.

General Household Survey (1993), London, HMSO.

Gershuny, Jonathan (1983) *Social Innovation and the Division of Labour*, Oxford, Oxford University Press, pp. 151–97.

Gershuny, Jonathan, Godwin, Michael and Jones, Sally (1994) 'The domestic labour revolution: a process of lagged adaptation' in Michael Anderson, Frank Bechhofer and Jonathan Gershuny (eds) *The Social and Political Economy of the Household*, Oxford, Oxford University Press, 151–97.

Giddens, Anthony (1984) *The Constitution of Society: Outline of the Theory of Structuration*, Cambridge, Polity Press.

Gilligan, Carol (1982) *In a Different Voice: Psychological Theory and Women's Development*, Cambridge, Mass., Harvard University Press.

Gilman, Charlotte Perkins (1898/1966) *Women and Economics: a Study of the Economic Relation Between Men and Women as a Factor in Social Evolution*, New York, Harper & Row.

Gilroy, Paul (1987) '*There Ain't No Black in the Union Jack': the Cultural Politics of Race and Nation*, London, Hutchinson.

Ginn, Jay and Arber, Sara (1994) 'Mid-life women's employment and pension entitlement in relation to co-resident adult children', *Journal of Marriage and the Family* November, 813–19.

——(1995) 'Exploring mid-life women's employment', *Sociology* 29 (1), 73–94.

Ginn, Jay, Arber, Sarah, Brannen, Julia, Dale, Angela, Dex, Shirley, Elias, Peter, Moss, Peter, Pahl, Jan, Roberts, Ceridwen, Ruberg, Jill (1996) 'Feminist fallacies: a reply to Hakim on women's employment', *British Journal of Sociology* 47 (1), 167–74.

Glendinning, Caroline (1990) 'Dependency and interdependency: the incomes of informal carers and the impact of social security', *Journal of Social Policy* 19 (4), 469–97.

Glucksmann, Miriam (1990) *Women Assemble: Women Workers and the New Industries in Inter-War Britain*, London, Routledge.

Goldthorpe, John (1980) *Social Mobility and the Class Structure in Modern Britain*, Oxford, Clarendon Press.

——(1983) 'Women and class analysis: in defence of the conventional view', *Sociology* 17 (4), 465–88.

Goodman, L.A. (1986) 'Some useful extensions of the usual correspondence analysis approach and the usual log-linear models approach in the analysis of contingency tables', *International Statistical Review* 54, 243–309.

Goot, Murray and Reid, Elizabeth (1975) *Women and Voting Studies: Mindless Matrons or Sexist Scientism*, Beverley Hills, Sage.

Gordon, David M. (1988) 'The global economy: new edifice or crumbling foundations?', *New Left Review* 168, 24–64.

Green, M. (1989) 'Generalisations of the Goodman association model B, the analysis of multi-divisional contingency tables' in A. Decarli, B. J. Francis, R. Gilchrist and G. H. H. Seeber (eds) *Statistical Modelling Lecture Notes in Statistics*, 57, New York Springer-Verlag, pp. 165–71.

Gregory, Jeanne (1987) *Sex, Race and Law: Legislating for Equality*, London, Sage.

Hakim, Catherine (1979) *Occupational Segregation: a Comparative Study of the Degree and Pattern of the Differentiation Between Men and Women's Work in Britain, the US and Other Countries*, Department of Employment Research Paper No. 9, London, HMSO.

——(1981) 'Job segregation: trends in the 1970s', *Employment Gazette* 89 (12), 521–9.

——(1987a) 'Homeworking in Britain: key findings from the national survey of home-based workers', *Employment Gazette* 95 (2), 92–104.

——(1987b) 'Trends in the flexible workforce', *Employee Gazette* 95 (11), 549–60.

——(1991) 'Grateful slaves and self-made women: fact and fantasy in women's work orientations', *European Sociological Review* 7, 101–21.

——(1992) 'Explaining trends in occupational segregation: the measurement, causes, and consequences of the sexual division of labour', *European Sociological Review* 8 (2), 127–52.

——(1993a) 'The myth of rising female employment', *Work, Employment and Society* 7 (1), 97–120.

——(1993b) 'Segregated and integrated occupations: a new approach to analysing social change', *European Sociological Review* 9 (3), 289–314.

——(1995) 'Five feminist myths about women's employment', *British Journal of Sociology* 46, 429–55.

—— (1996) *Key Issues in Women's Work: Female Heterogeneity and the Polarisation of Women's Employment*, London, Athlone.

Halford, Susan and Duncan, Simon (1991) *Implementing Feminist Politics in British Local Government*, Brighton, University of Sussex, Centre for Urban and Regional Research, Working Paper no. 78.

Hamilton, Cicely (1981) *Marriage as a Trade*, London, The Women's Press (Originally published in 1909).

Hanmer, Jalna, Radford, Jill and Stanko, Elizabeth (eds) (1989) *Women, Policing and Male Violence: International Perspectives*, London, Routledge.

Hanmer, Jalna and Saunders, Sheila (1984) *Well Founded Fear: a Community Study of Violence Toward Women*, London, Hutchinson.

Harrison, Brian (1978) *Separate Spheres: the Opposition to Women's Suffrage in Britain*, London, Croom Helm.

Harrop, Anne and Moss, Peter (1994) 'Working parents: trends in the 1980s', *Employment Gazette*, November, 343–51.

Hartmann, Heidi, I. (1976) 'Capitalism, patriarchy and job segregation by sex', *Signs* 1 (3), 137–69.

Harvey, David (1990) *The Conditions of Postmodernity: An Enquiry into the Origins of Social Change*, Oxford, Blackwell.

Hayden, Dolores (1981) *The Grand Domestic Revolution: a History of Feminist Designs for American Homes, Neighbourhoods and Cities*, Cambridge, Mass., MIT Press.

Heath, Anthony, Jowell, Roger and Curtice, John (1985) *How Britain Votes*, Oxford, Pergamon Press.

Hernes, Holga Maria (1987) 'Women and the welfare state: the transition from private to public dependence' in Anne Showstack Sassoon (ed.) *Women and the State: the Shifting Boundaries of Public and Private*, London, Hutchinson, pp. 72–92.

Hewlett, Sylvia (1986) *A Lesser Life: the Myth of Women's Liberation in America*, New York, Morrow.

Hills, Jill (1981) 'Britain' in Jill Hills and Joni Lovenduski (eds) *The Politics of the Second Electorate: Woman and Public Participation*, London, Routledge & Kegan Paul, pp. 8–32.

Hills, Jill and Lovenduski, Joni (eds) (1981) *The Politics of the Second Electorate: Women and Public Participation*, London, Routledge.

Holcombe, Lee (1983) *Wives and Property: Reform of the Married Women's Property Law in Nineteenth Century England*, Oxford, Martin, Robertson.

hooks, bell (1982) *Ain't I a Woman?* London, Pluto Press.

—— (1984) *Feminist Theory: From Margin to Center*, Boston, South End Press.

Hoskins, Catherine (1985) 'Women's equality and the European Community', *Feminist Review* 20, 71–88.

Hudson, Ray (1978) 'Spatial policy in Britain', *Area* 10, 359–62.

Hutton, Sandra (1994) 'Men's and women's incomes: evidence from survey data', *Journal of Social Policy* 23 (1), 21–40.

Hutton, Will (1995) *The State We're In*, London, Jonathan Cape.

Incomes Data Services (1982) *Part-time Workers*, Study 267, London, Incomes Data Services.

—— (1983) *Temporary Workers*, Study 295, London, Incomes Data Services.

—— (1984) *Craft Flexibility*, Study 322, London, Incomes Data Services.

Irwin, Sarah (1995a) *Gender and Household Resourcing: Changing Relations to Work and Family*, Leeds, School of Sociology and Social Policy Gender Analysis and Policy Unit Working Paper no. 12.

—— (1995b) *Rights of Passage: Social Change and the Transition from Youth to Adulthood*, London, UCL Press.

Jayawardena, Kumari (ed.) (1986) *Feminism and Nationalism in the Third World*, London, Zed Press.

Jeffreys, Sheila (1985) *The Spinster and her Enemies: Feminism and Sexuality 1880–1930*, London, Pandora.

Jenson, Jane (1989) 'The talents of women, the skills of men: flexible specialisation and women' in Stephen Wood (ed.) *The Transformation of Work? Skill, Flexibility and the Labour Process*, London, Unwin Hyman, pp. 141–55.

Jessop, Bob *et al.* (eds) (1991) *The Politics of Flexibility: 'Restructuring State and Industry in Britain, Germany and Scandinavia*, Aldershot, Elgar.

Jones, David R. and Makepeace, Gerald H. (1996) 'Equal worth, equal opportunities: pay and promotion in an internal labour market', *The Economic Journal* 106, 401–9.

Jonung, C. (1983) 'Patterns of occupational segregation by sex in the labour market' in G. Schnid (ed.) *Discrimination and Equalisation in the Labour Market: Employment Policies for Women in Selected Countries*, Berlin, International Institute for Management, Wissenschaftszentrum.

Jortray, Francois, Meulders, Daniele and Plasman, Robert (1991) *Evaluation of the Impact of the Single Market's Completion on Women's Employment in the Banking Sector* Brussels, Commission of the European Community.

Joseph, Gloria (1981) 'The incompatible menage a trois: Marxism, Feminism and Racism' in Lydia Sargent (ed.) *Women and Revolution: the Unhappy Marriage of Marxism and Feminism*, London, Pluto Press, 91–108.

Joshi, Heather (1990) 'The cash opportunity costs of childbearing: an approach to estimation using British data', *Population Studies* 44, 41–60.

Kandyoti, Deniz A. (1987) 'Emancipated but unliberated? Reflections on the Turkish case', *Feminist Studies* 13 (2), 317–38.

—— (1989) 'Women and the Turkish State: political actors or symbolic pawns' in Nira Yuval-Davis and Floya Anthias (eds) *Woman–Nation–State*, London, Macmillan.

—— (ed.) (1991) *Women, Islam and the State*, Basingstoke, Macmillan.

Kedourie, Eli (1966) *Nationalism*, London, Hutchinson.

Keeble, David (1978) 'Reply to Hudson', *Area* 10, 363–65.

Kelly, Joan (1984) *Women, History and Theory. The Essays of Joan Kelly*, Chicago, Chicago University Press.

Kimmel, Michael S. (1987) 'Men's responses to feminism at the turn of the century', *Gender and Society* 1 (3), 261–83.

Kirkpatrick, Jeanne J. (1974) *Political Woman*, New York, Basic Books.

Klein, Ethel (1984) *Gender Politics*, Cambridge, Mass., Harvard University Press.

Klingender, F. (1935) *The Condition of Clerical Labour in Britain*, London, Martin Lawrence.

Klug, Francesca (1989) '"Oh to be in England": the British case study' in Nira Yuval-Davis and Floya Anthias (eds) *Woman–Nation–State*, London, Macmillan.

Kuhn, Annette (1982) *Women's Pictures: Feminism and Cinema*, London, Routledge.

Kyrk, H. (1933) *Economic Problems of the Family*, New York, Harper & Brothers.

Kravdal, Oystein (1994) 'The importance of economic activity, economic potential and economic resources for the timing of first births in Norway', *Population Studies* 48, 249–67.

Labour Force Trends (1996), London, HMSO.

Labour Market Trends (1996), London, HMSO.

Lampard, Richard (1994) 'An examination of the relationship between marital dissolution and unemployment' in Duncan Gallie, Catherine Marsh and Carolyn Vogler (eds) *Social Change and the Experience of Unemployment*, Oxford, Oxford University Press, 264–98.

Lancaster Regionalism Group (1985) *Localities, Class and Gender*, London, Pion.

Lash, S. and Bagguley, P. (1987) 'Labour flexibility and disorganized capitalism', mimeo, Department of Sociology, University of Lancaster.

Lash, Scott and Urry, John (1987) *The End of Organized Capitalism*, Cambridge, Polity Press.

——(1994) *Economies of Signs and Space*, London, Sage.

Laslett, Peter (1977) *Family Life and Illicit Love in Earlier Generations: Essays in Historical Sociology*, Cambridge, Cambridge University Press.

Lawson, Annette and Samson, Colin (1988) 'Age, gender and adultery', *British Journal of Sociology* 39 (3), 409–40.

Lees, Sue (1986) 'Sex, race and culture: feminism and the limits of cultural pluralism', *Feminist Review* 22, 92–102.

LeGrand, Julian *et al.* (1992) 'Findings from the Welfare State Programme', paper presented to Welfare State Programme Seminar, STICERD, London School of Economics.

Lewenhak, Sheila (1977) *Women and Trade Unions: an Outline History of Women in the British Trade Union Movement*, London, Ernest Benn.

Liddington, Jill and Norris, Jill (1978) *One Hand Tied Behind Us: the Rise of the Women's Suffrage Movement*, London, Virago.

Lindley, Robert M. (ed.) (1992) *Women's Employment: Britain in the Single European Market*, London, EOC, HMSO.

Lipset, Seymour Martin (1980) *Political Man: the Social Bases of Politics*, London, Heinemann.

Lister, Ruth (1987) 'Future insecure: women and income maintenance under a third Tory term', *Feminist Review* 27, 7–16.

——(1990) 'Women, economic dependency and citizenship', *Journal of Social Policy* 19 (4), 445–68.

——(1992) 'Tracing the contours of women's citizenship a social policy perspective', paper presented to LSE Gender Group seminar, London.

Littleton, Christine A. (1987) 'Equality and feminist legal theory', *University of Pittsburgh Law Review* 48 (4), 1043–59.

Lorde, Audre (1981) 'An open letter to Mary Daly' in Cherrie Moraga and Gloria Anzaldua (eds) *This Bridge Called my Back: Writings by Radical Women of Color*, Watertown, Mass., Persephone Press, pp. 94–7.

Lovenduski, Joni (1986) *Women and European Politics: Contemporary Feminism and Public Policy*, Amherst, University of Massachusetts Press.

—— (1995) 'The gender gap in voting', paper presented at the conference 'A New Labour academic link', Birkbeck College London.

Lyotard, Jean-Francois (1978) *The Postmodern Condition: a Report on Knowledge*, Minneapolis, University of Minnesota Press.

McFarland, Alan (1978) *The Origins of English Individualism*, Oxford, Basil Blackwell.

McIntosh, A. (1980) 'Women at work: a survey of employers', *Employment Gazette* 88, 1142–49.

McIntosh, Mary and Weir, A. (1982) 'Towards a wages strategy for women', *Feminist Review* 10, 5–20.

MacKinnon, Catharine (1989) *Toward a Feminist Theory of the State*, Cambridge, Mass., Harvard University Press.

McLoone, James and O'Leary, Maire (1989) *Infrastructures and Women's Employment* CREW, European Commission.

McNally, F. (1979) *Women for Hire: a Study of the Female Office Worker*, London, Macmillan.

227

McRobbie, Angela and Nava, Mica (eds) (1984) *Gender and Generation*, London, Macmillan.

Manley, P. and Sawbridge, D. (1980) 'Women at work', *Lloyds Bank Review*, pp. 129–40.

Mann, Michael (1986a) 'A crisis in stratification theory? Persons, households/families/lineages, genders, classes and nations' in Rosemary Crompton and Michael Mann (eds) *Gender and Stratification*, Cambridge, Polity Press, pp. 40–56.

——(1986b) *The Sources of Social Power*, Volume 1, *A History of Power from the Beginning to A.D. 1760*, Cambridge, Cambridge University Press.

——(1987) 'Ruling class strategies and citizenship', *Sociology* 21 (3), 339–54.

Marcus, Tobi (1996) 'Family friendly employment policies', from unpublished PhD thesis in progress, University of Bristol.

Mark-Lawson, Jane and Witz, Anne (1990) 'Familial control or patriarchal domination? The case of the family labour system in 19th century coal mining' in Helen Corr and Lynn Jamieson (eds) *The Politics of Everyday Life: Continuity and Change in Work and the Family*, London, Macmillan, pp. 117–40.

Mark-Lawson, Jane, Savage, Mike and Warde, Alan (1985) 'Gender and local politics: struggles over welfare policies' in Linda Murgatroyd, Mike Savage, Dan Shapiro, John Urry, Sylvia Walby, Alan Warde and Jane Mark-Lawson (eds) *Localities, Class and Gender*, London, Pion, pp. 195–215.

Marquand, David (1988) *The Unprincipled Society: New Demands and Old Politics*, London, Fontana.

Marshall, Gordon, Newby, Howard, Rose, David and Vogler, Carolyn (1988) *Social Class in Modern Britain*, London, Hutchinson.

Marshall, T.H. (1950) *Citizenship and Social Class*, Cambridge, Cambridge University Press.

——(1965/1975) *Social Policy in the Twentieth Century* (4th edn), London, Hutchinson.

——(1981) *The Right to Welfare*, London, Heinemann.

Martin, Jean and Roberts, Ceridwen (1984) *Women and Employment: a Lifetime Perspective*, London, HMSO.

Massey, Doreen (1984) *Spatial Divisions of Labour: Social Structures and the Geography of Production* London, Macmillan.

Massey, Doreen and Meegan, Richard (1982) *The Anatomy of Job Loss: the How, Why and Where of Employment Decline*, London, Macmillan.

Mayall, Berry (1990) 'The division of labour in early child care – mothers and others', *Journal of Social Policy* 19 (4), 299–330.

Meulders, Daniele and Plasman, Oliver (1990) 'The impact of the single market on women's employment in the textile and clothing industry: summary report of the expert network "Women in Employment"', *Social Europe*, Supplement, 2/91.

Meehan, Elizabeth and Sevenhuijsen, Selma (eds) (1991) *Equality Politics and Gender*, London, Sage.

Melby, Kari (1992) Personal communication.

Middleton, Chris (1988) 'Gender divisions and wage labour in English history' in Sylvia Walby (ed.) *Gender Segregation at Work*, Milton Keynes, Open University Press, pp. 55–73.

Middleton, Lucy (ed.) (1978) *Women in the British Labour Movement*, London, Croom Helm.

Mies, Maria (1986) *Patriarchy and Accumulation on a World Scale: Women in the International Division of Labour*, London, Zed Books.

Milkman, R. (1976) 'Women's work and the economic crisis: some lessons of the great depression', *Review of Radical Political Economy* 8 (1), 73–97.

Mill, John Stuart (1869) *The Subjection of Women*, London, Longman.

Miller, Robert Lee, Wilford, Rick and Donaghue, Freda (1996) *Women and Political Participation in Northern Ireland*, Aldershot, Avebury.

Millett, Kate (1977) *Sexual Politics*, London, Virago.

Mincer, Jacob (1962) 'Labor force participation of married women: a study of labor supply' in National Bureau of Economic Research *Aspects of Labour Economics: a Conference of the Universities*, National Bureau Committee for Economic Research, Princeton, Princeton University Press.

—— (1966) 'Labor-force participation and unemployment: a review of recent evidence' in Robert Gordon and Margaret Gordon (eds) *Prosperity and Unemployment*, New York, John Wiley.

Mincer, Jacob and Polachek, Solomon (1974) 'Family investments in human capital: earnings of women', *Journal of Political Economy* 82 (2), S76–S108.

Mitter, Swasti (1986) *Common Fate, Common Bond: Women in the Global Economy*, London, Pluto Press.

Moghadam, Valentine (1990) 'Revolution engendered: women and politics in Iran and Afghanistan', paper presented to the International Sociological Association Conference, Madrid.

Moraga, Cherrie and Anzaldua, Gloria (eds) (1981) *This Bridge Called my Back: Writings by Radical Women of Color*, Watertown, Mass., Persephone Press.

Morgan, Robin (ed.) (1985) Sisterhood *is Global: the International Women's Movement Anthology*, Harmondsworth, Penguin.

Morrell, Caroline (1981) *Black Friday and Violence against Women in the Suffragette Movement*, London, Women's Research and Resources Centre.

Morris, Lydia (1990) *The Workings of the Household: a US–UK Comparison*, Cambridge, Polity.

—— (1994) *Dangerous Classes: the Underclass and Social Citizenship*, London, Routledge.

National Economic Development Office (NEDO) (1986) *Changing Working Patterns: How Companies Achieve Flexibility to Meet New Needs*, London, National Economic Development Office.

Natti, Juko (1993) 'Temporary employment in the Nordic countries: a "trap" or a "bridge"?', *Work, Employment and Society* 7 (3), 451–64.

Naylor, Kate (1994) 'Part-time working in Great Britain – an historical analysis', *Employment Gazette* 102, pp. 472–85.

Nelson, Barbara J. (1984) 'Women's poverty and women's citizenship: some political consequences of economic marginality', *Signs* 10 (21), 209–31.

New Earnings Survey 1970, 1974, 1977, 1981, 1986, 1991, 1995, London, HMSO.

NOMIS (1971) Census of Employment, National Online Manpower Information Service, Manpower Services Commission; available from Department of Geography, University of Durham, Science Laboratories, South Road, Durham DH1 3LE.

—— (1981) Census of Employment, National Online Manpower Information Service, Manpower Services Commission; available from Department of Geography, University of Durham, Science Laboratories, South Road, Durham DH1 3LE.

Norris, Pippa and Lovenduski, Joni (1995) *Political Recruitment: Gender, Race and Class in the British Parliament*, Cambridge, Cambridge University Press.

Nowotny, Helga (1994) *Time*, Cambridge, Polity.

Obbo, Christine (1989) 'Sexuality and domination in Uganda' in Nira Yuval-Davis and Floya Anthias (eds) *Woman–Nation–State* London, Macmillan.

OECD (1980) 'Women's employment during the 1970s recession' in A. H. Amsden (ed.) *The Economics of Women and Work*, Harmondsworth, Penguin, pp. 359–85.

Offe, Claus (1987) *Disorganised Capitalism*, Cambridge, Polity Press.

Office of Population Censuses and Surveys (OPCS) (1995) *General Household Survey 1993*, London, HMSO.

—— (1996a) *Labour Force Trends*, London, HMSO.

—— (1996b) *Living in Britain: Results from the 1994 General Household Survey*, London, HMSO.

Okin, Susan Moller (1989) *Justice, Gender, and the Family*, New York, Basic Books.

Oldfield, Sybil (1989) *Women Against the Iron Fist: Alternatives to Militarism, 1900–1989*, Oxford, Blackwell.

Oppenheimer, Valerie K. (1970) *The Female Labor Force in the United States: Demographic and Economic Factors Governing its Growth and Changing Composition*, Berkeley and Los Angeles, Cal., University of California Press.

Pahl, Jan (1989) *Money and Marriage*, London, Macmillan.

Pahl, Ray (1991) 'Foreword' to Bryan Turner (ed.) *Citizenship, Civil Society and Social Cohesion*, Swindon, ESRC.

Pankhurst, Sylvia (1977) *The Suffragette Movement: an Intimate Account of Persons and Ideals*, London, Virago (originally published in 1931 by Longman).

Parmar, Pratibha (1982) 'Gender, race and class: Asian women in resistance' in Centre for Contemporary Cultural Studies, University of Birmingham, *The Empire Strikes Back: Race and Racism in 70s Britain*, London, Hutchinson.

Parsons, David (1992) 'Developments in the UK tourism and leisure labour market' in Robert M. Lindley (ed.) *Women's Employment: Britain in the Single European Market*, London, Equal Opportunities Commission, HMSO, pp. 101–12.

Pateman, Carole (1988) *The Sexual Contract*, Cambridge Polity Press.

—— (1991) 'Women and citizenship', paper presented to LSE Gender Group Seminar, London.

Penn, Roger, Rose, Michael and Rubery, Jill (eds) (1994) *Skill and Occupational Change*, Oxford, Oxford University Press.

Phizacklea, Annie (1990) *Unpacking the Fashion Industry*, London, Routledge.

Pilcher, Jane (1995) *Age and Generation in Modern Britain*, Oxford, Oxford University Press.

Piore, Michael and Sabel, Charles (1984) *The Second Industrial Divide: Possibilities for Prosperity*, New York, Basic Books.

Plumwood, V. (1993) *Feminism and the Mastery of Nature*, London, Routledge.

Pollert, Anna (1987) 'The "flexible firm": a model in search of reality (or a policy in search of a practice?)', *Warwick Papers in Industrial Relations*, No. 19, Coventry, Warwick University.

—— (ed.) (1991) *Farewell to Flexibility?* Oxford, Blackwell.

Randall, Vicky (1982) *Women and Politics*, London, Macmillan.

Reid, M. (1934) *The Economics of Household Production*, New York, John Wiley & Sons.

Rees, Teresa (1992) *Women and the Labour Market*, London, Routledge.

Reskin, Barbara F. and Hartmann, Heidi I. (eds) (1986) *Women's Work, Men's Work: Sex Segregation on the Job*, Washington, DC, National Academy Press.

Reskin, Barbara and Roos, Patricia (1990) *Job Queues, Gender Queues: Explaining Women's Inroads into Male Occupations*, Philadelphia, Temple University Press.

Rex, John and Tomlinson, Sally (1979) *Colonial Immigrants in a British City: a Class Analysis*, London, Routledge.

Rhode, Deborah L. (1989) *Justice and Gender: Sex Discrimination and the Law*, Cambridge, Mass., Harvard University Press.

Robinson, Olive (1988) 'The changing labour market: growth of part-time employment and labour market segmentation in Britain' in S. Walby (ed.) *Gender Segregation at Work*, Milton Keynes, Open University Press, pp. 114–35.

Robinson, Olive and Wallace, J. (1984) *Part-time Employment and Sex Discrimination Legislation in Great Britain: a Study of the Demand for Part-time Labour and of Sex Discrimination in Selected Organizations and Establishments*, Department of Employment Research Paper No. 43, London, HMSO.

Rogers, Barbara (1980) *The Domestication of Women: Discrimination in Developing Societies*, London, Kogan Page.

Roseneil, Sasha (1995) *Disarming Patriarchy: Feminism and Political Action at Greenham*, Buckingham, Open University Press.

Rowbotham, Sheila (1972) *Women, Resistance and Revolution*, Harmondsworth, Penguin.

—— (1981) 'The trouble with "patriarchy"' in Feminist Anthology Collective (eds) *No Turning Back: Writings from the Women's Liberation Movement 1975–1980*, London, The Women's Press, 72–8.

Rubery, Jill (ed.) (1988) *Women and Recession* London, Routledge.

Rubery, Jill, Humphries, Jane and Howell, Sara (1992) 'Women's employment in textiles and clothing' in Lindley, Robert M. (ed.) *Women's Employment: Britain in the Single European Market*, Equal Opportunities Commission, London, HMSO, pp. 81–100.

Ruddick, Sara (1989) *Maternal Thinking*, Boston, Beacon Press.

Rutherford, Sarah (1996) 'Gender and organisational culture', from unpublished PhD thesis in progress, University of Bristol.

Sahgal, Gita and Yuval-Davis, Nira (eds) (1992) *Refusing Holy Orders: Women and Fundamentalism in Britain*, London, Virago.

Sainsbury, Diane (ed.) (1994) *Gendering Welfare States*, London, Sage.

Sarlvik, Bo and Crewe, Ivor (1983) *Decade of Dealignment: the Conservative Victory of 1979 and Electoral Trends in the 1970s*, Cambridge, Cambridge University Press.

Saunders, Peter (1990) *A Nation of Home Owners*, London, Unwin Hyman.

Savage, Mike (1987) 'Spatial mobility and the professional labour market', University of Sussex Working Paper in Urban and Regional Studies.

Sawer, Marian (1990) *Sisters in Suits: Women and Public Policy in Australia*, Sydney, Allen & Unwin.

Sayer, Andrew (1984) *Method in Social Science: a Realist Approach*, London, Hutchinson.

Scott, Alison MacEwen (ed.) (1994) *Gender Segregation and Social Change*, Oxford, Oxford University Press.

Schreiner, Olive (1978) *Woman and Labour*, London, Virago (originally published in 1911 by Fisher Unwin).

Segal, Lynne (1987) *Is the Future Female? Troubled Thoughts on Contemporary Feminism*, London, Virago.

Sen, Amartya (1984) *Resources, Values and Development*, Oxford, Basil Blackwell.

—— (1985) *Commodities and Capabilities*, Amsterdam, North Holland.

Shiva, Vandana (1989) *Staying Alive: Women, Ecology and Development*, London, Zed Press.

Siltanen, Janet (1990) 'Social change and the measurement of occupational segregation by sex', *Work, Employment and Society* 4 (1), 1–29.

Siltanen, Janet and Stanworth, Michelle (eds) (1982) *Women and the Public Sphere: a Critique of Sociology and Politics*, London, Hutchinson.

Siltanen, Janet, Jarman, Jennifer and Blackburn, Robert M. (1992) *Gender Inequality in the Labour Market: Occupational Concentration and Segregation, a Manual on Methodology*, Working Paper IDP Women/WP-2, Geneva, International Labour Office.

Sklar, Kathryn Kish (1973) *Catherine Beecher: a Study in American Domesticity*, New York, W.W. Norton.

Skocpol, Theda (1992) *Protecting Soldiers and Mothers: the Political Origins of Social Policy in the United States*, Cambridge, Mass., Belknap Press of Harward University Press.

Smart, Carol (1984) *The Ties that Bind: Law, Marriage and the Reproduction of Patriarchal Relations*, London, Routledge & Kegan Paul.

——(1989) *Feminism and the Power of Law*, London, Routledge.

Smith, Anthony D. (1971) *Theories of Nationalism*, London, Duckworth.

——(1986) *The Ethnic Origins of Nations*, Oxford, Blackwell.

Smith, Susan (1989) *The Politics of 'Race' and Residence: Citizenship, Segregation and White Supremacy in Britain*, Cambridge, Polity Press.

Snell, Mandy (1979) 'The Equal Pay and Sex Discrimination Acts: their impact in the workplace', *Feminist Review* 1, 37–57.

Snell, Mandy, Glucklich, P. and Povall, M. (1981) *Equal Pay and Opportunities: A Study of the Implementation and Effects of the Equal Pay and Sex Discrimination Acts in 26 Organizations*, Department of Employment Research Paper No. 20. London, HMSO.

Social Europe (1993) Supplement 3/93, 'Occupational segregation of women and men in the European Community', synthesis report of the network of experts on the situation of women in the labour market, written by Jill Rubery and Collette Fagan.

Soldon, Norbert C. (1978) *Women in British Trade Unions 1974–1976*, Dublin, Gill & Macmillan.

Soothill, Keith and Walby, Sylvia (1991) *Sex Crime in the News*, London, Routledge.

Spellman, Elizabeth (1988) *Inessential Woman: Problems of Exclusion in Feminist Thought*, Boston, Beacon Press.

Spencer, A. and Podmore, D. (1987) 'Women lawyers: marginal members of a male dominated profession' in A. Spencer and D. Podmore (eds) *In a Man's World*, London, Tavistock.

Spender, Dale (1983) *Women of Ideas (and What Men Have Done to Them)*, London, Ark.

——(1984) *There's Always Been a Women's Movement This Century*, London, Routledge.

Stacey, Judith (1990) 'Feminism, postfeminism and contemporary Christians in the United States', paper presented to the International Sociological Association conference, Madrid.

Stacey, Margaret and Price, Marion (1981) *Women, Power and Politics*, London, Tavistock.

Standing, Guy (1989) 'Global feminization through flexible labour', *World Development* 17 (7), 1077–95.

Stanko, Elizabeth (1988) 'Keeping women in and out of line: sexual harassment and occupational segregation' in Sylvia Walby (ed.) *Gender Segregation at Work*, Milton Keynes, Open University Press, pp. 91–9.

Stanley, Liz (ed.) (1990) *Feminist Praxis: Research Theory and Epistemology in Feminist Sociology*, London, Routledge.

Stanworth, Michelle (1984) 'Women and class analysis: a reply to John Goldthorpe', *Sociology* 18 (2), 159–70.

Stewart, A., Prandy, K. and Blackburn, R.M. (1980) *Social Stratification and Occupations*, London, Macmillan.

Stone, Isabella (1988) *Equal Opportunities in Local Authorities: Developing Effective Strategies for the Implementation of Policies for Women*, Equal Opportunities Commission, London, HMSO.

Strachey, Ray (1978) *The Cause: a Short History of the Women's Movement in Great Britain*, London, Virago (originally published in 1928 by Bell & Sons Ltd).

Streeck, Wolfgang (1992) *Social Institutions and Economic Performance: Studies of Industrial Relations in Advanced Economies*, London, Sage.

Streeck, Wolfgang and Schmitter, Philippe C. (1992) 'From national corporatism to transnational pluralism: organised interests in the single European Market' in Wolfgang Streeck (ed.) *Social Institutions and Economic Performance: Studies of Industrial Relations in Advanced Economies*, Sage, London, pp. 197–231.

Summerfield, Penny (1984) *Women and Workers in the Second World War*, London, Croom Helm.

Taylor, Harriet (1983) *The Enfranchisement of Women*, London, Virago (originally published in 1851).

Taylor, Ian (1991) 'The experience of order and disorder in free market societies: New York and Manchester: a reply to Bryan Turner' in Bryan Turner (ed.) *Citizenship, Civil Society and Social Cohesion*, Swindon, ESRC.

Taylor-Gooby, Peter (1991) 'Welfare state regimes and welfare citizenship', *Journal of European Social Policy* 1 (2), 93–105.

Tinker, Irene (ed.) (1990) *Persistent Inequalities: Women and World Development*, New York, Oxford University Press.

Townsend, Alan (1986) 'Spatial aspects of the growth of part-time employment in Britain', *Regional Studies* 20 (4), 313–30.

Treiman, D. and Hartmann, H. (eds) (1981) *Women, Work and Wages: Equal Pay for Jobs of Equal Value*, Committee on Occupational Classification and Analysis, Assembly of Behavioural and Social Sciences, National Research Council, Washington, DC: National Academy Press.

TUC Annual Report (1945), London, TUC.

Turner, Bryan (1986) *Citizenship and Reformism: the Debate over Reformism*, London, Allen & Unwin.

——(1987) *The Body and Society*, Cambridge, Polity.

——(1990) 'Outline of a theory of citizenship', *Sociology* 24 (2), 189–217.

——(ed.) (1991a) *Citizenship, Civil Society and Social Cohesion*, Swindon, ESRC.

——(1991b) 'Prolegomena to a general theory of social order' in Bryan Turner (ed.) *Citizenship, Civil Society and Social Cohesion*, Swindon, ESRC.

Ungerson, Clare (ed.) (1990) *Gender and Caring: Work and Welfare in Britain and Scandinavia*, London, Harvester.

——(1990) 'Conclusion' to Clare Ungerson (ed.) *Gender and Caring: Work and Welfare in Britain and Scandinavia*, London, Harvester.

——(1991) 'Citizenship and caring – the routes to "carers" citizenship', paper presented to LSE Gender Group Seminar, LSE.

United Nations Development Project (UNDP) (1992) *Human Development Report 1992*, Oxford, Oxford University Press.

Urry, John (1990) *The Tourist Gaze*, London, Sage.

Vanek, J. (1980) 'Time spent in housework' in A. Amsden (ed.) *The Economics of Women and Work*, Harmondsworth, Penguin, pp. 82–90.

Vinnicombe, S. (1980) *Secretaries, Management and Organizations*, London, Heinemann.

Vogler, Carolyn (1994) 'Money in the household' in Michael Anderson, Frank Bechhofer and Jonathan Gershuny (eds) *The Social and Political Economy of the Household*, Oxford, Oxford University Press, 225–66.

Vogler, Carolyn and Pahl, Jan (1993) 'Social and economic change and the organisation of money within marriage', *Work, Employment & Society* 7 (1) 71–96.

Walby, Sylvia (1985) 'Spatial and historical variations in women's unemployment and employment' in The Lancaster Regionalism Group, *Localities, Class and Gender*, London, Pion, pp. 161–76.

—— (1986a) 'Gender, class and stratification' in Rosemary Crompton and Michael Mann (eds) *Gender and Stratification*, Cambridge, Polity Press, pp. 23–9.

—— (1986b) *Patriarchy at Work: Patriarchal and Capitalist Relations in Employment*, Cambridge, Polity Press.

—— (1988) 'Gender politics and social theory', *Sociology* 22 (2), 215–32.

—— (1989) 'Flexibility and the changing sexual division of labour' in Stephen Wood (ed.) *The Transformation of Work*, London, Hutchinson, pp. 127–40.

—— (1990) *Theorising Patriarchy*, Oxford, Blackwell.

—— (1992) 'Post-post-modernism? Theorizing social complexity' in Michele Barrett and Anne Phillips (eds) *Destabilizing Theory: Contemporary Feminist Debates*, Cambridge, Polity Press, 31–52.

—— (1994) 'Methodological and theoretical issues in the comparative analysis of gender relations in Western Europe', *Environment and Planning A* 26, 1339–54.

—— (forthcoming) *A History of Feminist Thought*, London, Sage.

Walby, Sylvia, Greenwell, June with MacKay, Lesley and Soothill, Keith (1994) *Medicine and Nursing: Professions in a Changing Health Service*, London, Sage.

Walkowitz, Judith R. (1980) *Prostitution and Victorian Society: Woman, Class and the State*, Cambridge, Cambridge University Press.

Wallerstein, Immanuel (1979) *The Capitalist World Economy*, Cambridge, Cambridge University Press.

Warde, Alan and Hetherington, Kevin (1993) 'A changing domestic division of labour? Issues of measurement and interpretation', *Work, Employment & Society* 7 (1), 23–45.

Watson, Sophie (ed.) (1990) *Playing the State: Australian Feminist Interventions*, London, Verso.

Watt, Shantu and Cook, Juliet (1991) 'Racism: whose liberation? Implications for women's studies' in Jane Aaron and Sylvia Walby (eds) *Out of the Margins: Women's Studies in the Nineties*, London, Falmer Press, pp. 131–42.

Watts, M. (1990) 'The sex ratio revisited', *Work, Employment & Society* 4 (4), 595–8.

Weedon, Chris (1987) *Feminist Practice and Poststructuralist Theory*, Oxford, Blackwell.

Weitzman, Lenore (1985) *The Divorce Revolution: the Unexpected Social and Economic Consequences for Women and Children in America*, New York, Free Press.

West, J. (1978) 'Women, sex and class' in A. Kuhn and A-M. Wolpe (eds) *Feminism and Materialism: Women and Modes of Production*, London, Routledge & Kegan Paul, pp. 220–53.

Westwood, Sallie and Bhachu, Parminder (eds) (1989) *Enterprising Women: Ethnicity, Economy and Gender Relations*, London, Routledge.

Wilson, Gail (1987) *Women and Money: the Distribution of Resources and Responsibilities in the Family*, Aldershot, Gower.

—— (1991) 'Liberty, caring and coercion: the case of elder abuse', paper presented to LSE Gender Group Seminar, London.

Wilson, William Julius (1978) *The Declining Significance of Race: Blacks and Changing American Institutions*, Chicago, University of Chicago Press.

—— (1987) *The Truly Disadvantaged: the Inner City, the Underclass and Public Policy*, Chicago, University of Chicago Press.

Wiltshire, Anne (1985) *Most Dangerous Women: Feminist Peace Campaigners of the Great War*, London, Pandora.

Winship, Janice (1985) '"A girl needs to be street-wise": magazines for the 1980s', *Feminist Review* 21, 25–46.

Witz, Anne (1992) *Professions and Patriarchy*, London, Routledge.

Women and Geography Study Group of the IBG (1986) *Geography and Gender: an Introduction to Feminist Geography*, London, Hutchinson.

Women's Trade Union Congress (WTUC) (1978) *Annual Report*, London, TUC.

Wood, Stephen (1982) 'Introduction' in S. Wood (ed.) *The Degradation of Work?* London, Hutchinson, pp. 11–22.

——(ed.) (1983) *The Degradation of Work?* London, Unwin Hyman.

——(ed.) (1989) *The Transformation of Work? Skill, Flexibility and the Labour Process*, London, Unwin Hyman.

Woolf, Virginia (1938) *Three Guineas*, London, Harcourt, Brace & Ward.

Wright, R. E. and Ermisch J. (1991) 'Gender discrimination in the British labour market: a reassessment', *The Economic Journal* 101, 508–22.

Yuval-Davis, Nira (1989) 'National reproduction and "The Demographic Race" in Israel' in Nira Yuval-Davis and Floya Anthias (eds) *Woman–Nation–State*, London, Macmillan.

Yuval-Davis, Nira and Floya Anthias (eds) (1989) *Woman–Nation–State*, London, Macmillan.

Ziltener, Patrick and Bornschier, Volker (1995) 'The politics of the "social dimension" in the Commission's project to revitalize Western European integration', paper presented at the Second European Sociology Conference, Budapest.

INDEX

Note: page numbers in italics refer to figures or tables where these are separated from their textual references.